general editor John M. MacKenzie

When the 'Studies in Imperialism' series was founded more than twenty years ago, emphasis was laid upon the conviction that 'imperialism as a cultural phenomenon had as significant an effect on the dominant as on the subordinate societies'. With more than fifty books published, this remains the prime concern of the series. Cross-disciplinary work has indeed appeared covering the full spectrum of cultural phenomena, as well as examining aspects of gender and sex, frontiers and law, science and the environment, language and literature, migration and patriotic societies, and much else. Moreover, the series has always wished to present comparative work on European and American imperialism, and particularly welcomes the submission of books in these areas. The fascination with imperialism, in all its aspects, shows no sign of abating, and this series will continue to lead the way in encouraging the widest possible range of studies in the field. 'Studies in Imperialism' is fully organic in its development, always seeking to be at the cutting edge, responding to the latest interests of scholars and the needs of this ever-expanding area of scholarship.

The harem, slavery and British imperial culture

Manchester University Press

AVAILABLE IN THE SERIES

Cultural identities and the aesthetics of Britishness ed. Dana Arnold

Britain in China
Community, culture and colonialism, 1900–1949 Robert Bickers

New frontiers
Imperialism's new communities in East Asia 1842–1952
eds Robert Bickers and Christian Henriot

The Arctic in the British imagination 1818–1914 Robert G. David

Imperial cities
Landscape, display and identity eds Felix Driver and David Gilbert

Science and society in Southern Africa ed. Saul Dubow

Equal subjects, unequal rights
Indigenous peoples in British settler colonies, 1830s–1910
Julie Evans, Patricia Grimshaw, David Phillips and Shurlee Swain

Scotland, the Caribbean and the Atlantic World, 1750–1820
Douglas J. Hamilton

Emigrant Homecomings
The return movement of emigrants, 1600–2000 Marjory Harper

Empire and sexuality
The British experience Ronald Hyam

Reporting the Raj
The Britsh press in India, c. 1880–1922 Chandrika Kaul

Silk and Empire Brenda M. King

Law, history, colonialism
The reach of empire eds Diane Kirkby and Catherine Coleborne

The South African War reappraised ed. Donal Lowry

Propaganda and empire
The manipulation of British public opinion, 1880–1960 John M. MacKenzie

The Other Empire
Metropolis, India and progress in the colonial imagination John Marriott

Guardians of empire
The armed forces of the colonial powers, c. 1700–1964
eds David Omissi and David Killingray

Female imperialism and national identity
Imperial Order Daughters of the Empire Katie Pickles

Married to the empire
Gender, politics and imperialism in India, 1883–1947 Mary A. Procida

Imperial persuaders
Images of Africa and Asia in British advertising Anandi Ramamurthy

Imperialism and music
Britain 1876–1953 Jeffrey Richards

Colonial frontiers
Indigenous–European encounters in settler societies ed. Lynette Russell

West Indian intellectuals in Britain ed. Bill Schwarz

Migrant Races
Empire, identity and K. S. Ranjitsinhji Satadru Sen

The Victorian Soldier in Africa Edward M. Spiers

Martial races and masculinity in the British Army, 1857–1914 Heather Streets

The French empire between the Wars
Imperialism, politics and society Martin Thomas

British culture and the end of empire ed. Stuart Ward

The harem, slavery and British imperial culture

Anglo-Muslim relations in the late nineteenth century

Diane Robinson-Dunn

MANCHESTER
UNIVERSITY PRESS
Manchester and New York

distributed exclusively in the USA by
PALGRAVE

Copyright © Diane Robinson-Dunn 2006

The right of Diane Robinson-Dunn to be identified as the author of this work has been asserted by her in accordance with the Copyright, Designs and Patents Act 1988.

Published by Manchester University Press
Oxford Road, Manchester M13 9NR, UK
and Room 400, 175 Fifth Avenue, New York, NY 10010, USA
www.manchesteruniversitypress.co.uk

Distributed in the United States exclusively by
Palgrave Macmillan, 175 Fifth Avenue,
New York, NY 10010, USA

Distributed in Canada exclusively by
UBC Press, University of British Columbia, 2029 West Mall,
Vancouver, BC, Canada V6T 1Z2

British Library Cataloguing-in-Publication Data is available

Library of Congress Cataloging-in-Publication Data is available

ISBN 978 0 7190 7329 8 paperback

First published by Manchester University Press in hardback 2006

This paperback edition first published 2014

The publisher has no responsibility for the persistence or accuracy of URLs for any external or third-party internet websites referred to in this book, and does not guarantee that any content on such websites is, or will remain, accurate or appropriate.

Printed by Lightning Source

For Brad

CONTENTS

Illustrations – page viii
Abbreviations – page ix
Preface and acknowledgements – page x
General editor's introduction – page xiii

1	Introduction	page 1
2	From desert caravans to Red Sea coasts: the British anti-slavery campaign in Egypt	31
3	Networks of support: English activism and slavery redefined	70
4	'The British Turk' and the 'Christian harem': imperial ideology in English gender politics	115
5	Islam in England	154
6	Conclusion	197

Appendices – 210
Select bibliography – 213
Index – 220

ILLUSTRATIONS

1 Sir William Allan, *Slave Market in Constantinople*, courtesy of the Fine Art Society, London   *page* 128
2 John Frederick Lewis, *The Harem*, courtesy of Birmingham Museums and Art Gallery   138
3 William Henry Quilliam in 'Eastern Dress', courtesy of Liverpool Public Record Office, Liverpool Libraries and Information Services   163
4 The Shah Jehan Mosque at the Oriental Institute, Woking, *Illustrated London News* (9 November 1889)   177

ABBREVIATIONS

ASR	*Anti-Slavery Reporter*
BFASS	British and Foreign Anti-Slavery Society
CD Acts	Contagious Diseases Acts
FO	Foreign Office Records
FOBPP	Foreign Office Records, British Parliamentary Papers
FOCP	Foreign Office Records, Confidential Print
LCM	London City Mission
LCMM	*London City Mission Magazine*
LPRO	Liverpool Public Records Office
IAQR	*Imperial and Asiatic Quarterly Review and Colonial Record*
IOR	India Public Records Office

PREFACE AND ACKNOWLEDGEMENTS

This book began as my PhD thesis, study for which was undertaken at Stony Brook University. However, my interest in this topic goes back to my undergraduate studies in English history, literature and politics at Oxford as part of an abroad programme. I became intrigued by a place in which so many people dedicated themselves to celebrating and recreating a very closed, private and traditional form of Englishness, yet which succeeded nevertheless in attracting countless students, scholars and visitors from around the world each year. Like Englishness itself, that place was simultaneously exclusive and inclusive. Prior to undertaking graduate studies, I developed a parallel personal, intellectual and later academic interest in Sufi mysticism, Islam and the Bahá'í faith. I hoped, therefore, to pursue a research project that would allow me to combine these two general areas of study by considering the role of Islam in English history, society and culture.

My exploratory trip to the archives was to look for any eighteenth- or nineteenth-century sources that might mention Islam: travel narratives, missionary writings, Foreign Office correspondence and reports, East India Company records, books, articles, letters and journals. I discovered that not only did the availability of materials referring to or in some way connected with that religion increase dramatically for the final three decades of the nineteenth century, but that there appeared to be some interesting relationships in the presentation and discussion of Islam by sources that otherwise would seem to have had little, if anything, in common. For example, while Orientalist writers and artists were creating images of the Muslim harem to entertain and delight an English audience, anti-slavery workers were encountering real harems in Egypt and making very different representations of them in the attempt to mobilise English women and men to support their cause. British officials were seeking to eliminate white slavery in Egypt and the surrounding areas at the same time as anti-vice activists were alerting the public to 'white slavery', or prostitution, in England. Finally, during a period when the British Government was beginning to assert itself in proximity to the centres of power in the Islamic world by occupying Egypt and attempting to reform that country, Muslims were establishing communities in England and presenting their religion as an elevating influence in English society. This book attempts to explain these historical developments and their significance.

I express my gratitude to Kathleen Wilson who directed my dissertation and was willing to support such an endeavour during the 1990s when few in the field considered Islam to be of importance to British imperial – much less English national – history. Her directed readings and her seminar 'Histories, Empires and Identities' introduced me to invaluable theoretical perspectives and analytical approaches. Her passion for her work, her commitment to both sophisticated and politically relevant scholarship, and her understanding of

PREFACE AND ACKNOWLEDGEMENTS

gender's centrality to the politics of nation and empire provided great inspiration. I thank Fred Weinstein for his insights, with regard particularly to the relationship between identity formation and social change, and the advances made in this field over the last three decades. My thanks go also to John Williams and Said Arjomand, the other members of my committee, who contributed to each phase of the writing of the dissertation and advised me on how to turn it into a book. I benefited greatly from the intellectual environment created by faculty and graduate students at Stony Brook. Carolyn Conley, advisor for my MA programme at the University of Alabama at Birmingham, provided me with a solid foundation in the history of Victorian England.

Several institutions contributed to this study. I received financial support from Stony Brook University, a series of faculty development grants from the University of Detroit Mercy and a grant from the Mellon Foundation. In addition, I thank the librarians, archivists and staff at the Rare Books and Special Collections Library at the American University in Cairo; the Beinecke Library at Yale University; the Bodleian Library of Commonwealth and African Studies at Rhodes House, Oxford University; the British Library; the Butler Library at Columbia University; the Dar Al-Kutub, the National Library and Archives of Egypt; the Fawcett Library, London; the Harlan Hatcher Graduate Library at the University of Michigan; Liverpool Public Record Office; Melville Library at Stony Brook University, New York; the English National Archives; the New York Public Library, particularly those in the Asian and Middle Eastern Division and the Schomburg Center for Research in Black Culture; and Special Collections in the main library of the University of Birmingham, England. In addition, I thank the staff at the London City Mission for allowing me to research that organisation's archive, and Nisar and Salme Suleimani for their hospitality and access to materials related to the Shah Jahan Mosque in Woking, England.

Professors, instructors and private tutors of Arabic have, over the years, contributed both to this project and to my understanding and appreciation of Islam in general. I am especially grateful to William Chittick, with whom I spent a year studying the Qur'an in Arabic; Azza Hassanein and Ragia Effat at the American University in Cairo; and Ilham Mahfouz for checking my translations. My thanks go to Beth Baron for her important scholarship on women and gender in nineteenth-century Egypt and for taking the time to check my transliterations from Arabic to Latin script. I have enjoyed many opportunities to practise the language informally with native speakers in Dearborn, Michigan, New York City and the Middle East. As an unexpected benefit, I have had the good fortune to be invited to a number of twentieth- and twenty-first-century harems and experienced this modern institution in its many forms, from the quiet, book-lined, Cairo apartment of Professor Ragia Effat to the elegant dinner parties of Detroit-based, Syrian-born artist Ilham Mahfouz, complete with a team of female valets to ensure the privacy of the guests.

I owe an incalculable debt both to the many scholars whose work has influenced my own and to my colleagues who, in faculty colloquia, conferences, seminars, discussion groups and informal conversations, have contributed their thoughts. In particular, I thank Kenneth Cuno and Gopalan Balachandran

PREFACE AND ACKNOWLEDGEMENTS

for their comments on chapters one and five, respectively; and Michael Barry for his literary insights. The work of the late Edward Said has been especially influential, particularly the advances made later in his career and documented in *Culture and Imperialism*. I had the pleasure of meeting him at the School of Oriental and African Studies, University of London, during the summer of 1997, and his lifetime of scholarship and encouraging words regarding this particular project have been a great inspiration.

I am appreciative of the support of my colleagues in the Department of History at the University of Detroit Mercy; their flexible scheduling and distribution of course loads have enabled me to divide my time during semesters between Detroit and my home in New York City and so finish this book. I thank also Amy Chinn, my research assistant, who with the help of Maryrose Patrick has spent the past year tirelessly checking and rechecking footnotes and doing preliminary copy-editing.

Finally, I thank my husband Henry Bradford Dunn. He has been by my side through every phase of this project. There are not words to describe what his years of love, support and devotion have meant to me.

GENERAL EDITOR'S INTRODUCTION

Egypt has long been regarded as a crossroads. A bridge between Africa and Asia, it has also, through the agency of the Nile, connected the Mediterranean to desert regions and sub-Saharan Africa. It has been close enough to Europe to inspire fascination as the centre of a great ancient civilisation, as a location of early Christianity, and as a notable region of Islamic culture and power. Consequently, Egypt attracted the interest of Napoleon and of his *savants*. The British saw it as a major route to India where their interests could be threatened in alarming ways. This became even more obvious after the opening of the Suez Canal in 1869, and the British were quick to establish their informal imperial power. Thereafter, and particularly after 1882, Egypt became a unique phenomenon within the British Empire. Neither colony nor protectorate (until the British formalised the latter status in 1914), it was nonetheless one of the most celebrated instances of British power. Although its British ruler had the apparently lowly title of consul-general, he – particularly in the guise of Evelyn Baring, Lord Cromer (1883–1907) – was nonetheless one of the major proconsuls of the high noon of empire.

As Diane Robinson-Dunn demonstrates in this book, it was also a major location for British anti-slavery activity. The British had been grappling for some decades with the tensions between the humanitarian concerns of the anti-slavery movement and their diplomatic and power objectives. Slavery had been abolished in India in 1843, by a ruling company that was under evangelical influence. Later, pressed on by the publications of David Livingstone and the agitations of his followers, the British had conducted an assault on the Omani–Swahili trade of the East African coast, partly through the operations of an anti-slavery naval squadron, partly through a series of treaties culminating in that of 1873 with the Sultan Barghash. But that dealt only with the slave trade and the British recognised that slavery was so woven into the social and economic fabric of Zanzibar and its dependencies that it was another two decades before they forced the abolition of the institution.

Egypt seemed to be an even more complex case. Still theoretically a dependency of the Ottoman Empire, it also had imperial ambitions of its own, not only in the Sudan, but also, on the eve of the partition of Africa, on the North-East African coast. It was also one of the most cosmopolitan societies of the entire Mediterranean and Middle Eastern worlds. But slavery in Egypt was mainly domestic rather than (as in Zanzibar) plantation. Even Cromer accepted that domestic slavery was a very different condition from that on plantations. Yet from a treaty of 1877, the British set about dealing with what they saw as the objectionable aspects of Egyptian slavery. The British and Foreign Anti-Slavery Society and various missionary interests combined in a campaign which the English saw as one of the principal benefits of their 'veiled protectorate'.

GENERAL EDITOR'S INTRODUCTION

But, as Robinson-Dunn penetratingly reveals, these bare facts offer merely a route into much more complex analyses. Bound up in this campaign were questions of identity, cultural relativism, race, gender and class. The protagonists of the anti-slavery agitation were almost inevitably unable to escape from the mores and perceptions of the period. Since a high proportion of Egyptian slaves were women, questions of their manumission became extensively connected with both conservative and liberal discourses of femininity in Britain. Moreover, the relationships between Christianity and Islam were characterised by sets of highly pluralistic commentaries that were expressed in a variety of shades of hostility and sympathy. And within Britain itself Islam had its adherents, its converts, and its intellectual and religious protagonists. The anti-slavery crusade unveils much about the society that generated it, as well as about the society against which it was directed.

Of course *othering* is seldom merely a bilateral matter. Responses to the other are invariably conditioned by perceptions of and relationships with other others. By the later nineteenth century, some British were identifying Muslims as a valuable counterpoise to a growing class of educated and nationalist Hindus in India. A developing interest in a conservative romanticism was moving towards anxieties to preserve traditional systems and hence to the system that what would come to be known as 'indirect rule'. Connections with Egypt and the *reputation* of Islam were closely bound up with both of these developments.

Today's political, popular and media perceptions of Islam and of Muslims, attitudes invoked in contemporary conflict and war, reveal that aspects of the issues analysed in this book remain pertinent in the modern world. Egypt is still pivotal within the Middle East, evidenced by its role within the negotiations of the Palestinian–Israeli dispute. All of this makes this book timely and relevant. Robinson-Dunn's acute dissection of the wider aspects of the anti-slavery campaign are informed by her considerable knowledge of Egypt, of Arabic and of Islam. This is a striking addition to an *interactive* imperial historiography.

John M. MacKenzie

CHAPTER ONE

Introduction

> How can our Christian voice appeal
> For foreign slaves alone?
> Our gentle sisters, true as steel,
> Fall bruised at Justice's Throne!
>
> Are there no Turks but Mussulmen?
> Have we no monsters here?
> Beneath the eye of Christendom
> Shall not oppression fear![1]

The above lines are from the poem *A Cry From The Depths: The British Turk*, published in the 1878 issue of the *Women's Suffrage Journal*. The term 'foreign slaves' refers to female slaves destined for the harem, and the poem reinforces the assumption that Islam requires the oppression and enslavement of women. This belief informed both contemporary British imperialist efforts to suppress slave traffic in Egypt and other Ottoman territories and the English identities that developed through this campaign. However, the author uses the phrase 'British Turk' to describe not a subject of the Ottoman Empire or even a Muslim but a tyrannous man from 'the depths' of east-end London. This is more than a rhetorical device used for dramatic effect to hold the reader's attention: it is a product of an imperial cultural system in which ideas about Islam not only helped to define Englishness and the imperial mission in British-occupied territories, but gave meaning to conflicts and divisions within English society, as in the case of *Cry From The Depths* which deals with class and gender tensions.

Whenever similar terms and ideas appear in different parts of the world linked politically or otherwise we say that *cultural exchange* takes place. What exactly does this phrase mean? How are ideas exchanged, and does the act of reproducing them in different contexts involve some type of mutation or transformation? What role do specific social circumstances play in this process? Finally, what is the relationship between the re-creation of ideas and other more concrete forms of political action taken by governments and individuals?

This book explores such questions in order to shed light on the formation of English national identities in relation to Islam as understood in the context of the British imperial mission. Such an approach is necessary if we consider identities not as structures or categories, but rather as cultural processes which occur in relationships, in this case imperial relationships.[2] I focus on the late nineteenth century, a period that marks a new departure in Anglo-Muslim relations in the context of the British Empire, both in England and abroad, shifting the ground on which British identity politics operated.

While the fluid and changing nature of the concepts *British* and *English* and their close relationship are central to this study, these terms are not used interchangeably: here the word *British* refers to the British Empire and the government responsible for administering it, including the individuals employed by that government, as well as to Her Majesty's subjects throughout the world; *English*, on the other hand, describes a national and cultural identity distinct from Great Britain and the rest of the Empire, but nevertheless dependent on the imperial mission for self-definition.[3]

Because no single project could begin to cover the countless contacts through which *Englishness* was defined in relation to Islam during the late nineteenth century, this study concentrates on certain historical developments that are especially interesting in light of the questions at hand. Chapters two and three discuss the role of the British Government and English activists respectively in the campaign to suppress slave traffic in Egypt and surrounding areas. Despite diverse backgrounds and opinions among members within these groups, and disagreements between them, government officials and British and Foreign Anti-Slavery Society (BFASS) members redefined English culture and proper English gender roles in similar terms. The two chapters combined provide an examination of the relationships between activism in England, the implementation of government policy in Egypt and imperial encounters, as well as the production of identities and ideologies associated with these efforts.

Chapters four and five expand on and add a critical dimension to the previous two by showing how beliefs about Englishness, English gender roles and Islam, which British officials and BFASS activists spoke of as obvious truths, were recreated and understood in very different ways in the metropole. Using materials such as feminist and women's writings, scholarly books and articles, anti-vice materials, and Christian and missionary publications, chapter four examines the debates regarding

INTRODUCTION

what was referred to in England as 'the woman question'. It focuses on the role of the harem, female slavery and the Muslim woman in defining the identities that informed these conflicts. Chapter five explains how the concept of the English nation as the centre of an empire helped to establish a place in England for Islam. The lives and writings of Muslims in that country contradicted the dominant discourses presented by anti-slavery advocates and others, as did the words of non-Muslims who sympathised with the faith. In light of the second half of the book, the anti-slavery activity discussed in the first half must be understood as not simply an effort to export English values or gender roles abroad, but a means through which these contested ideas were defined. This campaign, therefore, had as much to do with English domestic as it did with Egyptian and British imperial politics.

This book is a part of a growing field of scholarship which seeks to understand the development of English national identities in the context of British imperialism. Scholars such as Kathleen Wilson, Graham Dawson, Ian Baucom and Catherine Hall have explored the ways in which experiences of empire have impacted on formations of Englishness.[4] My work contributes also to the study of Orientalism by considering representations of Islam and the harem, a topic usually associated with literary and cultural studies, in relation to the more traditional historical narrative based on archival research and describing the unfolding of specific events and developments such as the implementation of British foreign policy.[5]

The primary contribution that this study makes to the field is that it illuminates the complex process whereby individuals, through political activities both in England and abroad, created English identities that were informed by their understandings of Islam during a critical period in the development of Anglo-Muslim relations in the context of the vast network of relationships which comprised the global cultural system known as the British Empire. The practice of understanding the West and Western identities in relation to the Orient or the Islamic East had existed since the Middle Ages.[6] However, certain political developments and the increased, more involved and more intimate contact between English people and both Muslims and Islam during the late nineteenth century complicated and even transformed methods of interaction. For example, any attempt to describe the newly established Muslim communities in England required original representations.

Contemporary identities informed by new understandings of the relationship between Englishness and Islam were not simply produced and then exchanged in a fixed and stable form like a product shipped from one imperial port to another. Rather their creation, re-creation and exchange were interdependent on one another, constituting one complex process. Through individual relationships historical actors developed their own beliefs about these ideas. They drew from existing representations of them and from ideological systems available within British imperial culture, such as, broadly speaking, Christianity, liberalism and social Darwinism, as well as their own creative and intellectual resources.[7] Their perspectives were mediated through concerns of class, gender, race, nation and religion, as well as through more organised loyalties such as to the British Government, the BFASS and specific religious or feminist associations. Historical actors were limited in that they had to make themselves understood by their contemporaries in light of their particular circumstances, but the ways in which they did so were not inevitable, predetermined or an obvious effect of a larger cause. As they expressed these new or continually changing identities verbally and through other types of action, they contributed to the larger cultural system, creating a dynamic between the local and the global or the specific situation and the British Empire as a whole.[8]

A definition of *Englishness* created in relation to Islam that emerged at any given time necessarily developed and was understood in the context of the multiple and even contradictory perspectives circulating throughout this cultural system. As a result the concepts around which individuals organised and defined themselves and others – concepts in which they had a great deal invested, emotionally and politically, and which made action not just meaningful but possible – must be understood as temporary, situational and incomplete creations, despite the illusion that they describe a permanent, essential truth.[9] This open-ended, amorphous quality contributed to the appeal and, therefore, the power of these identities, which could be redefined as circumstances changed, and the flexibility of these terms allowed heterogeneous individuals to particularise their own versions of them. For despite the underlying unity and stability implied by the terms *English*, *British* or *Muslim*, they were used to describe people with diverse interests, perspectives and concerns, as well as multiple ways of identifying themselves. Which of them would be given primacy at any given moment might depend on, for example, gender or class perspectives, and which would actually translate into political action and how would have been impossible to predict.[10]

The instability of the terms used to define identity as well as the continually fluctuating nature of the imperial cultural system as a whole belie the concrete material realities which often resulted from these ideas, as well as the obstacles and limitations experienced by individuals operating in this system. All had to work within the constraints of their particular situation or set of circumstances and within unequal power relationships. For example, the female slaves living in a harem or

INTRODUCTION

the freed slaves in Egypt had few options, and even anti-slavery advocates who worked on their behalf were uninterested in their perspectives. Similarly, most Muslim immigrants could do little to change the English public's perception of their religion. Even those with official authority, such as Sir Evelyn Baring, later Lord Cromer, who acted as Her Britannic Majesty's consul-general and agent in Egypt and had an entire military and administrative body responsible for implementing the imperial policies he formulated, had to conform to certain expectations. Had Baring decided to embrace Islam and let his new beliefs inform official decisions, to give an extreme example, he would have lost the confidence of his subordinates and been dismissed from his position.

Social conditions could, and did, impose limits on historical actors, who were restricted both by what their specific situations would allow and, of equal importance, by what they believed they would allow. However, individual agency came into play as well, and the tension between the roles of these two factors in identity formation runs throughout this work. The context may have provided opportunities and necessary support for how experiences were perceived and defined, but it did not guarantee that those experiences would be understood in one way rather than another.[11] The people discussed in this book operated within social constraints; nevertheless, they made individual decisions regarding their actions, and contributed unique perspectives and ways of identifying themselves to British imperial culture.

In this study I treat the British Empire not as an arena wherein different cultures interacted or even fused, but rather as a vast global and cultural system in its own right.[12] This system connected people from different continents, backgrounds and traditions, and was similar in many ways to the Atlantic world with which it intersected and overlapped.[13] To understand the Empire as a legitimate focus of analysis and a cohesive whole does not imply that any sort of unified outlook existed. For those who share a culture do not necessarily have the same beliefs, goals or interests; rather they have enough in common to allow them to engage in dialogue and compete to define issues according to their own concerns.[14]

While the idea of a centre with surrounding peripheries is very much a part of the ideology of imperialism and necessarily affected cultural production and exchange, the process of defining *Britishness*, *Englishness* and *Islam* though imperial encounters was not confined to the one area or to the other, but existed in a variety of ways in both places and continually crossed the boundary between the two. As a result, events in, for example, London influenced those in Cairo, and vice versa, and colonial interaction occurred in England as well as throughout British-occupied territories.[15] Similarly, because the borders that defined what was Eastern, Oriental or Islamic – usually, but not always, in opposition to what was Western, English or British – and created hierarchies based on these ideas were forged through multiple relationships within both England and Egypt as opposed to simply between the two, it is also necessary to understand borderland as existing everywhere in the Empire.[16]

To summarise, *identity* is a complex concept that has been used by many scholars in different ways, but for the purposes of this book it is a process that occurred in historical relationships in the metropole and peripheries of empire.[17] The process was characterised by continual creation, re-creation and exchange of ideas within the cultural imperial system. Despite the importance of social conditions, agency ultimately determined why certain perspectives or ways of understanding individual identities were accepted and other, equally plausible ones, were not. The appeal and power of these concepts had to do with their broad and flexible nature, which allowed them to include a variety of different, even contradictory, meanings and to change as historical circumstance changed.

In addition to the overall theme of the book, individual sections contribute to the understanding of certain historical developments. My work on the anti-slavery campaign in Egypt differs from previous studies on the topic both in terms of the specific details of the narrative and, more importantly, in exploring it in relation to the increasingly important role of Islam in British imperial politics and English identity formation during the late nineteenth century. This approach necessarily gives rise to new questions concerning efforts to transgress the boundaries of and to reform the Muslim harem.[18] By focusing on gender and imperialism in late nineteenth-century Egypt, the discussion helps to provide a context for recent scholarship on contemporary debates over the proper role of women in that society in relation to the growing movement for national independence.[19] Chapter two also expands and elaborates on the idea that British imperialists in Egypt hoped both to penetrate the forbidden space of the harem themselves and to take action that would have a profound impact on that space.[20]

Chapter five contributes to the history of Muslims and Islam in England by focusing on the critical but relatively unexamined period when that religion first was defined *both* as beyond the pale of true Englishness while nevertheless having a legitimate place in England as the centre of the Empire. The Muslims who lived in England, the focus of chapter five, were not the same people encountered by those who worked to suppress the slave trade in Egypt. In fact, the Muslims discussed in the different sections of the book reveal more about the diversity than the unity of the Islamic world.[21] However, my approach

INTRODUCTION

intends to examine different ways in which ideas about Islam developed and informed identities in the ever-changing imperial context of English national life during the late nineteenth century rather than to draw conclusions about Muslims in general. A focus on the creation of identities in a variety of situations and through historical developments both in England and Egypt provides an ideal way of exploring the relationship between British imperial identities and English national identities created through the imperial mission.

New imperial departures

It is fruitful to consider questions of identity, raised by the recent generation of colonial and postcolonial scholars, with regard to occupied Egypt because this area fitted squarely into the British imperial cultural system of the late nineteenth century. It was not a remote outpost, but an area of central importance, and the British methods of governing Egypt and the attitudes of Her Majesty's officers towards the Egyptians can best be described as *colonial*.

Egypt never officially became a colony, despite occupation, because the British Government could not afford to offend the other European powers which had a stake in that country. The image of internationalism had to be maintained, with citizens of France, Italy, Greece, Austria, Germany and other countries being employed in the service of the Egyptian Government. Any threat to this system could have provoked the combined force of the Russian and French navies against Britain's small Mediterranean fleet, thus jeopardising British access to the Suez Canal. However, despite the internationalist nature of the civil service in Egypt, the British still exercised considerably more control in the central administration than did any of the other powers; even the French, who had more influence than the rest, had a staff only half the size of the British, the majority in subordinate positions.[22]

Concern for international diplomacy as well as pressure from the 'little Englanders', or anti-imperialists, persuaded representatives of the British Government to downplay their involvement in Egypt despite the fact that foreign policy in that country was characterised by an aggressive, even colonial, approach.[23] The Egyptian Army was disbanded and replaced with British troops. Even while repeatedly promising to evacuate, British officials continued to take actions which only increased their power and expanded their role in Egyptian affairs. The occupation lasted seventy-two years and involved the British in the political, social, economic and judicial life of the country.

Sir Evelyn Baring governed with an autocratic style. While the *khedive* was allowed to retain his title and was publicly supported by the British, Baring was the real ruler.[24] He was accountable only to the British Government. British advisors were installed in key ministries, and all ministers, including Egyptian ones, were required to obey them, their failure to do so being grounds for dismissal. This system was known as the 'veiled protectorate', with Egypt officially becoming a protectorate in 1914.

The tension between the colonial nature of British rule in Egypt and efforts to maintain a radically different public image is apparent in the oft-quoted report of Lord Dufferin, the special envoy of Her Majesty's Government in Egypt and the ambassador to Istanbul. Dufferin stated that speedy evacuation was the goal, but he also emphasised that Egypt should be rehabilitated and reformed, and that European ascendancy should be maintained. Evacuation was hardly compatible with reforms of law and administration based 'on the Indian model', and Baring himself saw Dufferin's instructions as contradictory, stating that they 'forbade him to state in clear and positive terms the inevitable inference to be drawn from his own proposals', the necessity of a prolonged and involved British occupation.[25]

This reference to the Indian model is significant, for while, as I maintain, the Egyptian experience marked a new departure in terms of British involvement in the Islamic world dramatically different from previous encounters in South Asia, the Raj influenced the colonial nature of occupation. In this respect, Egypt and India, the latter the most celebrated colony in the Empire, had much in common, and many of the British officials in Egypt had served previously or spent time in India. The Indian experience provided the only real model for ruling people understood as having an ancient civilisation and deeply entrenched, stable forms of self-government.[26] As a result, during the course of the occupation, British and British–Indian institutions and methods, in areas ranging from education to public health, replaced Ottoman, French and Egyptian ones.[27] Similarly, efforts to reform the Egyptian legal and judicial system on an English model, which are discussed in chapter two, had a precedent in India.[28]

During his posting in India, Baring developed his basic theories regarding government in the East. He considered both Egyptians and Indians to be Oriental 'subject races' in need of leadership, and while Baring's extensive international experience taught him that the East and the West were not monoliths, he nevertheless understood the gulf 'which divides all Westerners from all Orientals' to be much wider than the internal divisions within these groups.[29] He believed that autocratic rule was necessary in both Egypt and India because the peoples of those countries were used to despotism, and while 'free institutions' may be able to thrive in England, he could not 'make a Western silk purse out of an Eastern sow's ear'.[30] While the colonial nature of the British administration in Egypt may have been downplayed by those who had an interest in promoting an image of internationalism, the colonial nature of the ideas and identities associated with Egypt's occupation could not be denied.

Baring's beliefs had much in common with the views of anthropologists, social scientists and others who addressed an English audience during the late nineteenth century. Darwin's theory of natural selection, which had become increasingly popular, assumed a gradual hierarchy distinguishing the inferior, or less evolved, from the superior or more evolved. English social Darwinists such as Herbert Spencer applied it to human relationships, justifying inequalities of all kinds, such as those based on race, class, religion, nationality and culture, and contending that entire societies were inferior and less morally or intellectually developed than others.[31] When applied to the imperial context this perspective defined British rule as a benevolent enterprise which gave colonised peoples a government far superior to what they would have had otherwise as well as a model which would help them to evolve, so that eventually they would be able to govern themselves effectively.

This perspective explains the official policy of occupation and reform followed by evacuation, for while modernisation was the goal, Anglicisation and modernisation were considered one and the same. The anti-slavery campaign represented one aspect of the British effort to reform Egyptian society according to an English model, which was itself redefined through this campaign, as the following chapters will show. Anti-slavery activity became synonymous with the 'civilising mission' and contributed to English hegemony abroad, which justified an aggressive colonial foreign policy.

The British would not have been as successful as they were without a certain degree of complicity among Egyptians themselves, for there were many who were willing to adopt the imperialist ideology and work within the British bureaucracy. Even before occupation Khedive Ismail declared: 'My country is no longer in Africa; we are now part of Europe. It is therefore natural for us to abandon our former ways and to adopt a new system.'[32]

The fact that such an approach was taken in the late nineteenth century contradicts the common assumption that although imperialism in the early 1800s was characterised by attempts to reform occupied countries, later attitudes towards colonised peoples were based on maintaining authoritarian rule while preserving the existing culture as much as possible.[33] It also contradicts the generally accepted interpretation that the British were drawn into Egypt by internal crises and 'forced' to stay, and that they 'muddled and drifted with events' rather than imposed their will.[34] For in the case of the anti-slavery campaign the effective suppression of the trade required considerable time, effort and resources as well as the motivation and ability to overcome resistance to their goals in the country itself. Such an endeavour was orchestrated not by reluctant, uncertain individuals, but rather by people who saw themselves as reformers and bearers of civilisation, and who worked with the intention of having a profound impact on Egyptian society. Both in terms of actual policies pursued and identities formed in relation to them, the British experience in late nineteenth-century Egypt was essentially imperial.

A significant portion of this book deals with British efforts to eliminate slavery in Egypt and surrounding areas during the late nineteenth century, from the activities of government officials and BFASS activists to the role of this issue in English gender politics, and then finally how the words and actions of Muslims in England and those sympathetic to Islam in that country challenged the dominant discourses of the movement. I have chosen to focus on this campaign because it represents an unprecedented action that occurred during a critical period in the development of Anglo-Muslim relations and in the context of an imperial cultural system in flux. It was both a result of and a contributor to the increasing importance of Islam within the British Empire, examination of which helps to shed light on the formation of Englishness and the British imperial mission in relation to ideas about Islam during this time, highlighting the central role that gender played in this process, from domestic relationships in Egypt and England to the international political arena.

While the British had a history of abolitionist activity with respect to slavery in places such as the West Indies, the United States and Brazil, it did not prepare them for these new encounters.[35] Similarly, even though the Indian model was influential in many ways, it was of limited value when it came to contesting Muslim authorities close to their centres of power and in an area with a highly concentrated Muslim population: A number of al-Azhar's scholars, recognised as some of the most important in the Islamic world, opposed the British agenda; in Mecca even Ottoman fermans, or imperial edicts, regarding slavery were resisted or ignored; and the Ottoman sultan, whose administration required the service of hundreds of slaves, was regarded as a religious as well as political leader. In addition, Cairo, Mecca and Istanbul were key areas for slave-trading. Finally, the Islamic powers of the Mediterranean had been a source of fear and wonder for English people throughout the seventeenth and early eighteenth centuries, and even as late as the early nineteenth century, the Government was reluctant to use excessive force in this important strategic and commercial area.[36]

INTRODUCTION

In light of these considerations, the British decision to occupy Egypt and initiate an anti-slavery campaign involved entering new political and ideological territory. It would, therefore, require a redefinition of the British role and imperial mission in respect of Muslim practices.

Further complicating this situation and marking it as a new departure in imperial politics, both in terms of the history of anti-slavery activity and Anglo-Muslim relations, was the fact that slavery in Egypt during this period was closely associated with the harem, the women's and children's quarters in the Muslim home. Efforts to suppress it necessarily involved the British in the private, domestic lives of Egyptians, defining proper and improper family relationships, and thereby their own national identities, in gendered terms. The literal meaning of 'harem', or *harim*, is 'inviolable': it is from the same root as the word used to refer to sacred spaces, such as the inside of a mosque. Likewise, the domestic harem was a sanctuary from the outside world, entry to which was forbidden to men who were not members of the immediate family. Female slaves, destined for the harem, were in demand because of their reproductive capabilities as well as their productive labour.[37] Once sold, they would become servants, concubines, or wives.[38]

British interest in the harem and the plight of the female slave reflects shifting power relationships in the Mediterranean. Prior to 1750, fears of Muslims in this region were expressed in narratives that included the forced sodomy of captured British seamen, with almost no reference to the fate of females also sold into slavery in North Africa. However, with Ottoman decline and British ascendancy, and the presumed safety of the latter's soldiers and sailors, came a new interest in the harem and stories highlighting not male but female vulnerability.[39]

When the British invaded Egypt in 1882 they found themselves governing, for the first time, a relatively unified Muslim society closely linked to centres of power and authority in the Islamic world. Baring himself noted that while India's Muslims were strong numerically, they constituted a religious minority living among a majority five times their size, while Egypt, in comparison, had a 'smaller but more compact body of Moslems, who are more subject to the influences of their spiritual leaders'.[40] In addition, anti-slavery activity challenged certain Muslim practices and traditions, and ultimately the religious and legal system which regulated them. While some Muslims were willing to assist British efforts, believing that they were compatible with and even in the true spirit of their religion, and many Muslims, including those discussed in chapter five, did not own slaves and had no interest in preserving the institution of slavery, British officials encountered considerable resistance from both religious authorities and a number of their followers who opposed those efforts in the name of religion. With the occupation of Egypt and the accompanying anti-slavery efforts, the British began to play a more involved role in the Islamic world, asserting their influence and challenging authorities in close proximity to the centres of power.

Muslims of British-occupied Egypt had inherited centuries'old traditions of Islamic jurisprudence concerned with the status, rights and obligations of slaves and freed slaves. For example, during the thirteenth century, debates addressing topics such as marriage between a freed slave woman and a slave man; whether a woman's status as slave or free should be the primary factor in determining the terms of divorce, and what happens to a female slave when the foetus she is carrying is given freedom, were summarised by Muhammad al-Qurtubi, a respected figure in the history of Islamic legal scholarship, whose writings were considered authoritative and were consulted by later generations in Egypt and elsewhere.[41] In addition, Islamic law placed limits on the rights of the master with respect to his female slaves.[42] For example, they could not be forced into prostitution, and once a slave became pregnant with her master's child she could not be resold; moreover, the child would be free and have inheritance rights.[43] According to Islamic jurisprudence, regardless of the particular interpretation or school of thought, the female slave of the harem could not be treated in an arbitrary manner: despite her obvious disadvantages and position of inferiority, she remained squarely within the pale of the Muslim family and the legal system.

Islamic law requires masters to treat their slaves humanely, and efforts were taken throughout the Ottoman Empire, including Egypt, to prevent cruelty towards them. In 1846 the Ottoman Sultan closed the slave market in Istanbul because slaves were being mistreated. This action was entirely an Ottoman initiative and part of a larger programme of reform. Other fermans which placed restrictions on the slave trade, such as one issued in 1847, were justified to their subjects in part as a measure to prevent abuse, and soon after taking office Khedive Ismail issued a proclamation stating that slaves treated cruelly will be freed in accordance with Islamic law.[44] One British Embassy official in Istanbul even remarked that Ottoman police officers, who usually resented British interference, showed 'goodwill and zeal' when dealing with cases of cruelty to slaves and even used their private influence to persuade their masters to free them.[45]

Many Muslims believed that their religion provided a moral framework that would promote justice and discourage cruelty or oppression whether or not slave-owners were made accountable for their actions in public or before a court of law. Under Islam slaves were renamed *raqiq*, a term that connotes tenderness, poverty and need, in order to remind

INTRODUCTION

owners of their slaves' vulnerability and of their own duty to treat them with kindness and mercy;[46] and the devout Muslim slave-owner, conceiving God to be all-knowing and all-powerful, would believe that he or she ultimately would have to answer to God regarding the treatment of slaves. In addition, the *Qur'an* encourages marriage to slaves and considers class differences less important than religious ones, stating that 'a believing slavegirl is better than an idolatress'.[47]

Finally, a tradition of liberating slaves according to Islamic principles existed in Egypt. Nineteenth-century records of the religious courts document individuals who bought slaves for the purpose of liberating them, declaring them free *Li-Wajhi*, or for the sake of God – a practice engaged in also by the khedives. In addition, slaves who were not given immediate emancipation might be promised freedom after a certain amount of time or upon the death of their master.[48]

Despite this indigenous tradition of emancipation and the above guidelines, cruelty towards and exploitation of slaves existed in nineteenth-century Egypt. Raids to capture slaves could be brutal, and traders and owners did not always respect the legal rights of slaves or the Qur'anic verses regarding them. The above-mentioned Ottoman initiatives to prevent cruelty are exceptional. In general the Government and legal system had a very limited influence over slave-owners regarding their slaves and rarely attempted to monitor their actions. Yet prominent Muslim authorities were reluctant to abolish slavery on the grounds that just as they could not allow what Muhammad had forbidden so they could not forbid what he had allowed. For them abuse of what they considered an essentially just system did not constitute grounds for replacing it by substituting Muslim laws with Western or English laws.[49]

Slavery was recognised as legitimate and was even defended by these Muslims, but not because Islam encourages it – on the contrary, the Qur'an repeatedly praises the freeing of slaves as a meritorious act. It was accepted rather because believers understood that the religious and legal system in place created a just and humane society for slaves as well as slave-owners. Different conceptions of justice and varying views as to who should enforce it remained at the heart of the conflicts through which new identities were forged between British anti-slavery workers and those who resented their influence.

While officially the British tried to suppress slave-trading of all kinds and referred simply to 'slavery' as opposed to 'harem slavery', they realised that the majority of slaves in Egypt and the surrounding areas were destined for the harem. In 1838, female slaves in Cairo outnumbered the males by a ratio of six to one.[50] As Appendix 1 shows, the majority of slaves (8,507 of 14,135, or 64 per cent) manumitted by British authorities

[13]

between 1877 and 1897 were female.[51] This is a large percentage considering that it was much more difficult for a female slave to escape from the harem and seek manumission than it was for a male slave to escape his master. Statements by British officials support these numbers. For example, they would make comments such as that recently liberated slaves were 'as usual' mostly female; one noted that 'the overwhelming majority' of the slaves seeking refuge at Her Majesty's embassy in Turkey were female;[52] another stated that the 'large majority of slaves in Egypt are women'.[53] The British consul in Damascus mentioned that three-quarters of the slaves imported to the area were girls between the ages of 10 and 14 years, and officials would report discovering slave caravans comprising just women and children.[54]

While British officials usually did not include age as a category on the lists of the slaves they manumitted, they frequently mentioned children in their reports and correspondence, and were they to be taken into consideration when analysing table 1.1's data would increase the percentage of slaves destined for the harem. For children were much in demand: they were inexpensive to keep, and they could learn the language and be trained in the ways of the household from an early age. British officials regularly encountered slave *dhows* in the Red Sea filled entirely with children, as well as young slaves in groups of 50–100 aboard steamers; and one BFASS contact reported a caravan bound for Egypt proper consisting of 100 slaves, all of a 'tender age'.[55]

The harem- and female-oriented slave trade in Egypt and the surrounding areas was reflected in the prices of slaves. The highest prices went not to the strongest and hardest-working slaves, but rather to those who would seem to make the best wives or concubines. Attractive young women and girls were the most expensive and were referred to as 'slaves of choice'. For example, one British official noted that while the price for most slaves ranged between $8 and $50, a beautiful Abyssinian girl could be sold for $300.[56] Circassian women were so expensive that they were regarded as a luxury or a status symbol for the harems of the wealthy *pashas* and *beys*. Female slaves would decrease in value with age,[57] yet they were almost always more expensive than the males, regardless of age, background or area of origin: an ordinary female slave could demand an average of 20 per cent more money than a male slave.

In addition to women and children who would reside in the harem, eunuch slaves were procured to guard it. One British official called them 'necessary adjuncts' of the harem and concluded that even if slavery were eliminated, demand for eunuchs would continue.[58] Reports of the prices of eunuchs further support the idea that the kind of slavery practised in Egypt had much to do with domestic life. An

INTRODUCTION

ordinary male slave cost between $20 and $100, but the eunuch could cost $250;[59] similarly, a young boy, once turned into a eunuch, could be sold for 5–8 times his original price.[60] While a number of religious authorities condemned the practice of castrating boys for the purpose of maintaining a supply of eunuch slaves, the Muslim man's right to have such a guard for his harem was assumed, and when one British official suggested levying a heavy tax on men who employed eunuchs he was told that such a measure would be too great a shock to the 'social prejudices' of the Egyptians.[61]

The actual numbers of these slaves are difficult to determine from Foreign Office and other available records, and British officials could not always be sure which male slaves were eunuchs. Most reports simply listed females and males, with occasional reference to the 'third sex'. The reports that do mention the number of eunuchs confirm their importance, as they could comprise 10–20 per cent of all slaves found in a newly liberated group.[62] Richard Burton estimated that not less than 8,000 of these slaves were imported annually into Egypt and Turkey.[63]

Male slaves functioned in capacities other than that of eunuch harem guard: some became agricultural labourers and personal servants or assistants; others were absorbed into the military–administrative system.[64] Often young slave boys would serve a master in exchange for food and shelter with the understanding that upon reaching adulthood they would enter the workforce as free men. The province of Isna in Upper Egypt was exceptional because therein existed a form of agricultural slavery which had more in common with New World slavery, although on a much smaller scale, than it did with the slavery practised throughout the rest of Egypt.[65] In this area male slaves were in greater demand than elsewhere; and as male slaves were not confined to the harem, they could be monitored more easily and liberated by the British than could females. Officials who assisted them did not have to worry about offending Egyptian men by interfering with their private domestic lives. However, despite the advantages of suppressing this form of slavery, the British showed comparatively little interest in it; in fact, Baring rejected proposals to focus on eliminating only male slavery, noting that such a strategy would be 'hardly worthwhile'.[66]

Because ordinary male slaves as well as women, children, and eunuchs were sold, I refer simply to slavery and the slave trade throughout the book, as do most of the contemporary letters, reports and articles on the topic. However, unless otherwise indicated, these terms refer to a slavery that was female- and harem-oriented and was understood as such by those involved in it and in its elimination. The importance that this aspect of Egyptian slavery had for the British can hardly be overemphasised, for as the chapters that follow illustrate, in

[15]

the context of this campaign the woman of the Muslim harem became a focal point for a number of gender tensions and concerns within the British imperial system. Historical actors worked on her behalf, defined themselves and their mission in relation to her, and used ideas about her to promote competing versions of proper English gender roles.

This brief introduction to the salient issues surrounding the campaign to suppress slavery in late nineteenth-century Egypt would not be complete without addressing the issue of race. For the way that race was understood in this context both distinguished activities there from previous anti-slavery work and informed the process through which new identities were created. Even when officials did not specifically refer to themselves in terms of race, to label slaves in that way gave credence to a global imperial ideological system that included all of humanity and impacted on identity politics in England as well as Egypt.

In Egypt slaves were labelled by skin colour and divided into four categories, which affected their status and treatment: *al-bayda'* (white), *al-samra'* (brown), *al-habashiyya* (Abyssinian or Ethiopian), and *al-sawda'* (black).[67] British officials employed a similar system, but classified slaves into three categories instead of four: 'white', or 'Circassian'; 'Abyssinian', or 'Galla'; and 'Negro', 'black' or sometimes 'Nubian'. These terms almost always appear on reports or references to specific cases of manumitted slaves, and they influenced both policy and the actions of individuals who dealt with slave traffic. When referring to slaves, I use the terms that the British used – 'Abyssinian', 'white', and 'black'.[68] (For the sake of simplicity I will not include quotation marks every time.)

The way that race functioned in late nineteenth-century Egypt was, as with identities in general, far more complex, fluid and situational than the labels themselves would seem to indicate. They did not simply reflect obvious truths but were, with effort, imposed on and adopted by diverse individuals. As one schoolteacher in Cairo related, 'the variety of races and complexions among the crowds here is at first quite bewildering, but in time the eye learns to distinguish each of the principal ones, at least'.[69] In addition, physical appearance was only one, and often not the most important, marker of race. For example, one influential nineteenth-century ethnologist understood race in terms of religion, political institutions, customs and language, as well as physical type, ranking cultural characteristics as more important than physical ones and insisting that language provided 'the most reliable indicator of racial affinity'.[70]

Because of the unstable and multidimensional nature of race, it functioned in a variety of ways simultaneously in the British imperial cul-

INTRODUCTION

tural system, within the metropole and the peripheries as well as between them. For example, British and Egyptian officials agreed that certain physical characteristics should serve as the primary indicators of race when labelling slaves and freed slaves, creating a bond between the two groups and reinforcing this belief system in their own societies.[71] Yet the British also considered the Egyptians to be 'Oriental subject races', not so much because of their appearance as because of their institutions and political system. Similarly, while the Circassian slave was not English and would not have been considered a part of the Anglo-Saxon race because of her culture, language and beliefs, her white skin nevertheless served as a marker of race, signifying difference from those around her and a certain affinity with the English. White slaves were often described as resembling English women, and the Circassian slave served as a powerful image that shocked English audiences and helped to highlight the connections between anti-slavery efforts abroad and gender politics in their own country, a theme explored in the following chapters.

White female slaves came primarily from Circassia but also from Georgia, Eastern Europe and Russia. While some were captured during raids, others were sold into slavery by their poverty-stricken families in the hope that they would eventually marry a Turk or an Arab able to provide for them financially or else be selected for the imperial harem. Unlike slavery in the New World, where the label 'white' was considered incompatible with slave status, Ottoman and Egyptian authorities regarded white slavery as legitimate, and even made efforts to protect it from British influence. The khedive initially tried to exempt white slaves from the Anglo-Egyptian convention signed in 1877, but finally, after much negotiation, agreed to include them in the convention's annex, with the stipulation that the trade in white slaves could continue for seven years after the slave trade in general had been abolished.[72] Similarly, only the trade in black and Abyssinian slaves was prohibited by the 1880 convention with the Ottoman Empire.

White slavery was an especially sensitive issue because of class concerns, and British officials understood the necessity of diplomacy and tact when approaching authorities on the subject. White slaves were owned primarily by the wealthy and the powerful – the very people with whom the British were trying to negotiate slave-trade agreements – often being the wives and mothers of such men. One British official noted that the wife of the grand vizier had been a Circassian slave and that 'ladies in a still more exalted position had belonged to the same class'. He went on to explain that he would have been 'guilty of a gross impropriety' had he expressed his belief in the debasing consequences of a practice so much a part of the domestic life of the elite.[73]

Because white slaves were usually bought and sold with the understanding that they would become wives or concubines of their masters and mothers of the latter's children as opposed to servants, this form of slavery was seen as especially private by British officials and by local authorities who objected to imperial interference. In this respect certain Victorian ideas about the feminine domestic sphere and the importance of the divide between public and private life had much in common with the secluded harem, in which the *hudud*, or sacred boundaries, separated the female members of the family from the marketplace and the city streets.[74]

Often the buyers as well as the slaves were women. One British official explained that while men trade in black slaves, 'great ladies' do the same with Circassian slaves. In fact, it was common for a lady to buy a young female slave, and educate and socialise her in elite roles so that she could be married to a relative or a promising young man. This practice strengthened female social networks through mutually dependent relationships in the domestic sphere. The official went on to admit, however, that he did not really understand this practice because 'it is not easy to penetrate the mysteries of the harem'.[75]

While the white slave had a certain political and symbolic significance for both British and Egyptian officials, the majority of slaves were not classified as white. Abyssinian slaves were taken from the east coast of Africa, although many believed that their ancestors originally came from the Yemen. British officials described these women as tall with 'straight' features, and they were much in demand and could be among the highest-priced slaves. Black women came from the Sudan and other areas of Central and Southern Africa.[76]

British officials working to suppress the slave trade in Egypt and surrounding areas often regarded black slaves as subject to greater exploitation and oppression than the others. This attitude was a result in part of the horrifying slave raids in which all the men in an African village were slaughtered, and the women and children forced to embark on a miserable journey that left many of them dead. Black slaves moreover came closest to a contemporary English idea of how a slave looked, an idea which had already become a part of British imperial culture through representations made by anti-slavery workers during the earlier part of the century.

The anti-slavery campaign in late nineteenth-century Egypt, an unprecedented effort which involved British officials in the most private areas of the Muslim home and undermined religious authorities in a predominantly Muslim country close to the centres of power for that religion, occurred during the period when Islam was beginning to acquire a more prominent place in England. English people came into contact with the faith on a scale never before experienced. Thousands of books, articles, letters and speeches by both Muslims and non-Muslims were published on that topic for an English-speaking audience. In addition, Muslims began to establish communities in England and actively engage in politics there as well as in the Empire. It was during that period that a mosque was erected in the town of Woking, near London.

These two developments in England and in Egypt were not causally related: far more immigrants came from South Asia than from the Middle East, and British anti-slavery activities hardly would have inspired Muslims to travel to England. However, the fact that they occurred during the same period was not a coincidence, but was a reflection of the increasing importance of Islam in the British Empire. For imperial political and economic opportunities and concerns drew Muslims to England, inspired English interest in Islam and prompted British involvement in Egypt. During this period, British officials even referred to their own Government as a Muslim power.[77] It is therefore necessary to examine English identity formation in relation to Islam during this critical period.

In order to do so, it is necessary also to consult a variety of sources, including official documents such as Foreign Office records and correspondence as well as writings and visual representations of different types typically employed in the discourse on identity formation. For the historical narrative has an essential place in studies of empire and identity, and too often it is ignored in this field of scholarship. Examining the efforts of British officials to suppress the slave trade in Egypt, and taking into consideration both the policies dictated and their manner of implementation, reveal how these individuals created and expressed their national, gendered and imperial identities through their actions. For them words were secondary: as chapter two shows, for example, how they treated female slaves and freed female slaves over a thirty-year period in the course of the campaign communicates more about their attitudes than does what they actually said about them.

In addition, the systems of meaning created by British officials, as participants in a global imperial culture, impacted on processes of identity formation in England: The more outspoken of their contemporaries, discussed in subsequent chapters, were keenly aware of the implications of activities in Egypt for ideas about proper gender relationships, Englishness and Islam. BFASS activists, feminists, reformers and those sympathetic to that religion constructed positions informed by efforts abroad, as they responded to, engaged with and even worked to counter the assumptions of officialdom. To consider their representations without taking into account the complex dynamics between their formation and related developments in British foreign policy would be to present a fundamentally incomplete picture.

The British Empire, the British Isles and Englishness

Since the 1970s historians have been re-conceptualising the British past by challenging the common practice of assuming that the English story alone adequately covers the history of the British Isles and of the nations and cultures within them.[78] Therefore, it is important to discuss briefly how this work relates to that field and treats Englishness and Britishness with respect to current concerns.

I use the term *British* to refer to the Empire, its administrative apparatus, and a global imperial culture; it also describes the British State and its institutions: the crown, Parliament and the armed forces. During the late nineteenth century people residing in the British Isles and British-occupied territories around the world could claim a British identity and feel loyalty to that State and its Empire. Yet most had other ways of defining themselves, ways which often they considered to be of greater importance. British subjects might regard themselves as first and foremost Irish, Scottish, Welsh or Muslim, for example, without posing a threat to the State.[79] In fact, imperial participation and accomplishments provided a means through which to assert Scottish and Welsh identities.[80] The resilience of the Empire as a global system during this period had to do with its ability to accommodate different nations, cultures and persuasions. In addition, while it may have promoted English hegemony in some cases and primacy in others, it did not require or even allow everyone living within its borders to become *English*.[81]

British subjects had *composite* identities and which part of these identities would have primacy at any given time depended on the specific circumstances and the actions of individuals.[82] War and other crises could generate loyalty to the State, as could employment in the army, the navy, the Government or the East India Company. A sense of Britishness often assumed primacy for those who resided among people with whom they did not share a common national or cultural bond: for example, the retinues of British embassies; Scots, Irish, Welsh and English settlers in the British colonies or occupied territories; and Muslims in Victorian England. In such cases, the term *British* described people whose situations seemed to have more to do with the British State and the global imperial cultural system associated with it than with local developments or distinctions.[83]

People from every part of the British Isles contributed to the imperial project and to the campaigns discussed in this book. Ideas about the

INTRODUCTION

British mission developed as a result of the efforts of individuals who considered themselves Scottish, Welsh and Irish, as well as those who saw themselves as English.[84] Yet their assistance did not preclude the creation of *English* identities through these movements. English people did not always give others credit for imperial accomplishments and often regarded the British Empire and its institutions as their own.[85] It is the purpose of this book to explore the process of English identity formation in relation to the new imperial departures of the late nineteenth century with respect to Muslims and Islam.

With the notable exception of W. H. Quilliam and his Manx identity, discussed in chapter five, the sources here used to explore the anti-slavery campaign in Egypt, the gender debates in England and the Muslim presence in that country communicate contemporary ideas about Englishness in relation to Britishness, but say almost nothing about other national identities in the British Isles. A worthwhile project or projects for future research would be to mine the archives in Scotland, Ireland and Wales asking similar questions about the Empire, the nation, identity and Islam. Such an approach would be especially interesting given both the complex relationships between religious and national identities in the United Kingdom and the nineteenth-century trend towards convergence among the nations of the British Isles during this time of imperial expansion.[86]

This book focuses on English identity development, yet it is not Anglocentric in the traditional sense, for one of the marks of Anglocentric history has been to take Englishness for granted.[87] My approach involves looking critically at this process and considering it in the light of, and indeed as dependent on, a larger imperial culture. I see it not as fixed and stable but as continually contested, redefined and understood in relation to specific polices and actions, as well as what was considered un-English. I examine both the shifting borders within the country and experiences and influences from abroad. For these reasons the work shares common ground with the 'new British history.'

Notes

1 *A Cry From The Depths: The British Turk*, poem published in the *Women's Suffrage Journal*, 9 (October1878), 173.
2 Any attempt to reify identities by treating them as categories is problematical because their boundaries are inconstant. The social process of defining group identities in terms of categories is characterised by both 'the reality of inconstancy and the denial of this reality': Immanuel Wallerstein, 'The Construction of Peoplehood: Racism, Nationalism, Ethnicity', in Etienne Balibar and I. Wallerstein (eds), *Race, Nation, Class: Ambiguous Identities*, trans. Chris Turner (London: Verso, 1991), p. 77. The understanding of identity as manifesting itself in human relationships as opposed to existing in society as a structure or a category was proposed by E. P. Thompson in *The Making of the English Working Class* (London: Victor Gollancz,

1963), p. 9. Thompson's ideas are especially relevant considering that class and imperial identities have much in common especially in terms of defining power relations, and, as this study will show, they often overlapped and informed one another. Philip Dodd describes Englishness as a relationship rather than a category, noting that the 'definition of the English is inseparable from that of the non-English': 'Englishness and the National Culture', in Robert Colls and Philip Dodd (eds), *Englishness: Politics and Culture 1880–1920* (London: Croom Helm, 1986), p. 12.

3   Because of the close connection between Britishness and Englishness, discussion of these ideas can sometimes be confusing. For example, while the British and Foreign Anti-Slavery Society welcomed members from the British Isles, the British Empire and the world (hence its name), the organisation was in fact London-based and often self-consciously represented an English point of view, even associating the anti-slavery cause with Englishness. The difficulty that the Victorians had in maintaining clear and accepted distinctions between Englishness and Britishness testifies to the importance of examining the formation of national identity in relation to the Empire. This issue is discussed in more detail on pp. 20–1.

4   Kathleen Wilson, *The Island Race: Englishness, Empire and Gender in the Eighteenth Century* (London and New York: Routledge, 2003) and *The Sense of the People: Politics, Culture and Imperialism in England, 1715–1785* (Cambridge: Cambridge University Press, 1995); Graham Dawson, *Soldier Heroes: British Adventure, Empire and the Imagining of Masculinities* (London and New York: Routledge, 1994); Ian Baucom, *Out of Place: Englishness, Empire, and the Locations of Identity* (Princeton, NJ: Princeton University Press, 1999); Catherine Hall, *Civilising Subjects: Metropole and Colony in the English Imagination, 1830–1867* (Chicago, IL, and London: University of Chicago Press, 2002) and *White, Male and Middle-Class: Explorations in Feminism and History* (Cambridge: Polity Press, 1992). Also see Inderpal Grewal, *Home and Harem: Nation, Gender, Empire, and the Cultures of Travel* (Durham, NC, and London: Duke University Press, 1996); Antoinette Burton, *Burdens of History: British Feminists, Indian Women, and Imperial Culture, 1865–1915* (Chapel Hill and London: University of North Carolina Press, 1994); and John M. MacKenzie, *Propaganda and Empire: The Manipulation of British Public Opinion, 1880–1960* (Manchester: Manchester University Press, 1984).

5   This enormous field was pioneered by Edward Said's *Orientalism* (New York: Pantheon Books, 1978).

6   The representation of the East and Islam in the West during earlier periods has been well covered in recent scholarship: in addition to Said, see Norman Daniel, *Islam and the West: The Making of an Image* (Oxford: Oneworld Publications Ltd, 1993 [1960]) and *The Arabs and Mediaeval Europe* (London: Longman, 1975); Nabil Matar, *Islam in Britain 1558–1685* (Cambridge: Cambridge University Press, 1998).

7   Donald Woods Winnicott discussed how individuals invent meaning, as well as finding it in society at large: 'The Use of an Object and Relating Through Identifications', in *Playing and Reality* (London: Tavistock Publications, 1971); Benedict Anderson emphasises the necessity for creativity in the process of identity formation when he explains that the nation must be imagined because it can never be experienced directly – no one person can know everyone else in a nation: *Imagined Communities: Reflections on the Origin and Spread of Nationalism* (London: Verso, 1983), p. 15.

8   The relationship between the development of ideas and other forms of social action is explored throughout the book. It is of critical importance, for, as Gerald Platt observed, 'meaningless action never occurs', and while ideas do not dictate what people will do, individuals are forced to give their actions meaning in terms that are culturally available: 'Thoughts on a Theory of Collective Action: Language, Affect, and Ideology in Revolution', in Mel Albin (ed.), *New Directions in Psychohistory* (Lexington, MA: Lexington Books, 1980), p. 80. I paraphrase Gordon Wood, 'Ideology and the Origins of Liberal America', *The William and Mary Quarterly: A Magazine of Early American History and Culture*, 44 (July 1987), 628–40, at 631. Similarly, Pocock and Ashcraft have discussed how political ideologies render social action

INTRODUCTION

meaningful: J. G. A. Pocock, *Virtue, Commerce and History: Essays on Political Thought and History, Chiefly in the Eighteenth Century* (Cambridge: Cambridge University Press, 1985); and R. Ashcraft, *Revolutionary Politics and Locke's Two Treatises of Government* (Princeton, NJ: Princeton University Press, 1986), pp. 5–6.

9   The fluidity of identity has been addressed by a number of scholars: for example, Alberto Melucci understands identity as necessarily 'rooted in the present to deal with the fluctuations and metamorphoses': A. Melucci, *Nomads of the Present: Social Movements and Individual Needs in Contemporary Society*, ed. John Keane and Paul Mier (Philadelphia, PA: Temple University Press, 1989), p. 114; also see Melucci, 'The Process of Collective Identity', in Hank Johnston and Bert Klandermans (eds), *Social Movements and Culture* (Minneapolis: University of Minnesota Press, 1995), vol. 4, pp. 41–63. Similarly, Richard Handler has warned scholars not to reify identity but to treat it with as much suspicion as they would concepts such as *ethnic group* and *nation*. He notes that groups do not have 'essential identities' nor are they 'bounded objects'; instead identities should be understood as 'symbolic processes that emerge and dissolve in particular contexts of action': 'Is "Identity" a Useful Cross-Cultural Concept?' in John Gillis (ed.), *Commemorations: The Politics of National Identity* (Princeton, NJ: Princeton University Press, 1994), pp. 27–40, at 27 and 30. Finally, William Bloom notes the influence of shifting social, political and economic realities on the process of identity transformation as the individual redefines loyalties in an attempt to 'maximise psychological security': *Personal Identity, National Identity and International Relations* (Cambridge: Cambridge University Press, 1990), p. 71.

10 Fred Weinstein focuses on heterogeneity and the absence of predisposition in the formation of identities in *History and Theory After the Fall: An Essay on Interpretation* (Chicago, IL, and London: University of Chicago Press, 1990). These issues, as well as the situational nature of identity, are discussed also by Gerald Platt in 'Thoughts on a Theory of Collective Action', pp. 69–94.

11 Miguel Cabrera relates this idea in 'On Language, Culture, and Social Action', *History and Theory*, 40 (December 2001), 82–100.

12 As Edward Said's work has shown, modern imperialism is responsible for setting in motion a 'globalized process' characterised by the 'overlapping experience of Westerners and Orientals': *Culture and Imperialism* (New York: Alfred A. Knopf, 1993), p. xx.

13 For example, see David Armitage and Michael Braddick (eds), *The British Atlantic World, 1500–1800* (New York: Palgrave Macmillan, 2002); Joseph Roach's 'circum-Atlantic world', or 'oceanic interculture', described as a 'vortex in which commodities and cultural practices changed hands many times', in *Cities of the Dead* (New York: Columbia University Press, 1996), pp. 4–5; Paul Gilroy's transcultural, international, black Atlantic, in *The Black Atlantic: Modernity and Double Consciousness* (Cambridge, MA: Harvard University Press, 1993); D. W. Meinig's 'transoceanic network' connecting three continents while 'lacing itself ever more deeply and complexly into the body of Europe', in *The Shaping of America: A Geographical Perspective on 500 Years of History* (New Haven, CT, and London: Yale University Press, 1986), vol. 1: *Atlantic America, 1492–1800*, p. 74. Also of interest regarding exchange through mutual appropriation of meaning and re-contextualisation of ideas and objects within a global colonial culture, see Nicholas Thomas, *Entangled Objects: Exchange, Material Culture, and Colonialism in the Pacific* (Cambridge, MA: Harvard University Press, 1991).

14 Rick Fantasia and Eric Hirsch, 'Culture in Rebellion: The Appropriation and Transformation of the Veil in the Algerian Revolution', in Hank Johnston and Bert Klandermans (eds), *Social Movements and Culture* (Minneapolis: University of Minnesota Press, 1995), pp. 144–59.

15 Inderpal Grewal states the importance of understanding that spaces of colonial encounter were in the metropole as well as the periphery in *Home and Harem*, p. 4, and Antoinette Burton examines colonial contacts in Victorian England by focusing on three Indian travellers in *At the Heart of the Empire: Indians and the Colonial*

Encounter in Late-Victorian Britain (Berkeley: University of California Press, 1998). Other scholars, such as Ian Baucom and Susan Thorne, have shown how colonial alterity was projected onto peoples and areas that had existed in England for generations. Baucom focuses on the urban centres, which were seen as imperial spaces encroaching upon and destroying rural England, while Thorne examines the 'uneven and complex intersection' of the discourses relating to the 'heathen' abroad and the labouring poor living in English cities and towns: Baucom, *Out of Place*, pp. 55–62; and Thorne, '"The Conversion of Englishmen and the Conversion of the World Inseparable:" Missionary Imperialism and the Language of Class in Early Industrial Britain', in Frederick Cooper and Ann Laura Stoler (eds), *Tensions of Empire: Colonial Cultures in a Bourgeois World* (Berkeley: University of California Press, 1997), pp. 238–62, at 241.

16 Michael Taussig explains how 'all the land is borderland' when constructing identities in the colonial context. His discussion of the ways in which those who identified themselves with the West and those who did not have engaged in creative dialogues, not despite but because of their distorted images of each other, helps to illustrate the essentially mercurial and open-ended nature of cultural representation, as well as the circular process of exchange which characterises imperial relationships: *Mimesis and Alterity: A Particular History of the Senses* (New York and London: Routledge, 1993), p. 249; chapters 15 and 16 are especially interesting in this respect.

17 In recent decades a wealth of scholarship has been produced on the topic of identity in both the psychological and the historical sense. These two fields have much in common, and the former is helpful for historians interested in understanding nationalism. For a discussion of developments in these related fields see Lewis D. Wurgaft, 'Identity in World History: A Postmodern Perspective', *History and Theory: Studies in the Philosophy of History*, 34 (1995), 67–85.

18 Miers, Erdem and Beachey have discussed or given more general accounts of British efforts to suppress the slave trade in Egypt and surrounding areas: Suzanne Miers, *Britain and the Ending of the Slave Trade* (London: Longman, 1975); Y. Hakan Erdem, *Slavery in the Ottoman Empire and its Demise, 1800–1909* (London: Macmillan, 1996); and R. W. Beachey, *The Slave Trade of Eastern Africa* (New York: Harper & Row, 1976).

19 Leila Ahmed explains that because nineteenth-century Egyptians were concerned with reforming their society in order to compete with the West, the issue of the role and status of women emerged as a subject for debate on a scale not seen since the rise of Islam: *Women and Gender in Islam: Historical Roots of a Modern Debate* (New Haven, CT, and London: Yale University Press, 1992), p. 128. Thomas Philipp also explores the links between feminism and nationalism during this period and explains how nationalist arguments were used by those with radically different views or agendas regarding feminism and women's emancipation in Egypt: 'Feminism and Nationalist Politics in Egypt', in Lois Beck and Nikki Keddie (eds), *Women in the Muslim World* (Cambridge, MA: Harvard University Press, 1978), pp. 277–94. Beth Baron shows how both men and women participated in these debates, and that the 'women's awakening', or the rise of a female literary culture during the late nineteenth century, provided a foundation for the active role that women would play in politics and public life during the twentieth century: *The Women's Awakening in Egypt: Culture, Society, and the Press* (New Haven, CT, and London: Yale University Press, 1994).

20 A number of scholars have commented on this desire: see, for example, Timothy Mitchell, *Colonising Egypt* (Cambridge: Cambridge University Press, 1988), p. 112.

21 A study which calls attention to diversity rather than unity in Islam presents a more accurate portrayal of the historical reality. Aziz Al-Azmeh notes that 'there are as many Islams as there are situations that sustain it': *Islams and Modernities* (London: Verso, 1993), p. 1. Also see the collection of essays on this increasingly important topic in Abdul Aziz Said and Meena Sharify-Funk (eds), *Cultural Diversity and Islam* (New York: University Press of America, 2003).

INTRODUCTION

22 William M. Welch, *No Country for a Gentleman: British Rule in Egypt, 1883–1907* (New York: Greenwood Press, 1988), p. 52.
23 'Umar bin Salim 'Umar Babakur discusses European but especially British and French involvement in Egypt during the nineteenth century, focusing on their economic and political interests in the area and contemporary debates regarding the nature of the occupation and the proper course of action: *al-Tanafus al-Urubbi Hawla Hawd al-Nil wa 'Alaqat dhalika bi-Istirdad al-Sudan* (Alexandria: Dar al-Wafa' li-Dunya al-Tiba'a wa al-Nashr, 2002), pp. 15–52. The transliteration from Arabic to Roman script is based on the *International Journal of Middle East Studies*' guide, except when referring to names and terms commonly used in English or a source in which the Arabic has already been transliterated. Also, all spellings not in quotations have been modernised.
24 Baring's role and importance in British-occupied Egypt can hardly be overstated, and they have been acknowledged by previous historians, even by those whose work does not focus on him. For example, Welch explains that Baring 'towers above other Anglo-Egyptians as the uncrowned king of Egypt' and that writing a history without discussing him would be 'like a priest giving a sermon without reference to God': *No Country for a Gentleman*, p. xi.
25 Peter Mansfield, *The British in Egypt* (London: Weidenfeld & Nicolson, 1971), pp. 56–7; the Earl of Cromer, *Modern Egypt* (New York: Macmillan, 1908), vol. 1, p. 342.
26 The fact that the British Empire had no other precedent in ruling a people with these characteristics is addressed by Bernard Cohn in *Colonialism and its Forms of Knowledge: The British in India* (Princeton, NJ: Princeton University Press, 1996), pp. 57–8. Robert Tignor discusses the influence of the Indian experience on Egypt in *Modernization and British Colonial Rule in Egypt, 1882–1914* (Princeton, NJ: Princeton University Press: 1966). He explains that in India the British took responsibility for their rule and governed directly, while in Egypt they tended to conceal their power by operating through existing institutions and administrators. However, towards the end of the century their rule became more direct and obvious.
27 Robert Tignor, 'The "Indianization" of the Egyptian Administration Under British Rule,' *American Historical Review*, 68 (April 1963), 636–61.
28 Despite the study of Indian traditions and law codes in creating a legal system based on an '"ancient Indian constitution"', by the late eighteenth century English law had become the law of the land: Bernard Cohn, 'Law and the Colonial State in India', in *Colonialism and its Forms of Knowledge*, pp. 57–75.
29 The Earl of Cromer, 'The Government of Subject Races', *Edinburgh Review* (January 1908), reprinted in Earl of Cromer, *Political and Literary Essays, 1908–1913* (London: Macmillan, 1913), pp. 3–53, at 40.
30 Cromer, 'The Government of Subject Races', p. 25. This type of language functioned as an 'apparatus of power' in the imperial context: Homi Bhabha, 'The Other Question: Difference, Discrimination, and the Discourse of Colonialism' in Houston Baker Jr, Manthia Diawara and Ruth Lindeborg (eds), *Black British Cultural Studies: A Reader* (Chicago, IL, and London: University of Chicago Press, 1996), pp. 87–106, at 92. For an in-depth discussion of Baring's approach to governing India, on the one hand, and Egypt, on the other, see Roger Owen, 'The Influence of Lord Cromer's Indian Experience on British Policy in Egypt 1883–1907', in Albert Hourani (ed.), *Middle Eastern Affairs*, no. 4, *St Antony's Papers*, no. 17 (Oxford: Oxford University Press, 1965), pp. 109–39.
31 For example, Edward B. Tylor presented a theory of intellectual and moral evolution which he applied to cultures in *Primitive Culture: Researches into the Development of Mythology, Philosophy, Religion, Art and Custom* (London: John Murray, 1871), 2 vols. For discussion of the application of Darwin's ideas to social theory see Greta Jones, *Social Darwinism and English Thought: The Interaction Between Biological and Social Theory* (New Jersey: Humanities Press, 1980), pp. 140–59.
32 Quoted in Mansfield, *The British in Egypt*, p. 11. For more on the British occupation and rule in Egypt see: Mansfield, *The British in Egypt*; Afaf Lutfi al-Sayyid, *Egypt and Cromer: A Study in Anglo-Egyptian Relations* (New York: Praeger, 1969);

Tignor, *Modernization*; Welch, *No Country for a Gentleman*; and Ahmad Turbiyyn, al-fasl al-khamis 'Misr min Ihtilal Baritani ila Thawra (1919-1887)', *Tarikh Misr wa al-Sudan al-Hadith wa al-Mu'asir* (Beirut: Muwassasat al-Risala, 1994).

33 Francis Hutchins is the best-known historian to present this idea. His *The Illusion of Permanence: British Imperialism in India* (Princeton, NJ: Princeton University Press, 1967) deals specifically with India, but because he maintains that this change in attitude resulted not from events abroad but rather from the political situation in England, his argument would apply to other areas of imperial expansion as well.

34 Ronald Robinson and John Gallagher, *Africa and the Victorians: The Official Mind of Imperialism* (London: Macmillan, 1961), pp. 159, 120. Robinson and Gallagher are not the only historians to downplay the British initiative regarding imperialism: an entire generation of scholars, including Hutchins (note 34), shared this attitude.

35 The following historians contrast the European slave trade with that of Arab and Islamic North Africa, commenting on differences of culture, religion, and the treatment and experiences of slaves: Muhammad Razuq, 'Qadiyat al-Riqq fi Ta'rikh al-Maghrib,' *Majallat al-Buhuth al-Tarikhiyya*, 8:2 (July 1986), 269–89; Jamal Zakriya, Shawqi al-Jamal; and Salah al-Hamarna, *Mas'alat al-Riqq fi Ifriqiyya: Buhuth wa Dirasat* (Tunis: al-Munazzama al-'Arabiyya li al-Tarbiya wa al-Thaqafa wa al-'Ulum, 1989), pp. 19–70. In addition, 'Imad Ahmad Hilal describes in detail the role of slavery in nineteenth-century Egypt, from the origins of the slaves and the slave trade to their contributions to their status and position in both society and the Islamic judicial system in *al-Raqiq fi Misr fi al-qarn al-tasi' 'ashara* (Cairo, 1999). Muhammad Mukhtar addresses these same issues, but in an overview of slavery in Egypt from the rise of Islam until the early twentieth century, in *Bughyat al-Marid fi Shira' al-Jawari wa Taqlib al-'Abid: al-Awda' al-Ijtima'iyya li al-Raqiq fi Misr 642-1924* (Cairo: Khalid Mukhtar and Muhammad Mukhtar, 1997).

36 Linda Colley notes that dependence on certain Mediterranean powers meant that London would 'look the other way' when subjects were attacked by corsairs. In addition, she maintains that the British Royal Navy's mere bombardment of Algiers in 1816 rather than a full-scale military occupation and colonisation exhibits restraint rather than aggression in light of the circumstances and both internal and external pressures: *Captives: Britain, Empire and the World, 1600–1850* (London: Jonathan Cape, 2002), pp. 106–34, at 98; discussion of Algiers is on pp. 132–3.

37 Recently the harem and female slavery have been seen by Western scholars in a less negative light than in the past. For example in *Slavery and Abolition in the Ottoman Middle East* (Seattle and London: University of Washington Press, 1998), p. 25, Ehud Toledano remarks on the 'currency, legitimacy, and respectability' of this form of slavery. Moreover, his article 'Shemsigul: A Circassian Slave in Mid-Nineteenth-Century Cairo' offers a glimpse into the life of a female slave, showing that despite her position of disadvantage she had a sense of her worth and was able to assert herself within the framework of the legal system: see Edmund Burke (ed.), *Struggle and Survival in the Modern Middle East* (Berkeley: University of California Press, 1993), pp. 59–74.

38 The Qur'an allows a man to have four wives as long as he is able to treat them equally. Like seclusion and veiling, polygamy (or, more distinctively, polygyny) was practised both before and after the rise of Islam. One justification for it was the larger number of women than men due to warfare. However, 'marry such women as seem good to you, two, three, four; but if you fear you will not be equitable, then only one' often is interpreted by modern Muslim legal scholars as forbidding polygamy because complete equality among wives is impossible. All quotations of the Qur'an are from *The Koran Interpreted*, trans. A. J. Arberry (New York: Touchstone, 1996), vol. 1, p. 100.

39 Colley explains this transition and its political significance, noting that during the earlier period for every one reference to heterosexual sex in British discussions of Barbary and Ottoman captivity there were at least five to sodomy: *Captives*, pp. 127–30, at 128.

40 Earl of Cromer, *Modern Egypt*, vol. 2, p. 141.

INTRODUCTION

41 Muhammad al-Qurtubi, *Bidayat al-Mujtahid wa Nihayat al-Muqtasid*, 9th edn (Beirut: Dar al-Ma'arifa, 1988), vol. 2, pp. 42, 62, 373–4.
42 Islamic law refers to *shari'a*, which is often translated as general good order; it also may be used to mean way or path. It is not a law code but a vast body of literature, including the Qur'an, *hadith* relating the words and deeds of Muhammad, and the writings of prominent jurists and legal scholars. Which texts are used and in what manner depends on the particular school of thought, and within Sunni Islam alone there are four principal schools. In addition, each generation of jurists must engage in *ijtihad*, or effort in interpretation, in order to reconcile revelation, legal traditions and the needs of current circumstances. Finally, local customs impact on the way that any given law is put into practice. The flexible and even latitudinarian nature of *shari'a* has made it viable in very different parts of the world and over centuries. During the nineteenth century Islamic jurists and scholars in Egypt and throughout the Ottoman Empire believed in the necessity of *ijtihad* to meet the challenges posed by Western legal systems: see Aziz Al-Azmeh, 'Blasphemy and the Character of Islamic Law', in *Islams and Modernities*, pp. 10–14, and '*Shari'a*', in C. E. Bosworth, E. van Donzel, W. P. Heinrichs and G. Lecomte (eds), *The Encyclopaedia of Islam*, new edn (Leiden: Brill, 1997), vol. 9, pp. 321–28.
43 It was also possible for her to have a contract with her master, which would allow her eventually to buy her freedom. Mukhtar, *Bughyat al-Marid fi Shira' al-Jawari wa Taqlib al-'Abid*, pp. 50–8.
44 Hilal, *al-Raqiq fi Misr*, pp. 352–3.
45 Foreign Office Records, Confidential Print, Public Record Office (henceforth FOCP) 541/26, Hugo Marinich, Second Dragoman in Her Majesty's Embassy, 30 July 1884.
46 Mukhtar, *Bughyat al-Marid fi Shira' al-Jawari wa Taqlib al-'Abid*, pp. 37–8.
47 The word which Arberry translates as 'slavegirl' in this verse can also be used to refer to someone of lowly birth; the word for idolatress comes from the root *sharik*, meaning partner – in this case, one who believes that God has partners, i.e. a polytheist: *The Koran Interpreted*, vol. 1, p. 58.
48 Hilal discusses the different forms of both immediate and delayed liberation and the circumstances surrounding them; he understands these practices as constituting an emancipation movement in their own right: *al-Raqiq fi Misr*, pp. 200–10.
49 'Abd al-Salam al-Tirmanini makes the point that no society is without such abuses by likening apartheid, drug-trafficking and forced prostitution, all of which can be found in the modern Western world, to the injustices of slavery during previous centuries: *al-Riqq Madihu wa Hadiruhu* (Kuwait: al-Majlis al-Watani al-Thaqafa wa al-Funun wa al-Adab, 1979), pp. 193–247.
50 In *The Slave Trade*, p. 122, Beachey states that there were 12,000 black female slaves in Cairo and only 2,000 black male slaves, an estimate that does not include the Circassian slaves, almost all of whom were female.
51 One British official estimated that 60–2 per cent of slaves manumitted by the bureau in Upper Egypt were female, and that the percentage of females was 70–5 per cent for the bureau at Cairo: FOCP 541/22 Ralph Borg, Vice Consulate, Cairo, 23 August 1878. During 1880, 2,083 slaves manumitted were not labelled by sex, though I have concluded that the 1,901 who became domestic servants were women, and the 182 who went into the army were men because those occupations almost always were assigned on the basis of gender. The circumstances surrounding manumission are discussed in chapter two; generally, manumission occurred if slaves were found in the possession of a slave trader, had been recently bought or sold, or could prove that they had been treated cruelly.
52 FOCP 541/48, George Goschen to Earl Granville, August 1880.
53 FOCP 541/29, Sir E. Baring to the Marquis of Salisbury, April 1889.
54 Foreign Office Records, British Parliamentary Papers (FOBPP), Vice-Consul Jago to Sir A. H. Layard, February 1880 (vol. 58, p. 264); FOBPP refers to Foreign Office records that became British parliamentary papers available to the general public for a printing fee.

55 FOBPP, Enclosure 5 in letter from Mr Mason to Mr Malet, November 1880 (vol. 58, p. 125).
56 FOBPP, Mr Sakakini to Mr Malet, June 1880 (vol. 58, p. 75).
57 FOBPP, Captain F. Hunter, 'Notes on the Slave Trade as Carried on in the Red Sea and Gulf of Aden', November 1877 (vol. 57, p. 5).
58 FOBPP, Mr Malet to Earl Granville, March 1881 (vol. 59, p. 21).
59 FOBPP, Hunter, 'Notes on the Slave Trade' (vol. 57, p. 5).
60 FOCP 541/49, Consul Burton to Earl Granville, February 1881.
61 FOBPP, Mr Cookson to Earl Granville, July 1881 (vol. 59, p. 44). The practice of employing eunuchs existed prior to Islam, and many Muslims have maintained that their religion forbids it: see, for example, Sayyid Amir Ali, 'Bondage (Slavery)', *The Spirit of Islam: A History of the Evolution and Ideals of Islam with a Life of the Prophet* (London: Chatto & Windus, 1964 [1891]), p. 267; and more recently Mukhtar, *Bughyat al-Marid fi Shira' al-Jawari wa Taqlib al-'Abid*, p. 136. There are a number of different spellings of the name Sayyid Amir Ali. In *The Spirit of Islam* it appears as Syed Ameer Ali. I have used the former spelling throughout the book for consistency and to avoid confusion.
62 FOCP 541, Vice-Consul Muhammad to Acting Consul Razzach, September 1890; FO 84/2144, August 1891; and FOCP 541/41, January 1892.
63 FOCP 541/49, Consul Burton to Earl Granville, February 1881.
64 Egypt had been ruled for approximately 600 years by the *mamluks*, an elite group of soldiers who had been white slaves. Gabriel Baer notes that while they were no longer a ruling class by the time of British occupation, during the first half of the nineteenth century a number of them still occupied important positions in the army and the Government: *Studies in the Social History of Modern Egypt* (Chicago, IL, and London: University of Chicago Press, 1969), p. 161. The common practice of buying male slaves in order to train them to serve as military commanders or civilian administrators in the Ottoman Empire was known as *kul* slavery (see Toledano, *Slavery and Abolition*, pp. 20–53), a form of slavery that declined in importance in nineteenth-century Egypt as officers and soldiers increasingly were recruited through conscription and trained in schools modelled on the European system.
65 FOBPP, Schaefer, Director of the Slavery Department, to Sir E. Baring, February 1887 (vol. 60, p. 9). Occasionally significant numbers of slaves would be manumitted from this area, and Baer is justified in his statement that agricultural slavery was 'not uncommon': *Studies in the Social History of Modern Egypt*, p. 165. Overall, however, Egyptian slavery was harem-oriented or harem-driven.
66 Foreign Office Records (FO) 84/1672, Sir E. Baring, June 1884.
67 These categories appear in the court records: see Judith Tucker, *Women in Nineteenth-Century Egypt* (Cambridge: Cambridge University Press, 1985), p. 167.
68 For discussion of racial categories as cultural creations developed through relationships, as opposed to an accurate way of describing essential or biological differences, see Margo Hendricks and Patricia Parker (eds), *Women, 'Race' and Writing in the Early Modern Period* (London and New York: Routledge, 1994); and Henry Louis Gates Jr (ed.), *'Race', Writing, and Difference* (Chicago, IL: University of Chicago Press, 1986).
69 M. L. Whately, *Ragged Life in Egypt*. (London: Seeley, Jackson & Halliday, 1863), p. 23.
70 George Stocking, *Victorian Anthropology* (New York: Free Press, 1987), p. 51. 'Culture and race developed together, imbricated within each other' in the nineteenth-century imperial context: Robert Young, *Colonial Desire: Hybridity in Theory, Culture and Race* (London and New York: Routledge, 1995), pp. 27–8.
71 Eve Troutt Powell has examined the political significance of race, Sudanese slavery and the Sudan with regard to Egyptian national and cultural identity in the context of British imperialism in *A Different Shade of Colonialism: Egypt, Great Britain, and the Mastery of the Sudan* (Berkeley and Los Angeles: University of California Press, 2003). For discussion of race in the Middle East see Bernard Lewis, *Race and Slavery in the Middle East: An Historical Enquiry* (Oxford: Oxford University Press, 1990).

INTRODUCTION

72 FOCP 541/21, Mr Vivian to the Earl of Derby, April 1877.
73 FO 84/1324, Elliot to Granville, October 1870.
74 The word hudud, the plural of *hadd*, is often used to describe the limits or boundaries set by God, though it may refer also to the division between the harem and the outside world. Timothy Mitchell has observed that while nineteenth-century Europeans often attempted to divide space at home and abroad into the 'bourgeois interior and the public exterior', a similar and even more rigid practice already existed in Middle Eastern towns where 'the interior world of women and the family' was separated from the 'male world of the marketplace and mosque': *Colonising Egypt*, p. 55. However, the ideologies that separated the English domestic sphere and the Muslim harem from public life were not universally accepted; nor did they always reflect reality. For example, see Leonore Davidoff and Catherine Hall, '"The Nursery of Virtue": Domestic Ideology and the Middle Class', in *Family Fortunes: Men and Women of the English Middle Class, 1780–1850* (Chicago, IL: University of Chicago Press, 1987), pp. 149–92. Tensions regarding gender and efforts to maintain the idea of a fixed divide between public and private were especially pronounced in England during the late nineteenth century. As Judith Walkowitz explains, the streets of London became 'contested terrain', with women transgressing established boundaries, forcing themselves into public spaces and participating in debates about that most private of subjects, sexuality: *City of Dreadful Delight: Narratives of Sexual Danger in Late-Victorian London* (Chicago, IL: University of Chicago Press, 1992), p. 11.
75 FO 84/1370, Mr Elliot, 30 August 1873.
76 For discussion of the numbers of slaves exported from 'Africa' to Egypt during and prior to the period here studied, and the difficulties involved with this type of research, see Ralph Austen, 'The Mediterranean Islamic Slave Trade Out of Africa: A Tentative Census', *Slavery and Abolition: A Journal of Comparative Studies*, 13 (April 1992), 214–48.
77 For example, Lytton to Salisbury, 21 May 1877, Lytton Papers, Letters Despatched 1877, vol. 2, pp. 405, 519–20, quoted in P. Hardy, *The Muslims of British India* (Cambridge: Cambridge University Press, 1972), pp. 118–19. This idea was echoed throughout the period and sparked debate regarding the proper course of action regarding British foreign policy in Europe and the Middle East, a concern addressed and perhaps best expressed in a 1913 article by Lord Cromer: 'We are constantly being reminded that King George V is the greatest Mohammedan ruler in the world, that some seventy millions of his subjects in India are Moslems, and that the inhabitants of Egypt are also, for the most part, followers of the Prophet of Arabia. It is not infrequently maintained that it is a duty incumbent on Great Britain to defend the interests and to secure the welfare of Moslems all over the world because a very large number of their co-religionists are British subjects and reside in British territory': 'England and Islam', *Spectator* (23 August 1913). The article appears in the *Spectator* unsigned, but was published in Lord Cromer's *Political and Literary Essays*, pp. 407–15.
78 In 1974, J. G. A. Pocock called for a 'new' British history that would cover not only England but Wales, Scotland, Ireland, the British colonies, the Empire, and the Commonwealth: 'British History: A Plea for a New Subject,' *New Zealand Journal of History*, 8 (April: 1974), reprinted in *Journal of Modern History*, 47 (December: 1975), 601–21. Similarly, Hugh Kearney describes the Anglocentric approach to British history as a 'strait-jacket' for those in other areas of the British Isles: 'Four Nations or One?' in Bernard Crick (ed.), *National Identities: The Constitution of the United Kingdom* (Oxford: Blackwell, 1991), pp. 1–6, and *The British Isles: A History of Four Nations* (Cambridge: Cambridge University Press, 1989); and Alexander Grant and Keith Stringer (eds), *Uniting the Kingdom? The Making of British History* (London and New York: Routledge, 1995), especially David Cannadine's historiographical discussion, 'British History as a "New Subject": Politics, Perspectives and prospects', and Pocock's article revisiting this topic, 'Conclusion: Contingency, Identity, Sovereignty'.
79 Laurence Brockliss and David Eastwood explain that national identities were not a

threat to the Union as long as they were not used to promote its dismemberment: 'Introduction: A Union of multiple identities', p. 6; in addition, along with Michael John, they note that the nineteenth-century inhabitants of the British Isles had multiple allegiances and that their 'primary identity was seldom' British: see Brockliss, Eastwood and John, 'Conclusion: From Dynastic Union to Unitary State: The European Experience', p. 207, in L. Brockliss and D. Eastwood (eds), *A Union of Multiple Identities: The British Isles, c.1750–c.1850* (Manchester and New York: Manchester University Press, 1997). The British Muslim statesman is discussed in chapter five.

80 John MacKenzie, 'Essay and Reflection: On Scotland and the Empire', *International History Review*, 15 (1993), 661–880, and 'Empire and National Identities: The Case of Scotland', *Transactions of the Royal Historical Society*, 6th series (Cambridge: Cambridge University Press, 1998), vol. 8, pp. 215–31.

81 Brockliss and Eastwood describe the relationship between England and the other nations in the British Isles during the nineteenth century as characterised by the 'political and cultural primacy of the English' rather than by hegemony: *A Union of Multiple Identities*, p. 2. British anti-slavery ideology associated with efforts in occupied Egypt promoted English hegemony, as this book maintains.

82 Brockliss and Eastwood use the phrase 'composite identity' to describe Britons in the United Kingdom: *A Union of Multiple Identities*, p. 2.

83 A number of scholars have explored questions of British identity and loyalty in respect of the United Kingdom. Kearney explains that a British history existed 'over and above our "multi-national" history' and that therefore the answer to the question '"four nations or one" should be perhaps "four nations and one"'; yet he notes the inherent shortcomings of the term 'nation', given the divisions based on culture, class and gender within nations. 'Four Nations or One?' in Crick, *National Identities*, pp. 3–4. Eastwood, Brockliss and John refer to Britain as a 'Unionist state', in part because of its flexible nature which has allowed it to include multiple identities, distinct nations and changing circumstances: 'A Union of Multiple Identities', pp. 1–8, and 'From Dynastic Union to Unitary State', pp. 193–212. Similarly, Keith Robbins has described the United Kingdom as 'unified but not uniform': 'An Imperial and Multinational Polity: The "Scene from the Centre", 1832–1922', in Grant and Stringer, *Uniting the Kingdom?* p. 253.

84 British subjects from Scotland, Ireland and Wales served in the Government, the armed forces and the East India Company, and they settled in colonial territories. Jim Smyth explains that by the end of the eighteenth century Scottish and Irish national identities were 'articulated within a sturdy British superstructure', because what previously had been an English empire became a British one: *The Making of the United Kingdom, 1660–1800: State, Religion and Identity in Britain and Ireland* (London: Longman, 2001), pp. 161–3, at 163.

85 This attitude had much to do with what Grant and Stringer call the 'magnetic pull' from the 'political centre of gravity in southern England', which has existed for centuries: 'Introduction: The Enigma of British History', in *Uniting the Kingdom?*, p. 7. As Crick has noted, while the Scots and others in the British Isles may have had a dual sense of identity, most English people did not – for them, to be British was to be English: 'The English and the British', in *National Identities*, p. 97. Keith Robbins refers to the English tendency of claiming British institutions as their own citing the British museum as an example: *Great Britain: Identities, Institutions and the Idea of Britishness* (London: Longman, 1998), p. 284.

86 Grant and Stringer understand British history in terms of 'convergence and divergence', noting that the nineteenth century was one of the most British centuries due to economic and political expansion: 'The Enigma of British History', in *Uniting the Kingdom?*, p. 11.

87 Smyth notes how English power, confidence and sense of self-assurance could discourage reflection on the issue of national identity, creating a 'blind spot' in English historiography – many scholars simply regarded England 'as given': *The Making of the United Kingdom*, p. 154.

CHAPTER TWO

From desert caravans to Red Sea coasts: the British anti-slavery campaign in Egypt

Introduction

Over the course of several decades, from roughly 1870 until 1900, the British became actively involved in suppressing slave traffic in Egypt and surrounding areas. Most slaves were female and destined for the harem. Because the campaign and its accompanying ideology contributed to efforts to establish English hegemony in Egypt and required the presence of British officials, it must be understood as part of the larger imperialist project associated with occupation of that country.[1] Officials were motivated by their loyalty to the Government as well as by what could be considered a moral perspective or interest based on the belief that slavery was a violation of individual liberty and that, as part of the British imperial mission, anti-slavery activity would help to reform or *civilise* Muslim society by restructuring relationships along a Western, or more specifically English model.[2]

However, no stable or universally accepted model of English or, for that matter, Muslim relationships existed.[3] Instead, through the anti-slavery campaign and encounters with Egyptians and the institution of the harem, British officials defined both Englishness and Islam in relation to each other, and did so in gendered terms. In certain situations, British officers and male Muslim authorities in Egypt worked together, assuming and reinforcing their shared beliefs in the justness and legitimacy of male authority in general. This assumption informed anti-slavery activity from the administrative structure to specific policies and practices. However, through conflicts that occurred in the course of the campaign, British officials also created a hierarchy between what they considered to be less evolved or less civilised Muslim patriarchal practices, associated with the harem and sanctioned by Islamic law, and English gender roles or English patriarchy. As a result, ideas about

Englishness and Islam were re-formed in relation to specific imperial political activities and developments.

Because this discussion of the campaign in Egypt is organised thematically as well as chronologically, a brief overview of British antislavery activity will help to avoid confusion. The ambassador, Lord Ponsonby, first proposed the elimination of slavery to Ottoman authorities in 1840 in response to pressure from the BFASS. The British soon realised that attempts to suppress slavery in this part of the world would differ from earlier abolitionist efforts in the Western hemisphere. As Ponsonby reported to the Foreign Secretary:

> I have mentioned the subject and I have been heard with extreme astonishment accompanied with a smile at the proposition for destroying an institution closely interwoven with the frame of society in this country, and intimately connected with the law and with the habits and even the religion of all classes ... I think that all attempts to effect your Lordship's purpose will fail, and I fear they might give offence if urged forward with importunity. The Turks may believe us to be their superiors in the Sciences, in Arts, and in Arms, but they are far from thinking our wisdom or our morality greater than their own.[4]

As a result of British and European pressure, several *fermans* – decrees of the sultan – were issued by the Ottoman Government limiting slave-trading, with one prohibiting the slave trade sent to the *valis* of Egypt, Tripoli and Baghdad in 1857. During the later part of the century, the British were able to play a more active role in Egypt and surrounding areas.[5] As elsewhere in North Africa, financial crisis and state bankruptcy were the prelude to imperial expansion. In 1876, the Caisse de la Dette Publique, governed by an English and French controller, was established to manage Egyptian finances and ensure that the bond-holders received payment, and the first treaty between the British and Egyptian Governments regarding the slave trade was signed in the following year. This convention established bureaus for the manumission of slaves and allowed British ships to patrol certain waterways searching for slave traders. The 1880 convention between Her Majesty's Government and the *Sublime Porte* made similar provisions for the prevention of the slave trade in Ottoman territories outside of Egypt.

After the occupation of Egypt in 1882, the British became much more aggressive in their efforts to suppress the slave trade in that area, eventually eliminating it for all practical purposes. They created a British-dominated administrative system to free slaves and punish dealers. In 1889, eleven European powers and several others, including the emperor of the Ottomans, signed a British-initiated anti-slavery convention. Finally, in 1895 Egyptian slaves were entitled to 'full and complete freedom' according to another convention between the British and Egyptian Governments.

The BFASS contributed both practically and ideologically to these efforts and to the work of British officials, initiating the campaign and generating support for it throughout the late nineteenth century. Beliefs about the essential immorality of slavery that British officials brought with them to Egypt had much to do with BFASS representations. BFASS members assisted officers, acted as their informants and established the Cairo Home for Freed Women Slaves. In addition, the relationship between officialdom and the activists was one of mutual assistance and reinforcement. The BFASS used Foreign Office correspondence and records to monitor and publicise the progress of the anti-slavery campaign. The following description of the activities and ideas of British officials represents, then, one part of an international movement involving the work of private citizens in England as well as government directives.

Initial efforts to suppress slave traffic

The convention between the British and the Egyptian Governments for the suppression of the slave trade was signed in Alexandria in 1877.[6] It prohibited the importation and transportation of slaves by land or by sea in Egypt and its dependencies, which included Egypt proper as far as Aswan and Egyptian possessions in Northern Africa and on the shores of the Red Sea. The suppression of the traffic in black and Abyssinian slaves came into effect almost immediately, while the sale of white slaves and the sale of slaves from family to family were to be banned in seven years. According to this treaty, British cruisers were given the right to patrol the Red Sea, the Gulf of Aden, the coast of Arabia, the eastern coast of Africa, and the maritime waters of Egypt and her dependencies. British officials could search Egyptian vessels suspected of slave-trading and detain them. While they were required to turn the vessels, cargo and crew over to Egyptian authorities, they kept the slaves in their custody until manumission could be secured.

Under this convention Egyptian officials, provincial *mudirs*, governors and prefects of police were responsible for suppressing slave trafficking in their areas of jurisdiction, and this included searching caravans on land and vessels on the Nile. Freed slaves would be sent to bureaus established by the convention at the governorships of Cairo and Alexandria, as well as in Upper Egypt and Lower Egypt, under the direction of the inspectors-general. These bureaus handled issues related to the enfranchisement of slaves, such as keeping a registry, making inquiries regarding slaves who wished to be manumitted and sometimes providing for newly liberated slaves until they could find employment and, in the case of children, be placed in schools. Slave-dealers were to be arrested and tried by a court martial or a 'competent Tribunal'.[7]

This treaty initiated an imperialistic approach regarding slavery in Egypt. It required British officials stationed in that country to enforce practices that were at odds with the indigenous power structure and the accepted customs and traditions. British officials understood these expectations. In fact, in 1877 all of Her Majesty's consular officers in Egypt were instructed to 'scrupulously watch over their loyal fulfilment [of the terms of the convention] by the local authorities, pointing out to them any instance of their violation'.[8] The underlying assumptions of the treaty and the role that it expected British officials to play had much in common with authoritarian approaches to imperial rule previously seen in India and elsewhere, albeit in new and unprecedented circumstances.

British officials were willing to adopt the role prescribed to them. Even before they arrived in Egypt, they had made commitments to follow orders and pursue the objectives of their Government. They were no doubt influenced by popular ideas about the British hero of the Empire who brought civilisation and beneficent rule to foreign peoples,[9] and their identification with this role, a sense of obligation to the Government and a belief in the essential immorality of slavery all played a crucial part in determining what actions they would take and how they would understand those actions.

Certainly these ideas were not new, and in retrospect the willingness of British officials to act on them and follow orders does not seem surprising. However, if we understand identities not as permanent truths but as temporary and situational creations around which diverse individuals orient themselves, then it becomes clear that the way in which they were redefined and implemented in Egypt was not inevitable. Officials chose to continue to honour previously made commitments. They may have come to that country with preconceived ideas, but they reconciled those ideas with their specific situations, encounters and activities, and in the process gave them new meaning.

The initial approach towards the Egyptians was cautious, but with the intention of making a profound impact. One official wrote that slavery is a deeply rooted institution and that its suppression represented a 'thorough revolution in a system to which they [the Egyptians] have been accustomed for centuries'. The British could expect only resistance, at least at first.[10] Diplomacy was therefore required, and one of the convention's attachments emphasised the importance of using 'reserve and tact in order not to cause annoyance'. The above-mentioned circular also warned them to be prudent and to avoid arousing 'Mussulman susceptibilities'.[11]

According to the terms of the convention, British officials could not manumit slaves who came to the consulate; they were limited to interviewing them in order to obtain their testimonies and then escorting them to Egyptian authorities, to whom they would speak on their behalf. This process was slow and time-consuming, usually involving one or two slaves at a time, and manumission not always was granted. Nevertheless, through these early encounters, both before and after the signing of the convention, British officials developed a sense of the importance of their new role in Egypt. One at Suez wrote that many slaves never would have been able to obtain their freedom without him, noting that a large number had travelled all the way from ports on the Red Sea, provinces in Lower Egypt and even Alexandria because his office represented their only hope of obtaining manumission.[12] In addition, British officials often provided for runaway slaves until employment could be found.[13] While they realised that the future prospects of manumitted slaves were never great, without such services their situation could be bleak indeed. For example, one British official noted that freed slaves were kept in offices near the prison and fed army food, which was a great improvement over the former policy of confining them in the prison itself.[14]

The convention allowed the British more power to suppress slave traffic on the Red Sea and other waterways than it did on land. On the recommendation of the Lords Commissioners of the Admiralty, the khedive appointed Captain George Malcolm, RN, to the post of the director-general of the Suppression of the Slave Trade in the Red Sea, giving him the responsibility of organising and superintending an Egyptian police force in the Gulfs of Suez and Aden, on the Red Sea and off the coast of Arabia.[15] By 1877–78 at least seven of Her Majesty's ships and one of its gunboats patrolled the Red Sea and nearby waterways. This area was especially important: for it was through the Red Sea that slaves were taken from the eastern coast of Africa to the Arabian peninsula and from there to Turkey, Persia and throughout the Middle East. Jiddah and Hudaydah were the two principal landing places, but slave traders found that travelling from one deserted area of the coast to another was the best way to avoid detection.[16]

Estimates of the numbers of slaves transported this way vary, but most sources agree that tens of thousands of them crossed the Red Sea in the course of a year, with some ports receiving more than 2,000 slaves annually. Prior to the signing of the convention, one British captain estimated that 25,000–30,000 slaves were imported into the Hijaz and the Yemen from the Red Sea each year.[17] According to the reports of the British officers who captured slave vessels, the overwhelming majority of them were children, primarily girls but boys as well, usually around 12–13 years. Children comprised more than half of the slave population of the Red Sea; the next largest group was women, followed by men and eunuchs. Most of these slaves were Abyssinians or Gallas.[18]

Despite the presence of British cruisers, the strategies used to ship slaves made detection difficult. They were transported by night in light 'drought' boats in groups of 20 or fewer, and rarely more than 100.[19] These boats were quick, easily manoeuvred and capable of outrunning a British cruiser, especially along the coast; the vessels themselves were inconspicuous and could blend easily with the life of the ports, engaging in fishing and pearl-diving and only transporting slaves when a profitable opportunity arose. Moreover slave traders could monitor the movements of British cruisers and plan their activities around them, an unintended consequence of the publicity surrounding British efforts in the Red Sea.[20] For these reasons, British officials achieved only limited success in the area: they regularly reported capturing slave traders, but also noted the difficulty of patrolling the hundreds of miles of desert coastline and the constant smuggling of slaves.

Experiences in the Red Sea helped to confirm the belief of British officials that they opposed an entire society. They reported that the slave trade in this area had local support and that whole tribes and other groups had a vested interest in seeing it maintained. One British captain explained that it existed with the acquiescence of Egyptian governors and other authorities, and therefore could be suppressed only by men outside of the local networks and power structures. He believed that a successful anti-slavery campaign would be so unpopular that it would cause riots, but that the British presence would act as a 'repressive force' and serve as 'a corrective to the lawlessness', stating even that 'a firm officer, with a sure hand, and one who did not understand being trifled with, would soon stop them and be respected by the Arabs. They thoroughly understand and appreciate a just man with a strong will and a ready hand.'[21]

The conflicts and difficulties which resulted from trying to suppress the slave trade did not bring British officials to question their actions. Rather they had expected such resistance and became convinced further of the importance of their role in Egypt and that they were different in fundamental ways from those around them, whether they referred to them as Egyptians, Muslims or Arabs. Even when these sentiments were not expressed, British officials understood that they were in Egypt and surrounding areas as subjects of Her Majesty, employees of the Government and part of a network of agents abroad acting in the national interest.

With the perception of difference came the desire to understand – not the kind of understanding that would foster sympathy, but one that could be used strategically: they wanted to learn about the people, the area and the local political networks. In order to do this, ship commanders maintained regular contact with British consuls, residents and other informers in the ports and along the coastline, as well as conducting investigations ashore. For example, Commander Washington of HMS *Vulture* was given a translator and instructed to visit Sawakin and Massowah in order to 'report on the slave trade and political matters in these ports'.[22] Similarly, Commander Morice Bey of HMS *Torr*, who patrolled the coast from Suez to Sawakin, went ashore and observed encampments of slaves and dealers. Later he stopped at Berbera harbour, toured the area and visited government offices, the hospital and even some mosques.[23]

The reports of these commanders give detailed descriptions of slave-trading and the role of local authorities in it. British officers monitored activity on the water, as well as along the coasts, and they required Egyptian vessels engaged in *legitimate* commerce to submit forms stating the details of their business on the Red Sea.[24] These activities were crucial to the development of new conceptions of Englishness in relation to Islam, for despite preconceived notions about the British mission or the soldier–hero of the Empire that officials may have had before arriving in Egypt, they still had to make them meaningful in relation to their new surroundings and circumstances. In the years following the 1877 convention, through observation and the collection of data, in addition to direct encounters, British officials began to create an image of themselves on the basis of a developing understanding of Egypt's people, society and culture.

British attempts to monitor steamer traffic provided additional opportunities for these kinds of observations, encounters and, ultimately, identity formation.[25] Gender relationships were central to this process, and while slavery in Egypt was female, or harem-oriented, in general, this was especially true of steamer traffic: almost all of the slaves travelling this way during the late 1800s were women. Foreign Office correspondence is full of individual reports of female slaves found aboard steamers, usually in groups of 2–3, but in some cases as large as 50. References to male slaves are much more difficult to find: for example, a report of slaves discovered during the pilgrimage season in 1873 shows 37 females and only 3 males, and the Foreign Office records confirm that slaves transported by steamer were 'principally women'.[26]

Methods of finding slaves aboard steamers were haphazard at best. British consuls had to rely on other passengers, guards and the passport superintendent to act as informants.[27] Just locating the slaves among the 5,000–6,000 passengers in the short time period that a steamer would be in port proved difficult; sometimes cargo had to be searched as well. Even when those presumed to be smuggled slaves were found, determining their status was still another matter; for, as British consuls frequently complained, the slave-dealer easily could obtain documentation certifying that they were his wives. In fact, under the Islamic legal system in nineteenth-century Egypt, it was possible for a man to marry four women, travel with them, divorce and sell them, and repeat the process. Occasionally a slave-dealer would be caught only after it was noticed that he had new wives every time he returned to Egypt.

Steamer traffic was yet another area where the slave trade was allowed to continue, for the most part unchecked, and this further contributed to the process of identity formation in opposition or contrast to the Egyptians. For British officials, their experiences aboard steamers served as proof that both Muslim laws and gender relationships needed reform, and that Egyptians were loyal to a system that protected slave-dealers. Therefore, only they could suppress the slave trade. They expressed these opinions openly, and Egyptian authorities responded to these criticisms by explaining that, while they required manumission papers or documentation of some kind for suspected slaves, they could not prevent abuse of the system.[28]

While the British concentrated much effort on suppressing slave-trading by sea, they also attempted to prevent the importation of slaves into Egypt by caravan. Slave caravans took a variety of routes, which changed constantly to avoid detection,[29] usually travelling by moonlight and avoiding large towns and roads. The sparsely populated area between the Nile and the Red Sea was ideal for slave traders because it was vast and empty, so that 'armies might be marched through it without being seen by a single Egyptian official'.[30] Sometimes the caravans would stop outside of Cairo, so slaves could be smuggled into the city a few at a time disguised as the slave-dealer's wives, daughters, or servants. One British official estimated that an average of 1,500 black slaves were imported by caravan into Egypt annually; he noted that 31 of the 71 recent manumissions at the bureau in Upper Egypt were 'fresh comers', or slaves who recently had arrived by caravan from Southern or Central Africa.[31]

Foreign Office correspondence regarding caravan traffic reflects a familiar pattern: while British officers did not expect cooperation from Egyptians, they nevertheless expressed frustration at Egyptian inability or unwillingness to assist efforts to suppress the slave trade. For these officers, opposition only confirmed the necessity of a British presence and contributed to the development of an understanding of themselves

THE ANTI-SLAVERY CAMPAIGN IN EGYPT

in contrast to those around them. For example, in 1877 a British official wrote from Banghazi to the Foreign Office that slave caravans had been arriving at Jalo, an oasis in the Libyan desert, an eight-day journey to the south.[32] Traffic continued, and even increased, despite an earlier confrontation with a local pasha and a group of sheikhs. The British official believed that the only solution was to station a military force of 100 men to occupy Jalo and search the incoming caravans. Although he realised that a British force would be impossible, he suggested that a British vice-consul accompany the troops because otherwise 'the commander would probably be unable to resist the temptation of rapidly making his future by closing his eyes to the slave-dealers' misdeeds'.[33] While he obtained a promise from the Ottoman Government that the matter would be considered, his time was largely spent monitoring and reporting caravan traffic, making representations to the local authorities and requesting manumission for individual slaves.

As this example illustrates, British officials who hoped to suppress the slave trade in Egypt had to negotiate with Ottoman as well as Egyptian authorities. While the Egyptian Government could enter into treaties with outside powers regarding its own territories, it remained a suzerain of the Ottoman Empire. In addition, national boundaries meant little to slave-dealers and important links in their trading networks existed outside of Egypt proper in areas under Ottoman control. British consuls in these territories were instructed to watch local authorities to ensure that they took action to suppress the slave trade according to the imperial fermans and vizieral orders. They had very little influence, however: for example, the British vice-consul in Damascus reported that in the previous year, twelve slaves had taken refuge at his consulate and only one of them had been granted freedom. He complained that there was an 'open disinclination shown by the authorities to attend to any consular interference, no matter how officiously and courteously expressed', and he resolved to tell runaway slaves to try to escape to Beirut because his lack of authority meant that he had become little more than a slave catcher.[34]

Because British cruisers had the right to search and detain only Egyptian ships, Ottoman vessels or vessels flying 'Turkish colours' were free to come and go as they pleased, and British commanders reported that these were used as the primary means of transporting slaves. Furthermore, according to the terms of the convention, the British could not search Egyptian vessels if they were in 'Turkish waters'. These factors proved to be such obstacles for Her Majesty's commanders that as early as 1878, roughly one year after signing the convention with Egypt, the foreign secretary, the Earl of Derby, stated that a treaty for the suppression of the slave trade in Turkey was a 'necessity'.[35]

During that same year the khedive, under British pressure, attempted to persuade the Porte to sign such a treaty with Great Britain.³⁶

The British had their much hoped for treaty in 1880 with the signing of a convention between Her Majesty's Government and the Sublime Porte in Istanbul. While many points of this convention simply restated the Porte's ferman of 1857, it gave the British a legal right to take an active role in the suppression of slavery in Ottoman territories, and what had been considered inappropriate interference hitherto now had official sanction. The convention forbade the transportation of black and Abyssinian slaves through Ottoman territories, by land or by sea, unless they accompanied their owners as domestic servants, and even those slaves were required to carry certificates stating the purpose of travel along with a personal description. African slaves found in the possession of a dealer would be liberated and persons engaged in this traffic or in the mutilation of children would be tried by 'competent' tribunals, Ottoman or otherwise depending on the situation.³⁷ British cruisers were allowed to visit, search and, if necessary, detain Ottoman vessels, and any vessel employing African slaves had to carry papers of documentation.³⁸

For British officials, the experiences in Ottoman territories during the early years of anti-slavery activity were similar to those in Egypt. The resistance to their agenda that they encountered served only to confirm the importance of their mission and the belief that as representatives of Her Majesty's Government they had a unique role to play in this part of the world. Their frustrations and difficulties in trying to exert an influence on the existing political system convinced them that they needed increased power and authority.

British officials encounter the boundaries of the harem

British officials used various strategies to suppress slave traffic by caravan, steamer and Red Sea slave dhow, but they saw one common obstacle to all of their efforts: the harem, and the seclusion and veiling that accompanied it. While the institution of the harem and Muslim gender relationships in Egypt were probably of little importance to most British officials prior to the period examined, anti-slavery activity made them issues of concern. One British consul asserted that the harem required slavery, stating that 'as long as Mahommedans of the richer classes continue to shut up their women, they must have slaves to wait upon them – for men cannot go into the harem'.³⁹ He, as well as other officers, complained that the veiling of women facilitated slave-trading, and smuggled slaves were often reported as travelling 'covered with veils', 'secluded' or 'concealed with yashmaks'.

Veiling was seen as an unwelcome barrier by officials who wished to question women travellers in an attempt to determine whether or not they were slaves. Even before the signing of the convention, one British officer suggested that female agents and a female interpreter should be hired to question these women, for under no circumstances could British men demand that a Muslim woman traveller remove her veil.[40] On at least two occasions, the Sublime Porte made an official complaint to the British Government regarding the treatment of Muslim women travelling through Malta. As one officer explained, even if they acted with 'perfect courtesy' and made no attempt to force the women to remove their veils, the request alone was regarded as 'extremely offensive'.[41]

The fact that the British could not enter the harems themselves remained a constant source of frustration. One British official believed that owners in his immediate area forced slaves into prostitution and that the only way to stop this practice would be to search the harems, but he could not because even the mere suggestion of doing so would be 'revolting to the people'.[42] After the elimination of the public slave market, the buying and selling of slaves took place primarily within the harem or the private domestic quarters, and so anti-slavery advocates expressed the desire to have access to this space in order to combat the slave trade effectively. British officials reported that while Muslim men were allowed into the private dwellings of the slave-dealers, European men were denied such access 'unless accompanied by the proprietor, in accordance with Moslem customs and etiquette', and that the failure of British officials to respect these customs would provoke 'fanaticism'.[43] British authorities repeatedly complained that local officials refused to raid the private houses of even well-known slave-dealers. Confirming these statements yet presenting an alternative perspective, a dispatch to the Sublime Porte from the vali of Banghazi refuted the argument that 'domiciliary visits' or visits to harems were a practicable and logical extension of efforts to suppress slavery, implied that British consular agents made inappropriate demands and defended the actions of local authorities who refused to allow a man's harem to be searched.[44]

British efforts to transgress the hudud, or the boundaries of the harems, and Egyptian efforts to maintain them sometimes erupted into violent confrontation. A resident of Zaila, a town on the coast of the Gulf of Aden, related that one British officer and his men not only interrogated residents of the town demanding to see their wives and servants but forcibly entered the harems, searching for slaves. The resident reported that this action greatly traumatised the inhabitants and caused three women to have miscarriages. He saw this as violation of moral as well as physical boundaries and concluded his report by saying that this incident was 'not agreeable to God nor the Prophet'.[45] Such a raid was, most likely, not an isolated incident: the British consul at Jiddah reported: 'Now and again . . . a man-of-war is dispatched to the offending village [where officials believed slave-trading took place], a few shells are fired, the village is burnt, the people fly'.[46]

In the course of suppressing the slave trade in Egypt and surrounding areas British officials came into contact with the boundaries of the harem. While positive representations of this institution were available within the British imperial cultural system, these officials were concerned with it only in relation to their own experiences and political agenda. They were not interested in considering the possible benefits of veiling or maintaining a strict division between private and public life, as did the English women who visited harems (see chapter four). To them these practices served only to frustrate their efforts and protect slave-dealers. Therefore, they considered the patriarchal relationship between the Muslim man and his harem, both the physical space and those who occupied it, as an obstacle to Egyptian progress and modernisation.

In this context, Muslim men who travelled with their harems were highly suspect. Often British officials would separate the women from the men for an unspecified amount of time. For example, in 1885 when the Ottoman Government formally complained on behalf of a man whose five female slaves travelling by steamer to Istanbul were detained in Crete, the British Embassy responded that women suspected of being slaves needed to be removed from the men who accompanied them for a considerable length of time, otherwise the women would be 'too much under the influence of fear to be free agents' and their testimonies worthless.[47]

Whether or not he had an intention of selling them, a Muslim man could lose his female slaves while travelling. One British official stated that anyone with slaves, 'as has every Musselman family', is forced to free them before embarking on a steamer.[48] In one case, a number of slaves travelling on an Ottoman steamer were seized from their owners by Egyptian authorities. While the travellers were known to be pilgrims and not slave-dealers, the justification for this action was that they probably would have sold the slaves anyway to pay for their trip.[49]

In their effort to suppress the slave trade, British authorities in at least several instances took legitimate wives away from their husbands. In one case Khelill Chelebi of Baghdad and his family were travelling by steamer to Mecca when his wife and four of his female slaves were seized by a British gunboat. All of them asked to be returned to him, but their requests were ignored inasmuch as British officials did not consider them free agents. The man eventually found three witnesses to testify that he and his wife Hussineh Bint Abdulla were married according to Muslim law. Despite these efforts, the women were detained by the authorities for ten months.⁵⁰ In a similar case, a traveller's two wives were taken from him by officials, and in order to find them he was forced to neglect his business, causing financial hardship, which he explained in a letter requesting compensation from the British Government. Perhaps the most surprising case involved Said Mohammed Bergunzi, who was travelling with his two wives and daughter from Suez to Bombay. Officials seized his wives and daughter, and arrested him as a slave trader, sentencing him to two years' hard labour.⁵¹

In a society in which wives could become slaves and slaves could become wives, the very decision to suppress slavery in this part of the world necessitated the British involving themselves in the private lives of Muslim families. As the correspondence and reports cited in this chapter show, officials were well aware of the implications of their approach and understood its potential for arousing opposition. In 1874, a group of British–Indian subjects on pilgrimage pleaded with the consul at Jiddah not to 'disturb family arrangements or dissolve family ties' while pursuing the Government's objective of suppressing the slave trade.⁵²

According to certain contemporary feminist perspectives, British policy would have appeared very progressive in terms of gender relations. After all the British in Egypt brought women's issues into the public sphere and advocated the importance of rights on the basis of liberal principles of individual freedom and autonomy, even at the expense of domestic harmony. In certain respects, British officials seemed to be pursuing the same agenda in Egypt as were feminists in Britain. However the former tended to be either indifferent to such activities in England or were opposed to them. For example, while Baring was one of the most influential men in Egypt in terms of ensuring the eventual success of the anti-slavery campaign – and he criticised the practices of seclusion and veiling – he also vehemently opposed the movement for women's suffrage in Britain.

What seems like a contradiction becomes logical if we understand that British officials had no intention of undermining male authority in Egypt. While they may have regarded the harem or patriarchal Muslim gender relationships as obstacles to necessary reform and their efforts to suppress the slave trade, they feared women's independence even more, and usually expressed those fears in moral terms. One reported the undesirability of allowing freed women slaves to 'follow their own inclinations', because such a policy would put them at the mercy of 'temptations which may cause moral ruin'.⁵³ Another opposed the practice of giving newly manumitted females complete freedom, stating that they only use their freedom for 'immoral purposes'. He assumed, regardless of the explanation, that any former female slave who refused a position in domestic service did so because she planned to prostitute herself.[54] A British official dismissed the statements of a woman from the Sudan who reported being beaten by her master's wife, noting that she was 'fond of exhibiting her wardrobe' and that 'her ideas of getting her own living became clear, and were not creditable'. She was manumitted, but placed in the harem of her former master's brother.[55]

The officials who were reluctant to give freed female slaves independence usually justified their position on moral grounds, but their real objection was to women's freedom. One British officer admitted that for a number of years officials had focused on the trade in African slaves, all but ignoring the Georgians and Circassians because they understood the traffic in these women to be similar to European prostitution:[56] it seems that prostitution could be considered legitimate as long as the women in question were under the control of a man. Similarly, Consul Barker rationalised his policy of dismissing nine-tenths of the slaves who sought manumission from him as 'trivial cases' by explaining that their living conditions were fair, they had adequate food and clothing, and so few opportunities existed for outside work that most likely they would become prostitutes if freed. He realised that his decision over whether or not to free them was a choice between allowing 'legalized rape [if they stayed with their masters] versus prostitution'.[57] His choice was not between any conception of morality or immorality but between granting or withholding independence for a considerable number of women in his immediate area. Once again, while British officials may have regarded the harem and Muslim male authority as obstacles to progress and less advanced than their own gender relationships, they considered them preferable to complete freedom for females.

The assumption that harem slaves would become prostitutes if freed had much to do with English prejudices based on class and race. For both concepts were used to define inferiority, and when applied to women usually they were associated with sexual depravity. During this same time period, authorities in England frequently assumed that working-class women were prostitutes.[58] Not only was the harem slave regarded as coming from an inferior class or social position, but because of her language, culture and possibly, although not necessarily, because of her physical characteristics, she was considered to be racially inferior as well. For the Victorians, racial difference meant a proclivity to promiscuity and a sexual drive that could not be controlled.[59] These ideas further reinforced the belief that the harem slave was morally suspect and should not be allowed complete freedom.

The fear that through anti-slavery activity British officials would give these women independence was exaggerated considerably, for officials admitted that even after manumission they could not be sure that they were not sending them back into slavery and that those who returned to their former masters did not do so under pressure. In one case a young girl who was to be sold near Larnaka was liberated and sent back to her parents in the Syrian mountains, the very people who had already sold her once.[60] Sometimes women who entered domestic service would find themselves reduced to the status of a slave, and while the Cairo Home for Freed Women Slaves was supposed to prevent this situation, it could not always do so. A traveller and resident of Cairo reported that when slaves were set free, they were divided among the local pashas and beys.[61] One Abyssinian slave was manumitted at Jiddah and then actually married to the master from whom she had tried to escape.[62]

By suppressing the slave trade while taking care to restrict female independence, British officials defined proper gender relationships both for Egyptians and for themselves. The ideal that they created was characterised by male authority but opposed to female slavery and was understood in contrast to the Muslim harem. If slavery was oppressive and if, as British officials believed, the harem was an obstacle to eliminating it and reforming Egyptian society, then the gender relationships that they presented as an alternative would be liberating. This ideal was a product of an imperial cultural system, for it developed through the implementation of an aggressive foreign policy and simultaneously contributed to the establishment of English hegemony in Egypt and the re-creation of English national identities defined in imperial and gendered terms.

An example helps to illustrate these processes. One British officer described an incident in which an escaped female slave with an injured ankle waded to a British ship in the Red Sea seeking protection. When others tried to persuade her to return she resisted, stating that she 'preferred being killed by Englishmen to returning to her master'.[63] This exaggeration is revealing. In a few words, the officer has made reference to the military presence of British ships patrolling the Red Sea, implying their importance, and depicts the Englishman and his authority, even when taken to the extreme, as preferable to that of the Muslim man.

British officials brought with them to Egypt familiar concepts about the necessity of male authority and female dependence, yet these ideas were far from uncontested or universally accepted in England.[64] Maintaining them in England required effort, and there is no reason to assume that they would have been reproduced under new circumstances abroad. Her Majesty's Government did not require those involved in the anti-slavery campaign to take measures to prevent female independence, and while these attitudes regarding women may have helped to create a bond between British officers and Muslim men, the same officials also aggressively pursued policies that they believed would generate conflict between the two groups and they even drew inspiration from and defined themselves through this conflict. Thus, while the nature of English patriarchy and its value were being debated and criticised in England itself, through the words and actions of individual officials in the course of anti-slavery activity and their encounters with the Muslim harem, that patriarchy was re-created and promoted as a noble ideal (see chapter four).

Challenging the Islamic social order in nineteenth-century Egypt

The identities associated with the imperial nation state that British officials created through the encounters and experiences involved in anti-slavery activity were understood not only in gendered terms and in opposition to the harem, but in relation to the Islamic legal system in place during the late nineteenth century: The British sought to abolish slavery and give manumitted slaves equal status before the law, a goal which repeatedly put them in direct conflict with Muslim authorities in and around Egypt. The motivation and justification for British policy had to do with a particular moral perspective based on nineteenth-century liberal ideals, which celebrated the freedom and autonomy of the individual. According to this belief system, cruelty was not the issue. Regardless of treatment, the status of slavery itself was a violation of the almost sacred principle of individual liberty and was considered inherently degrading and demoralising to both slave and master.[65] In one early encounter, Stratford Canning, the British ambassador to the Porte, responded to a defence of slavery in the Ottoman Empire by stating the argument was 'by no means destitute of truth, though offering no real compensation for the loss of personal liberty, and the moral degradation resulting from it to the slave, and reacting on the owner himself'.[66] Similarly, the British consul-general in Suez remarked on the difficulty of determining whether travelling children were slaves because 'they are so proud of being Islamicized that they . . . have certainly no idea that their position as a slave is a degrading one'.[67] To British officials the practice of slavery and slave status had to be eliminated regardless of the perceptions of the slaves.

During this period, the Egyptian judicial system was comprised of complicated networks of 40 independent courts organised into 4 distinct administrative structures.[68] Personal law, which included individual status, guardianship, marriage, divorce and succession, fell under the jurisdiction of the Muslim courts, referred to by the British as either the *qadi* or the *'medjelis'*. While the 1877 convention prohibited the slave trade, slavery itself had not been abolished, and, according to these courts, even slaves who had been manumitted could not marry or inherit without the consent of their former masters.

Because the Muslim courts in late nineteenth-century Egypt tended to be sympathetic to slave-owners and could aid and protect slave-dealers, British officials tried to check their power. In one case the British consul at Salonica reported that a well-known slave-dealer, who had just left Egypt, was turned over to the 'medjelis' by the authorities. Not only was he released, but he was allowed to keep the 8 female slaves who were travelling with him after he claimed that 2 were his wives and the rest were his servants. However, the man was re-imprisoned as soon as authorities discovered that the British consul had been informed of the situation.[69] British officials often commented that religious courts returned slaves to their masters as wives, and one reported that Muslim legal authorities knowingly issued marriage contracts for the sole purpose of allowing slave-dealers to legally transport 2–3 women at a time, usually by steamer, and then sell them.[70]

Until the turn of the century Muslim authorities in Egypt generally opposed the ultimate goal of the British campaign, the abolition of the legal status of slavery. In 1873, when the terms of the 1877 convention were being negotiated, the khedive warned British diplomats of the difficulties involved in trying to prohibit slavery in a Muslim country.[71] In 1882, he agreed to abolish slavery but only if he could persuade the religious authorities to issue a *fatwa* against it, which he could not do.[72] Baring expressed concern that abolition would provoke Muslims who did not own slaves to oppose the measure on principle.[73] Fears of 'Mahommedan fanaticism' were frequently stated; in fact, this phrase was used often to describe anyone who opposed British anti-slavery efforts.

The British attempted to influence the courts in Egypt indirectly. For example, the consular assistant in Cairo and Mrs Sheldon Amos of the BFASS went to hear a case tried in the qadi's court, and the assistant reported that their presence in the courtroom had a positive effect on the proceedings.[74] In that case, a black female slave who had escaped and obtained manumission was being taken to court by her former master for remarrying without his permission. He also claimed that she was already married to another man, although she denied it. The judge ruled that she would have to divorce both husbands simultaneously – clearly, she was not recognised as a free and equal citizen under the law. However, because the former slave was neither punished nor required to return to the man from whom she escaped, the outcome was considered a success for the anti-slavery cause.

The British, not surprisingly, had less of an impact on the Ottoman courts than on the Egyptian courts, but they took similar steps to monitor and influence those as well. A British officer at Her Majesty's Embassy in Istanbul hired a Muslim and former officer of the Porte, Osman, to assist the female slaves who came to the Embassy; he attended the Council of the Ministry of Police every day in order to watch the proceedings and defend the slaves' interests. Osman was given specific instructions on how to act and when to intervene. The British officer who employed him noted that the 'presence of this semi-official personage among the Council strongly tends to ensure a fair hearing' or rulings favourable to the anti-slavery cause.[75]

The most effective way that the British had of eroding the power of the Muslim courts in Egypt and surrounding areas was to establish alternative or additional judicial systems. British officers created naval courts along the coast of the Red Sea to try those on captured slavers according to British legal traditions. While the tribunals were Egyptian, they were given copies of the rules and regulations used to guide the British Admiralty and consular courts, and Captain Malcolm had judicial authority regarding slave-trading cases.[76] In 1883, just after the occupation, the native courts, also known as native or national tribunals, appeared in order to deal with all civil and criminal jurisdiction in matters concerning Egyptian subjects alone, except in cases regarding domestic relations and personal status, which were still handled by the religious courts.[77] Proceedings were conducted in Arabic, but a 'considerable number' of English and European judges sat on the bench.[78] In 1884 Baring reported that these tribunals, which had only just begun to work, would eventually gain public support and replace the qadi, noting that 'the day can not be far distant when the personal law of the Mahommedan will be subjected to the native courts'.[79] In that same year the sale of slaves between families was prohibited, creating another 'conflict between the new Courts and the Justice of the Cadi',[80] for the new Egyptian courts martial, which operated 'to some extent' under the supervision of English officers, usually tried these cases.[81]

British officials tried to use their military presence, especially after occupation, to undermine not only the qadi but other Egyptian courts that they feared fell under the influence of Islamic principles. One consul, from Sawakin, wrote that since the town was under British occupation and administration, pressure could be put on the local tribunals to force them to make the status of slavery illegal. He went on to propose the establishment of a system of 'judicial machinery', no doubt British-dominated, in order to compensate those who manumitted their slaves.[82] Similarly, while the Egyptian civil authorities exercised jurisdiction along with the British consular agent in Aswan, the British commandant could overrule judgments made by local bodies.[83]

Through conflicts with Muslim courts in Egypt and surrounding areas and measures to circumvent them, British officials claimed a role for themselves as the bearers of justice, believing that in respect of slavery justice was incompatible with Islamic traditions and that it could be brought to Egypt only through their institutions and influence. As Mr Vivian explained, the new Egyptian tribunals needed guidance in order to prevent them from committing 'some miscarriage of justice which might bring them into collision with Her Majesty's Government'. He concluded his report by stating that the Egyptian Government could 'never' carry out the terms of the convention without British assistance.[84]

British officials' relationship with Muslim legal authorities in Egypt and their efforts to erode the existing court system, as well as general frustrations experienced in the course of suppressing the slave trade with the intention of eventually abolishing slavery, led them to conclude that they could not rely fully on Muslims to cooperate with their polices or assist in their efforts. While they realised that it would have been politically impossible to take over the suppression of the slave trade completely and replace Egyptian with British officers, this strategy remained an ideal. One British consul-general reported that after accusing an Ottoman governor-general of connivance in the slave trade, he was given the explanation that slavery was 'bound up with Islamism'. He went on to state that high-ranking Muslims owned slaves and that 'every Mussulman here has a vital and paramount interest in upholding the abominable institution'.[85] Even Sir Richard Burton, the soldier–adventurer and scholar who had gone on pilgrimage to Mecca and was known for his understanding of and sympathy with Islam, stated that the khedive was 'too Moslem' to interfere with the institution of slavery.[86] The British consul at Jiddah went so far as to say that because Muhammad proclaimed the freeing of slaves to be a meritorious act, that 'every good Mohammedan is to purchase as many slaves as his means will permit, with the intention of gradually giving them their freedom', and that therefore Islam requires a constant supply of slaves.[87]

This statement has little to do with how Egyptian Muslims understood their faith with regard to slavery. In fact, such rhetoric is not so much an attempt to describe Islam as it is a reflection of the immediate conflict between Her Majesty's officers and those who resisted their attempts to reform Egyptian society and impose an alternative political and legal system. For British officials, these discourses gave meaning to the opposition they encountered, defined them as fundamentally different from the people among whom they were living and reassured them that their cause was just. It served to orient individuals from a variety of backgrounds and perspectives to a common mission and goal, and to identify with the imperial role that their Government prescribed for them.

Through the development of these ideas about Islam and the Muslim man described above, a certain image of the imperial hero was created, an Englishman whose love of liberty and commitment to individuality distinguished him from Muslims and even from other Europeans. One official commented that

> whatever Treaties may be made, I do not believe that the sincere co-operation of Mussulman officials can be expected . . . It is rare to find Mussulmans, however humane, who have any of the abhorrence of slavery, theoretical or practical, which influences many Englishmen, and other Europeans, in a somewhat less degree.[88]

Another stated that any efforts by Muslims to suppress slavery were merely to pacify the English and that '[t]he work, if it is to be done, must be done by England alone'.[89] While the British were willing to work with others, particularly the French and the Italians, they understood anti-slavery activity as a British initiative and – especially after the occupation of 1882 – a British project, and in the context of the campaign the activities of a diverse group of British officials came to represent Englishness itself.

For British officials engaged in the process of defining themselves and their anti-slavery agenda in opposition to Islam, no place could better symbolise the belief that slavery was integral to that religion than the city of Mecca. It was a centre for slave-trading and an area of opposition to British and British-influenced policy. In 1855–56, a holy war was proclaimed against the Ottomans in the streets of Mecca and throughout the Hijaz, in part as a response to anti-slave trade measures. While the revolt was eventually suppressed, this area was approached with great caution afterwards and was exempted from the Ottoman ferman of 1857 prohibiting the slave trade.[90] One British official referred to 'that holy city' as a 'grand emporium for slaves';[91] another gave a detailed account of slave-trading according to which the *sharif* of Mecca was involved, and he noted that during pilgrimage season in nearby Jiddah 'the pulse of all orthodox Islam' could be felt.[92] In 1876 Her Majesty's consul in Jiddah reported that slaves were openly brought to the city in daylight and that the owners were even charged a quarantine fee of 10 piastres per slave by local authorities on entering the town.[93]

The British tried to suppress slave-trading in Mecca by patrolling the Red Sea and key ports in the area, particularly Jiddah, and by targeting travelling pilgrims. Pilgrims especially were suspect because they could buy slaves cheaply at Mecca and sell them for 2–3 times the price in places such as Cairo or Alexandria. In a measure to prevent pilgrims from returning to Egypt with new slaves intended for sale while claiming them as personal servants, a circular, approved by the Council of Ministers and the khedive, was addressed to the 'Mudirs and Governors', instructing them to have all pilgrims who planned to leave the country obtain a certificate with a complete description of each servant travelling with them. This certificate would be registered and checked at the point of disembarkation by the local Bureau d'Affranchissement. Only slaves who had been registered previously would be allowed to enter Egypt. Attempting to monitor pilgrims was a difficult undertaking that required considerable human resources, as thousands of them left daily from Jiddah alone during the pilgrimage season.[94] Over the years British officials became more involved and more aggressive in this effort; at one point they even went beyond their legal power, according to the terms of the convention, by requiring pilgrims with slaves to produce manumission papers for them at Jiddah.[95]

The approach taken and attitudes developed by British officials to pilgrims and Muslims in general in the course of anti-slavery activity were essential to defining their role in Egypt. If justice was incompatible with slavery, then only the new courts that they had created could provide justice. If Egyptian Muslims were too sympathetic to the existing system, then only British, sometimes more broadly Western, officials could reform it. The idea of the backward Muslim man clinging to oppressive traditions made possible the obverse idea of the British officer struggling to bring liberty, progress and civilisation to Egypt.

Yet other discourses or ways of understanding Islam were available to the British in Egypt. Occasionally an officer would mention the Qur'an's instructions on kindness to slaves and the value of freeing them. Another would comment on the courtesy and support of British policy shown by the grand sharif of Mecca.[96] In a letter Baring reported consultations with religious authorities in Cairo who explained that in the future they might be able to use their influence to encourage the voluntary liberation of slaves in accordance with the teachings of Muhammad. Baring then quoted the British Muslim statesman Sayyid Amir Ali, who wrote for an English audience and argued that true Islam discourages slavery.[97]

Ahmad Shafiq, a contemporary of Sayyid Amir Ali, wrote a book in response to the anti-Islamic abolitionist discourse. In this book, as well as in his speech to the Egyptian Geographical Society, he argued that slavery has existed throughout world history, but that the teachings of Islam undermine it and attempt to make it as humane as possible. He maintained that in Egypt slaves generally are treated well: often slaves are freed and given dowries or other forms of compensation, and slavery has traditionally been an avenue of upward mobility, as in the case of the mamluks.[98] Considering that the French version of his book and the speech for the Egyptian Geographical Society were directed towards a Western audience, and they addressed the issue of the suppression of the slave trade during the time of British occupation, it would be surprising if British officials in Egypt were not aware of his arguments.

While mention of these alternative discourses and sympathetic references to Islam regarding the issue of slavery appear periodically throughout the collections of correspondence and reports, they are the exception rather than the rule and do not reflect British attitudes overall to the anti-slavery campaign. In fact, in his letter, Baring concluded that, despite its praiseworthy characteristics, 'if the Mahommedan law could not conform itself to the spirit of modern times, so much the worse for the Mahommedan law. It would have to go to the wall.'[99] British officials may have been exposed to contradictory understandings of Islam available in the larger cultural system, but they usually resolved this ambiguity by giving preference to the interpretation that best complemented their campaign and the overall imperial agenda. They seem to have decided that engaging with the complexity of the religion and the society was not compatible with the concerted and aggressive political action prescribed by their Government. In other words, during the course of anti-slavery activity, British officials chose to elaborate on certain representations and ignore others in order to create an understanding of Islam that reflected their imperial political goals, social circumstances and experiences in Egypt and surrounding areas.

The elimination of slavery in Egypt, 1880–1900

This discussion of British efforts to undermine the Islamic legal system and transgress the boundaries of the harem shows that certain attitudes and beliefs remained consistent throughout the anti-slavery campaign both before and after occupation. Yet after 1880, the situation began to change dramatically for British officials, who went from requesting cooperation from Egyptian authorities to orchestrating an extensive anti-slavery campaign, eliminating the institution for all practical purposes by the end of the century. If the vision of English justice and patriarchy that developed through initial efforts and frustrations seemed to them at first to be a worthy but almost impossible goal, it soon became a symbol of Egyptian progress and reform under British rule.

The new khedive publicly supported this ideal. After a failed attempt in 1879 to resist European dominance by dismissing the English and French ministers of his cabinet, the former khedive, Ismail Pasha, was replaced by his son Tawfiq. The new ruler owed his position to the

THE ANTI-SLAVERY CAMPAIGN IN EGYPT

influence of European powers, particularly the British and the French. Unlike his father, Tawfiq was monogamous and did not keep a large harem full of slaves. His monogamy was an important issue, considering that rumours of the former khedive and his mother regularly purchasing harem slaves served to impede British goals:[100] for if the khedive ignored his own decrees, Egyptian agents hardly could be expected to believe that their Government intended to honour agreements with the British.[101] Tawfiq, however, expressed disgust for the slave trade and support for its suppression: 'I trust, we may be able to do away with slaves in the harem. I hate the very idea of slavery, and am doing all I can to put it down: moreover, a harem is only wanted for many wives; with one wife there won't be any necessity for seclusion.'[102] His position contributed to the success of the anti-slavery campaign and the ideologies that developed through it.

The Egyptian Government took several new measures to suppress the slave trade. The Egyptian minister of foreign affairs began to issue reports of slaves liberated and dealers punished. Targeting the dealers had been a long-awaited goal of British officers who complained that freeing slaves did nothing to deter the dealers from selling them.[103] An office for the emancipation of slaves was established in Alexandria in an attempt to put an end to the common practice of forcing slaves seeking emancipation to return to masters who had filed false charges against them.[104]

In addition, Count Edward della Sala was appointed as the chief of the Service for the Abolition of the Slave Trade, also known as the Service for the Suppression of the Slave Trade. An Italian subject and professional military officer, Della Sala had served in the Austrian Army under the Emperor Maximilian in Mexico and under the ex-khedive. His background seemed to be an ideal compromise: for the Egyptians he was not connected with England or France, a matter of no small importance to the increasingly vocal nationalists, while for the British he was not Turkish, Arab or Muslim. Della Sala was given the title of colonel and all mudirs in the area were instructed to consider him a superior and obey his orders. He led a force of 436 men in patrolling the primary caravan routes west and southwest of Cairo by which slaves were brought into Egypt.[105]

By 1881 Della Sala's efforts began to yield results. He reported that slave traffic in his area was disappearing, noting that in the last four caravans he had searched nothing but dates and oil were found. He explained that not only had the terms of the slave trade convention become common knowledge, but he had caused panic in the local Bedouin communities and kept alive a general 'salutary fear'. He even went beyond his instructions to inspect caravans by making arrests in Cairo.[106]

In a campaign that depended on orienting officials around a certain ideal of masculinity associated with the imperial mission Della Sala served as a model: even though he was not English, British officials saw in him the traits that they believed Her Majesty's officers should have. They praised him for his 'energy' and 'character', and his aggressive tactics and success inspired admiration. He was promoted to the rank of brigadier-general and given the title of pasha.[107]

Della Sala was not the only Westerner to assume a title that had meaning for the Egyptians. Accomplished British officers did the same, for example Colonel Schaefer Bey and Baker Pasha. This strategy served to bolster their authority and promote their cause. However, these titles were not used for the sake of the Egyptians alone: they appear in Foreign Office correspondence and writings for an English audience. In that context, the terms helped to create an imperial masculine ideal, for like the soldier–adventurers who had portraits of themselves painted in 'Oriental dress' after returning to England, those who adopted foreign titles did so as a means of identifying themselves with the power of the 'other'.[108] If the Muslim man with his harem represented to them a primitive or brutal masculinity, then the British hero of the Empire who commanded the respect of these men on their territory and their terms would have had to have been equally if not more fearsome. Thus the notion of English masculinity created through anti-slavery activity was understood in relation to ideas about the Egyptian Muslim man, not only in opposition to him but through a certain degree of identification with him.

Della Sala also provides an example of the diversity of those involved in the anti-slavery campaign. While certain ideas regarding English hegemony and the nature of English national identity developed through it, many officials who contributed to the cause were not from England, but came from other areas of Britain, Europe and Egypt, and they assumed titles associated with authority in those different parts of the world. Those from Scotland, Ireland and Wales may have had distinct national identities that they reconciled with loyalty to the British State and their role in its administration in Egypt; but, unlike their English counterparts, they did not express them in the Foreign Office correspondence and reports examined. Even officers from England had diverse backgrounds and perspectives, and life and work in Egypt did not have the same meaning for all of them. Yet all who participated in this imperial project were able to identify with certain basic ideas that were redefined through the campaign, such as the need to eliminate slavery, the benefits of British rule and gender relationships characterised by male heroism and female dependence.

After 1882, the role of British officials expanded considerably, as the occupation of Egypt marked a turning point in the anti-slavery campaign, and for the first time they had real authority with which to pursue their agenda. No longer confined to the position of watchdog, they now had reason to believe that their efforts would be successful and that they, as British officers, would reform Egyptian society and gender relationships, and thus modernise the country as part of the imperial mission. The ideals that British officials had defined for themselves during the early period of anti-slavery activity were beginning to have an impact, translating into concerted action and the eventual elimination of slavery in Egypt.

Prior to occupation, British officials rarely mentioned abolishing slavery;they considered suppressing the traffic to be the most diplomatic and realistic strategy, believing that it would lead eventually to abolition by halting the supply: Mr Vivian, the diplomat who negotiated and signed the 1877 convention, described the document as 'providing for the suppression of the Slave Trade and eventually of slavery in Egypt'.[109] In part because focusing on the supply had not brought about the desired results and in part because of Britain's new position of power in Egypt, abolition became a goal. The khedive's British consul expressed the belief that the khedive should be 'pressed' on the subject, stating that 'as long as English troops remain there would be no danger'.[110]

After occupation, the administration of the anti-slavery campaign was put under British control. In 1883 Baker Pasha assumed responsibility for the Slave Trade Department.[111] A special bureau was created to take the place of the former Service for the Abolition of the Slave Trade (which had been disorganised during the insurrection), employing the police in the towns and the constabulary in the provinces. In addition, the Bureau of Manumission, which previously had been under the authority of the Egyptian governors, was transferred to the provincial commandant of the constabulary, so that inspectors would be able to better 'supervise and report' on the activities of the service.[112] As a result of these structural changes, anti-slavery work went from being British initiated to British-dominated.

The changes that accompanied British occupation did, in fact, have a profound effect. As Appendix 1 indicates, far more slaves were freed in the years after occupation than at any other time. As early as 1884 Baring stated that 'throughout the harems the means by which freedom may be obtained are well known' and that those who remained in a state of slavery did so voluntarily or because they were prevented physically from escaping.[113] Large numbers of liberated slaves continued to be reported during 1885-86. In addition, manumission returns and sentences given to those involved in slave-dealing were published in the major Arabic newspapers every month. This publicity deterred slave-dealers and prompted slaves in remote areas to write letters to the Anti-Slavery Department requesting manumission.[114]

Colonel Schaefer of the Slave Trade Department reported similar success. He explained that when he assumed responsibility for this department in 1883, there were 32 slave-dealers in Cairo, but that within 4 years 25 of them had been arrested and the others were either forced to leave the city or stop trading. He went on to explain how recent fraudulent sales helped anti-slavery efforts. In such a case, a freed slave would allow herself to be sold by a dealer only to run away from her new master the next day and collect her share of the profits from the sale. Occasionally the would-be buyers were arrested. These incidents created a feeling of insecurity regarding the buying of slaves and prompted some Egyptians to wonder whether or not there were any 'bonâ fide slaves' to be bought.[115]

In addition to these developments, after 1889 workers in the abolitionist cause could draw inspiration from the fact that they had the support of a formidable international community. In that year, an anti-slavery conference resulted in a treaty that was signed by, among others, eleven European powers and the emperor of the Ottomans.[116] It made certain demands on the Ottoman Government. For each power that signed the treaty agreed to punish slave-dealers, patrol caravan routes and monitor coastal areas in their territories. Each also had to provide for liberated slaves until they could support themselves, which included establishing a place of refuge for women and schools for children. In addition, specific reference was made to vigilance on the part of the participating powers whose laws recognised domestic, or female and harem-oriented, slavery.[117]

Continued efforts in the 1890s led to the demise of slavery in Egypt. The most significant event of this period was the signing of the 1895 convention between the British and Egyptian Governments, which declared that every slave on Egyptian territory was entitled to 'full and complete freedom' and could demand papers of enfranchisement. It also required the Department for the Suppression of the Slave Trade to have a special force at its disposal to 'keep watch over the roads leading from the Desert as well as the shores of the Red Sea'.[118] These measures were followed by two khedival decrees in 1896 detailing the penalties for buyers and sellers of slaves. While some smuggling continued, the slave trade had been suppressed effectively in Egypt. By 1899 that traffic was pronounced 'moribund' and in 1908 the home which had provided temporary shelter for freed female slaves in Cairo was closed because insufficient former slaves used it to justify its existence.[119]

What did the elimination of slavery at the end of the century mean? For the Egyptians it meant that the elite Ottoman or Ottoman–

Egyptian household characterised by harem slavery ceased to be a model of domestic social organisation. It was replaced by a new ideal, that of the middle-class home, which contemporary Egyptians believed would provide a foundation for the new nation.[120] Through the encounters and exchanges in the course of the anti-slavery campaign, Egyptians, like the British officials stationed among them, recreated identities for themselves understood in terms of both gender and the nation. Their identities were as multidimensional and as much an evolving process within an imperial cultural system as the English ones discussed in this chapter.

While a new model of *proper* domestic relationships eventually triumphed in Egypt, Egyptians did not simply adopt what British officials and others presented to them. For example, even though anti-slavery workers repeatedly criticised the harem, seclusion and veiling as corrupting to the country and as root causes of slavery, this institution and these practices continued to exist after abolition. Similarly, while the elimination of slavery brought a reassessment of female roles critical to the emergence of various feminist movements, interpretations of Islam informed most of the arguments presented by Egyptians who sought to improve the status of women.[121] Even the khedival house of Egypt, which British officials praised after the accession of Tawfiq as a reformed institution and an example of their positive influence in the country, in part because the khedive himself promoted this image to them, had not exchanged former traditions for British ones. For example, Tawfiq's subjects understood his monogamous lifestyle as no more than the expected consequence of having married a princess. His harem may have been smaller than his father's, but that change was the result of the weak Egyptian economy and the diminished political role of the khedival household during British occupation, not a desire to eliminate it.[122]

Similarly, while jurist and theologian Muhammad 'Abduh was on good terms with Cromer and supported the abolition of slavery, he nevertheless remained both a nationalist and a respected religious authority in Egypt. 'Abduh became grand *mufti* in 1899 and was influential in turning Egyptian public opinion against slavery. He pronounced that abolition was, in fact, in the true spirit of Islam. Yet far from wanting to Anglicise or Westernise, 'Abduh sought to interpret Islam in light of contemporary needs in order to establish it as the foundation for a progressive society and thus help to narrow the widening gap between religious and secular life in Egypt.[123]

The ways in which traditional practices and beliefs of Egyptian Muslims were reconciled with the eventual elimination of slavery in that country challenged the dichotomies between slavery and Islam on one hand and liberty and Englishness on the other. However, for British officials the eventual abolition of slavery served only to confirm the rightness of their mission, the importance of British rule, and the conceptions of Islam and English national identity that they had developed in the course of the campaign. Maintaining those ideas over a thirty-year period was as much a part of the process of identity formation as their original creation. For British officials chose to interpret each new success as reinforcing what they had already come to believe rather than as an opportunity to re-evaluate their understanding of the harem and Egyptian society as perhaps more complex and flexible than the ideology that they had developed recognised.

Conclusion

British officials stationed in Egypt during the late nineteenth century found themselves in unfamiliar circumstances. Neither they personally nor the British Government more generally had prior experience with an anti-slavery campaign in which the majority of the slaves were women and destined for the harem in an occupied country close to the centres of power of the Islamic world. Through new encounters, officials redefined and elaborated on previous understandings of the British imperial mission and their role in it, forming identities in relation to their current situation.

The 1877 convention between the British and Egyptian Governments for the suppression of the slave trade initiated this process. It put British officials into conflict with authorities in that country and gave them the responsibility of undermining accepted practices and customs. Instructions to these officials as well as correspondence among them indicate that they were well aware of what was expected and the opposition they would encounter from Egyptians opposed to their interference. The role that they adopted was essentially an imperial one influenced by earlier representations of the British hero engaged in a civilising mission. This image, loyalty to the Government and the belief in the immorality of slavery determined, to a great extent, the initial attitudes and approach of British officials to the Egyptians.

The power of this role lies in its flexibility. British officials came from a variety of backgrounds and perspectives. Not all were English – they hailed from other areas of the British Isles, the British Empire and Europe – yet they found meaning in a role that helped to define Englishness. In addition, this ideal was recreated in relation to the new circumstances surrounding the campaign in Egypt. For example, representatives of Her Majesty's Government had not always seen slavery and freedom as opposite, mutually exclusive, conditions.[124] Yet in this new context, the stance on the essential immorality of slavery, regardless of cruelty, which had become a part of English society primarily through BFASS representations, motivated British officials and informed their actions and how they presented themselves. Moreover, the temporary, situational and incomplete nature of this identity allowed individuals to reconcile their own understandings of it with the dominant imperial ideologies and the numerous new encounters and activities that took place in Egypt. This role continually evolved as the situation changed, and British officials went from cautiously observing their surroundings to negotiating with Egyptian authorities, to taking military and aggressive action.

In the years immediately after the signing of the 1877 treaty, British officials had very little power. They had to use care and diplomacy, and were limited to assisting Egyptian authorities, monitoring their actions and attempting to influence them. Nevertheless, the early years of the campaign proved a formative period for British officials, a time during which they experienced resistance to their political agenda. They expected such a reaction; it did not cause them to question their mission. Rather the conflicts between their goals and local interests served to define difference for them: those conflicts seemed to distinguish British officials from the Egyptian Muslim men they encountered and confirm that the former were engaged in an important civilising mission in Egypt, which they alone could accomplish, and that, therefore, they required greater power and authority in that country.

During the early years of the campaign, British officials also came into contact with the slave trade in Egypt and surrounding areas. They assisted individual slaves and monitored traffic on steamers, in caravans and along the coasts of the Red Sea. They studied the practices of slave-traders and gathered information about local networks in order to strategise. From their observations as well as the difficulties they encountered, they concluded that their campaign pitted them against not just the slave-traders but an entire society, which they would have to revolutionise using whatever force necessary.

Through the anti-slavery campaign in Egypt the harem, the women's and children's quarters of the Muslim home, acquired new meaning for British officials. Their previous ideas about this institution would have been based primarily on fantastical representations, literary, artistic or otherwise, intended to arouse and delight. However, after 1877 they encountered the hudud, or the boundaries of the harems, which frustrated efforts to monitor and suppress slave traffic. They resented the fact that they were not allowed within the private, domestic sphere, where slaves lived and slave-trading took place. Conflict erupted between British men who wanted access to this space and Muslim men who tried to prevent them from having it. Because Muslim gender and domestic relationships created barriers between females and males outside of the immediate family, British officials increasingly regarded them as obstacles to progress. They understood the harem in the light of their political concerns, dismissing alternative representations of the institution available in the British imperial cultural system.

Defining the harem and Muslim patriarchy played a crucial role in the process of identity formation that occurred through anti-slavery efforts, for a certain masculine ideal associated with Englishness and the British imperial mission developed in relation to them. On the one hand British officials considered Egyptian men to be less evolved, even primitive, in their treatment of women; on the other, these officials also realised that respect for the Muslim male could bolster their own position in Egypt and affirm beliefs that they brought with them about the legitimacy, even the necessity, of male authority. For they proudly assumed Egyptian masculine titles of honour such as pasha and bey, and took care not to promote female independence when freeing slaves. They were so intent on preserving a male governmental and administrative structure to combat the slave trade that they did not consider employing the female anti-slavery workers who lived in Egypt, even though they realised that these women would be able to, for example, question female travellers without their veils and have access to spaces that British officials did not. Thus the English hero of empire created by British officials in the course of anti-slavery activity was a male role which drew power from male authority in Egypt and images of masculinity in that country, even though it was understood in contrast to the Muslim man and his harem.

This ideal served several political functions in the imperial cultural system. For British officers it promoted a version of English patriarchy that seemed to protect women, liberate them from slavery and civilise Egypt. It therefore helped to justify and reinforce English hegemony and an aggressive imperialistic foreign policy in that country. It also presented a counter-argument to feminists in England who criticised the patriarchal gender roles in their society as inherently exploitative and oppressive, an issue that will be explored further in the following chapters.

For British officials, encounters with the Islamic legal system of late nineteenth-century Egypt played as important a role as did gender in the process of identity formation. Their agenda was based on the belief that justice was incompatible with slavery, which therefore positioned them in conflict with Muslim authorities who understood justice as primarily the responsibility of the owner to treat his or her slaves fairly and without cruelty, but not as an idea entailing abolition of the institution itself. Because the qadi, or Muslim courts, often showed sympathy to slave-owners and protected dealers, British officials tried to erode their power, using the threat of military force to influence them and establishing alternative court systems. Through these activities, British officials developed an understanding of themselves as the bearers of justice, and for them the attempt to suppress the slave trade and challenge the Islamic judicial system that sanctioned it meant becoming lovers of liberty.

From the point of view of British officialdom, Islam appeared to be so intimately linked with the slave trade that one could have scarcely existed without the other, and the place that best symbolised this association for them was Mecca, a centre of commerce and an area especially resistant to anti-slavery efforts. Extra British cruisers patrolled its nearby ports during the pilgrimage season and pilgrims were targeted as a group by officials who monitored steamer traffic. The Muslim man, whether in the form of pilgrim, religious authority or court judge, was considered suspect. British officials seem to have concluded that a simple ideology which outlined clear hierarchical distinctions between what they considered to be English justice on the one hand and Muslim tyranny on the other would promote unified and aggressive action in the face of opposition in a way that a more nuanced or sophisticated understanding of Islam and Egyptian society would not.

While British officials had defined their role in Egypt during the early years of anti-slavery activity, in the later period, particularly after the occupation in 1882, which marked a turning point in the campaign, their ideas began to have a significant impact. With increased authority they could pursue their goals openly and with less regard for diplomatic concerns. They established an extensive British-dominated administrative structure to suppress the slave trade: They took control of the Slave Trade Department and established new bureaus for the manumission of slaves. Officers searched caravans, patrolled the Red Sea and monitored steamer traffic more effectively than they could previously. An entire network of officials involved themselves in this project from the eastern coasts of Africa to Cairo and in areas beyond Egypt proper, such as Benghazi and Istanbul.

As a result of such measures, by the late 1890s the trading of slaves in Egypt ceased to exist for all practical purposes; the additional efforts and progress made were well publicised, and by the end of the century the ideal of the bourgeois home had replaced that of the Ottoman harem. Like the British officers who formed new gendered national identities on the basis of imperial encounters and experiences as well as previously held beliefs, the majority of Egyptians adopted the bourgeois household and the roles associated with it as the result of the

British anti-slavery campaign, but reconciled them with their own traditions, customs and interests. They did not simply imitate the British; in fact, they even understood these concepts in ways that challenged imperialist perspectives, often employing the ideal of the bourgeois home in Egyptian nationalist arguments.

Still, to British officials the accomplishment of their mission served to reinforce the beliefs that they had developed already in the course of anti-slavery activity regarding the superiority of their version of English masculinity and patriarchal gender relationships to existing Islamic practices. In other words, the eventual success of the anti-slavery campaign confirmed the identities that developed through it. However, it is important to emphasise that this result was not simply the logical outcome of abolition. In fact, the type of society that emerged in Egypt in the late nineteenth and early twentieth centuries contradicted the fundamental assumptions of British anti-slavery ideology. Its existence demonstrated that neither Islam nor the harem required slavery. Yet British officials chose not to reconsider their earlier judgements in light of the developing situation, and instead they continued to create roles for themselves that reflected their imperial political interests and concerns. As in the early years of anti-slavery activity, the process of identity formation involved choosing to take an interest in certain cultural influences and ignoring others.

As a group, British officials tended to be less creative than the historical actors discussed in the chapters following. They were more concerned with accomplishing the task at hand than in contributing alternative perspectives to the imperial cultural system. As a result, their ideas about English masculinity and national identity were closely connected to their social context and role in Her Majesty's service, following orders, pursuing government objectives and overcoming resistance in Egypt.

However, British officials did not have to perceive their situation or act in the way that they did. For example, they could have decided not to identify with their Government's political agenda. Just like the official who admitted to turning a blind eye to Circassian slaves travelling on steamers because they seemed to receive good care and treatment, British officials could have done the same for female slaves throughout Egypt. They could have likened Muslim patriarchal practices to their own and identified with the Muslim man on the basis of gender, as seen elsewhere in the campaign, assuming that for women maintenance was adequate compensation for loss of liberty as long as there were no obvious signs of cruelty. Had they decided to take this approach, the slave trade would never have been eliminated in the short time that it was.

Perhaps they could have taken the opposite tack, giving primacy not to their masculine or gendered identities but rather to a sense of national identity based on the principle of individual liberty. Abolitionists and other activists had for generations been making the case that to be English meant cherishing certain rights, liberties and freedoms, and feminists had argued that it was positively un-English not to apply these ideas to women as well as to men. Had the British officials who associated their efforts with Englishness adopted this perspective, they would have freed as many slaves as possible without taking precautions to limit the number of independent women that would result. After all their Government did not instruct them to concern themselves with this issue, and even if this policy had created conflict with Muslim men British officials expected conflict in Egypt and often drew inspiration from it.

Despite these alternative possibilities and the diversity among British officials, the overwhelming majority of them chose to suppress female slavery while maintaining a version of patriarchal authority. These historical actors sifted through the various influences available to them within the imperial cultural system. They took previous ideas about patriarchal gender roles and recreated them in the light of new circumstances and in relation to their continually developing understandings of the harem, Islam and the position of the British Government in Egypt. They emphasised and elaborated on certain aspects of these ideas and dismissed others. They also favoured some ways of identifying themselves over others, for example gender or nation, which could change depending on the specific situation. Through individual agency they formed an ideology that made sense of and shaped their experiences in Egypt.[125] In addition, both their words and actions had resonance in England, as the following chapters explain.

Notes

1 I use the term *hegemony* to describe a consensual relationship between the rulers and the ruled on the basis of certain moral and intellectual perspectives, a relationship which legitimises the social order. In this case, ideas about English cultural superiority served to justify British political and economic power in Egypt. However, it is important to understand that these beliefs were never more than partially accepted among even Anglicised and Westernised elites, and they were met with considerable resistance by others in Egyptian society. While the concept of hegemony used in this way has much to with the writings of Antonio Gramsci, one important difference remains: Gramsci understood it as a 'willed and knowing deception' imposed on the governed by the governing; British officials, however, did not think that they were presenting a false sense of reality to the Egyptians. Rather, like BFASS supporters (discussed in chapter three), they believed in the superiority of their values and pursued policies that reinforced this perspective: *Antonio Gramsci: Selected Writings 1916–1935*, ed. David Forgacs (London: Lawrence & Wishart, 1988), p. 196.

THE HAREM, SLAVERY AND BRITISH IMPERIAL CULTURE

2   To attempt to reform a society on an English model should not be confused with trying to turn the people who live in it into English men and women. Even the Anglicised Indian of the British Empire was seen as a 'mimic man' or 'almost the same [as the Englishman] but not quite': Homi Bhabha, 'Of Mimicry and Man: The Ambivalence of Colonial Discourse', *The Location of Culture* (London and New York: Routledge, 1994), pp. 85–92.
3   As chapter four shows, *proper* English gender roles were contested fiercely during this period, and through anti-slavery activity British officials entered these debates presenting a certain ideal as the norm. For discussion of Victorian masculinities see James Eli Adams, *Dandies and Desert Saints* (Ithaca, NY, and London: Cornell University Press, 1995).
4   FO 195/108, Lord Ponsonby to Lord Palmerston, Secretary of State for Foreign Affairs, December 1840.
5   For discussion of Egypt in the nineteenth century and British influence in that country see the following: Ahmad 'Abd al-Rahim Mustafa focuses on the period between the establishment of the Caisse de la Dette Publique and the British occupation in *Misr wa al-Mas'ala al-Misriyya min 1876 ila 1882* (Cairo: Dar al-Ma'arif bi-Misr, 1966); J. C. B. Richmond, *Egypt 1798–1952: Her Advance Towards a Modern Identity* (London: Methuen, 1977); 'Abd al-Ghafar Muhammad Husayn covers Egyptian history from the eighteenth century until the British occupation in *Bina' al-Dawla al-Haditha fi Misr* (Cairo: Dar al-Ma'arif, 1981); Afaf Lutfi al-Sayyid Marsot, *A Short History of Modern Egypt* (Cambridge: Cambridge University Press, 1985); and 'Abd al-'Azim Ramadan gives an overview of political and economic developments in the country during the nineteenth and twentieth centuries in *Awraq fi Ta'rikh Misr* (Cairo: al-Hay'a al-Misriyya al-'Amma li al-Kitab, 1995).
6   The summary of the terms of the convention includes annex A and an attached ordinance issued and published by the khedive as required by article 5 of the convention.
7   *Convention entre les gouvernements britannique et égyptien pour la suppression de la traite des esclaves*, FOBPP, 1877.
8   FOBPP, 'Circular Addressed to Her Majesty's Consular Officers in Egypt', August 1877 (vol. 56, p. 35); the same circular is in FOCP 541/21.
9   Graham Dawson discusses images of imperial masculinity in Victorian England in *Soldier Heroes: British Adventure, Empire and the Imagining of Masculinities* (London and New York: Routledge, 1994).
10 FOCP 541/21.
11 FOBPP, 'Circular Addressed to Her Majesty's Consular Officers in Egypt', August 1877 (vol. 56, p. 35).
12 FO 84/1371, Mr West to Mr Vivian, July 1873.
13 Sometimes they would pay the expenses from their own pockets and then later request compensation from their superiors, and at other times they would arrange for slaves to be temporarily housed with friends or marry soldiers in the army: FOBPP, The Governor-General of the Coast of the Red Sea to Riaz Pasha, October 1880 (vol. 58, p. 107).
14 FOBPP, Mr Malet to Earl Granville, January 1881 (vol. 59, p. 1).
15 FOBPP, Mr Vivian to the Earl of Derby, September 1877 (vol. 56, p. 39); FOBPP, Chérif Pasha to Mr Vivian, September 1877 (vol. 56, p. 40); FOBPP, Sir J. Pauncefote to Mr Vivian, November 1877 (vol. 56, p. 50); and FOCP 541/21, November 1877.
16 Groups of slaves would travel from Jiddah to Mecca or northwards to the Hijaz: FOBPP, Acting Consul Burrell to Mr Goschen, September 1880 (vol. 58, p. 272).
17 FO 84/1412, Captain Beyts to the Earl of Derby, June 1875.
18 FO 84/1472 and FO 84/1371, July 1873; later FO letters and reports corroborate these estimates.
19 On rare occasions British officials discovered vessels holding over 200 or even 300 slaves.
20 FOBPP, Mr Vivian to Chérif Pasha, April 1877 (vol. 56, p. 18).

21 FOBPP, Captain Malcolm to the Marquis of Salisbury, July 1878 (vol. 57, p. 24); the same document is in FOCP 541/22.
22 FOBPP, Consul Beyts to the Earl of Derby, March 1877 (vol. 56, p. 252).
23 FO 84/1472, Morice Bey's reports, 1877.
24 FOBPP, 'Passenger Certificates', December 1877 (vol. 56, p. 55) and FO 84/1472.
25 Exact numbers of slaves who travelled by steamer are difficult to determine. During the years 1872–73, 663 were detained by British officials in Malta alone. One common route involved bringing slaves from Central Africa overland to Tripoli where they would then board steamers to Istanbul via Malta. Alexandria, Suez, and Smyrna were all key ports as well. Sources relating to slave traffic by steamer and its suppression can be found throughout Foreign Office correspondence; the FO 84 series from the early 1870s is especially helpful.
26 FO 84/1427, October 1873.
27 British consuls could initiate investigations aboard steamers, but usually the matter would have to be turned over to the local authorities.
28 FO 84/1354, July 1872. While this particular reference dates from before the signing of the convention, British attitudes regarding the issue of slave traffic via steamer described above continued and even intensified after 1877.
29 Common routes included travelling north from the Sudan and then along the Nile to Aswan; coming from the west and crossing the Libyan desert to Assiout; and moving northwards from oasis to oasis just west of Cairo. Richard Burton reported a 'small but vigorous' branch of slave traffic northwest of Cairo: FOBPP, Consul Richard Burton to Earl Granville, April 1880 (vol. 58, p. 62).
30 FOBPP, 'Memorandum by Mr A. B. Wylde Regarding Slave Trade in the Soudan and its Red Sea Coast', September 1878 (vol. 57, p. 151).
31 FOBPP, Vice-Consul Borg to Mr Vivian, August 1878 (vol. 57, p. 33).
32 These slaves were destined for Tripoli, Banghazi, Cairo, and Istanbul.
33 FOBPP, Consul Henderson to the Earl of Derby, September 1877 (vol. 56, p. 233).
34 FOBPP, Vice-Consul Jago to Sir H. Elliot, December 1876 (vol. 56, p. 240).
35 FOBPP, the Earl of Derby to Mr Layard, March 1878 (vol. 57, p. 113).
36 FOCP 541/22, Julian Pauncefote, January 1878.
37 The Ottoman Government accepted responsibility for ensuring that freed slaves had some means of supporting themselves.
38 British cruisers had this right in the Red Sea, the Gulf of Aden, off the coast of Arabia, in the Persian Gulf and off of the east coast of Africa, as well as in 'Ottoman maritime waters when no constituted authorities exist'.
39 FOBPP, Acting Consul Barker to Mr Layard, Salonica, October 1877 (vol. 56, p. 245); the same document is in FOCP 541/21.
40 FOBPP, the Earl of Derby to Sir H. Elliot, June 1876 (vol. 55, p. 149).
41 FO 84/1450, June 1876; FO 84/1412, Mr Elliot to the Earl of Derby, December 1875; and FOCP 541/20, December 1875.
42 FOBPP, Memorandum, Zeila, February 1878 (vol. 57, p. 12); the same document is in FOCP 541/22.
43 FOCP 541/27, Consul Jago to the Marquis of Salisbury, July 1887.
44 FOBPP, Dispatch from the Vali of Bangazi to the Sublime Porte, c.1880 (vol. 58, p. 255). British authorities were, however, able to request police searches of the private quarters of known slave-dealers in Ottoman territories after 1889: FOCP 541/30, Memorandum by Mr Marinich on the Slave Trade in Turkey, 1889; and FO 84/2144 Memorandum from Dragoman Marinich, March 1891.
45 FOBPP, Enclosure No. 65, Abubekr Pasha of Zaila to Hasan Ali Rajab Ali, not dated but enclosed in letter dated December 1878 (vol. 57 p. 49); the same document is in FOCP 541/22.
46 FOBPP, Consul Jago to Mr Wyndham, February 1885 (vol. 60, p. 77).
47 FOBPP, Consul Sandwith to Sir W. White, September 1885 (vol. 60, p. 76). Fifteen days was the suggested amount of time, although in practice this varied: FOBPP, 'Circular Vizirial Order to the Provincial Authorities', October 1884 (vol. 60, p. 83).
48 FO 84/1354, September 1872.

49 FO 84/1370, March 1873. As these examples suggest, British officials could exert influence on Egyptian authorities in matters related to slave traffic via steamer even before the 1877 convention, and their power in this area only increased after its signing.
50 FOBPP, Declaration of Khelill made at the British Consulate-General at Baghdad, April 1878 (vol. 57, p. 129); the materials related to the case printed in FOBPP before and after this document are also helpful.
51 It is unclear from the correspondence how this case was resolved; however, as the matter was brought to the attention of both British and Ottoman authorities, it is unlikely that the man in question had to serve the entire two-year sentence: FO 84/1370, October 1873.
52 FOCP 541/20, December 1874.
53 FOBPP, Vice-Consul Borg to Mr Vivian, August 1878 (vol. 57, p. 33), and Lieutenant-Colonel Schaefer to Sir E. Baring, February 1887 (vol. 60, p. 10).
54 FOBPP, Vice-Consul Borg to Mr Cookson, July 1881 (vol. 59, p. 45).
55 FOBPP, 'Return of Slaves Who Have Sought Refuge in Her Majesty's Consulate at Jeddah, or Who Have Been Manumitted Through the Intervention of Her Majesty's Consul, During the Quarter Ended September 30, 1881' (vol. 59, p. 134).
56 FO 84/1370, February 1873.
57 FO 84 1675, Consul Baker to Sir E. Baring, November 1884.
58 Judith Walkowitz, *Prostitution and Victorian Society: Women, Class and the State* (Cambridge: Cambridge University Press, 1980).
59 Robert Young, *Colonial Desire: Hybridity in Theory, Culture and Race* (London and New York: Routledge, 1995), p. 181.
60 FOCP 541/22.
61 This informant made a report to Charles Allen, secretary of the BFASS: FOBPP, Mr Allen to Earl Granville, June 1880 (vol. 58, p. 81).
62 FOBPP, 'Return of Slaves' (vol. 59, p. 133).
63 FOBPP, Admiralty Reports, Lieutenant Bremer to Captain Foot, September 1881 (vol. 59, p. 52).
64 Mary Poovey has examined the fundamentally 'uneven' and unstable nature of gender ideology in Victorian England, showing how it was constantly in the process of being constructed, revised and challenged: *Uneven Developments: The Ideological Work of Gender in Mid-Victorian England* (Chicago, IL: University of Chicago Press, 1988).
65 These beliefs had become a part of English society primarily through the work of the BFASS and other anti-slavery activists.
66 FOBPP, Sir Stratford Canning to Viscount Palmerston, July 1849 (vol. 39, p. 403).
67 FO 84 /1371, Mr West to Mr Vivian, July 1873.
68 For discussion of the Egyptian judicial system during this period see Jasper Yeates Brinton, *The Mixed Courts of Egypt* (New Haven, CT, and London: Yale University Press, 1968); and Byron Cannon, *Politics of Law and the Courts in Nineteenth-Century Egypt* (Salt Lake City: University of Utah Press, 1988).
69 FO 84/1370, November 1873.
70 FOBPP, Memorandum from Colonel Schaefer to M. de Martino, February 1887 (vol. 60, p. 15).
71 FO 84/1370, Sir H. Elliot, July 1873.
72 FO 84/1618, 1882.
73 FOBPP, Sir E. Baring to Earl Granville, February 1884 (vol. 60, p. 3).
74 FOBPP, Memorandum by D. A. Cameron, Consular Assistant, February 1885 (vol. 60, p. 12); the same document is in FO 84/1721.
75 FOCP 541/26, Memorandum by Hugo Marinich, Second Dragoman in Her Majesty's Embassy, July 1884.
76 FOCP 541/22, March 1878. Captain Malcolm had the title of the director-general of the Suppression of the Slave Trade in the Red Sea.
77 Egypt already had a class of 'secular legalists' serving the mixed courts created in 1875–76; these were courts with both European and Egyptian judges responsible for

THE ANTI-SLAVERY CAMPAIGN IN EGYPT

trying cases involving non-Egyptian parties on the basis of French law: Brinton, *The Mixed Courts of Egypt*.
78 Brinton, *The Mixed Courts of Egypt*, p. 158.
79 FOBPP, Memorandum by D. A. Cameron, Consular Assistant, February 1885 (vol. 60, p. 12–13); and FO 84/1672, Sir E. Baring to Lord Granville, February 1884.
80 Quotation of FOBPP, Mr Egerton to the Marquis of Salisbury, August 1885 (vol. 60, p. 19); the reference to convicting slave-traders through the new system is from FOCP 541/50, Schaefer to E. Baring, April 1886.
81 FOCP 541/50, Sir E. Baring to the Earl of Roseberry, April 1886. According to the 1877 convention, a 'competent tribunal' must try these cases. Foreign Office correspondence reveals that the phrase 'competent tribunal' was decided on only after a variety of suggestions were considered by both representatives of the British and Egyptian governments, and was chosen most likely because of its ambiguity: that way the convention would be signed, but resolving a difficult issue could be postponed for seven more years.
82 FO 84/1675, Baker to Granville, February 1884.
83 FOBPP, Lieutenant-General Sir F. Stephenson to Sir E. Baring, May 1885 (vol. 60, p. 14).
84 FOCP 541/21 and FOBPP, Mr Vivian to the Earl of Derby, October 1877 (vol. 56, pp. 46–7).
85 FOBPP, Consul Dupuis to Sir A. H. Layard, June 1880 (vol. 58, p. 231).
86 FOBPP, Consul Richard F. Burton to Earl Granville, May 1880 (vol. 58, p. 64).
87 FOCP 541/47, Consul Zohrab to the Marquis of Salisbury, May 1879.
88 FOCP 541/25, Memorandum by Lynedoch N. Moncrieff, February 1882.
89 FOCP 541/47, Consul Zohrab to the Marquis of Salisbury, May 1879.
90 Ehud Toledano, *The Ottoman Slave Trade and its Suppression: 1840–1890* (Princeton, NJ: Princeton University Press, 1982), pp. 129–35.
91 FOCP 541/20, Extract from Captain Beyts' Council Report, 1875.
92 FOBPP, 'Memorandum Respecting the Soudan Littoral Contraband Trade', October 1885 (vol. 60, p. 21).
93 FOBPP, the Earl of Derby to Sir H. Elliot, July 1876 (vol. 55, p. 159).
94 FOBPP, Consul Beyts to the Earl of Derby, March 1876 (vol. 55, p. 165).
95 FOCP 541/27, Consul Cameron to Sir E. Baring, January 1887.
96 FOCP 541/22, Commander Powlett to Rear Admiral Corbett, April 1878, and FOBPP, Vice-Consul Wylde to the Earl of Derby, February 1878 (vol. 57, p. 135).
97 For discussion of Sayyid Amir Ali see chapter five. The nature of true Islam was a concern and matter for debate in late nineteenth-century Egyptian society. For example, the writings of individuals who criticised the status quo and offered strategies for reform, such as Jamal al-Din al-Afghani, Muhammad 'Abduh, and Qasim Amin, became well known. For discussion of these individuals and others who presented alternative interpretations of Islam during this period see Albert Hourani, *Arabic Thought in the Liberal Age 1798–1939* (Oxford: Oxford University Press, 1962).
98 Ahmad Shafiq, *al-Riqq fi al-Islam*, translated from French into Arabic by Ahmad Zaki (Cairo, 1892), pp. 96–100. A report on the speech for the Egyptian National Geographic Society is in the Arabic scientific journal, *Al-Muktataf*, 41 (Cairo, 1892), 495–7.
99 FO 84/1672, Sir E. Baring to Lord Granville, February 1884.
100 Beachey notes that Ismail's mother had three hundred Circassian slaves, and that his favourite Circassian concubine had fifty Circassian and thirty Abyssinian slaves: *The Slave Trade of Eastern Africa* (New York: Harper & Row, 1976) p. 130. Cited from Emine Tugay, *Three Centuries: Family Chronicles of Turkey and Egypt* (London: Oxford University Press, 1963), pp. 179, 191.
101 FO 84/1371, Mr Vivian to Granville, July 1873.
102 Baron De Malortie, *Egypt: Native Rulers and Foreign Interference* (London: William Ridgeway, 1883), p. 203, quoted by Kenneth Cuno in 'Ambiguous Modernization: The Transition to Monogamy in the Khedival House of Egypt', in

Beshara Doumani (ed.), *Family History in the Middle East: Household, Property, and Gender* (Albany: State University of New York Press, 2003), pp. 247–70, at 253.
103 One such report noted that a recent inquiry found 4 men guilty of trading in slaves; they were punished with 3 years' penal servitude with their legs 'in irons': FOBPP, Moustapha Fehmy, the Minister for Foreign Affairs, to Mr Malet, December 1880 (vol. 58, p. 128). In an effort to publicise the Egyptian Government's new vigilance, circulars issued to local governors were printed in the *Moniteur Égyptien*: FOBPP, Mr Malet to Earl Granville, November 1880 (vol. 58, p. 98).
104 FOBPP, Mr Cookson to Earl Granville, June 1881 (vol. 59, p. 43).
105 FOBPP, Correspondence, 1880 (vol. 58, pp. 56–66).
106 FOBPP, Count della Sala to Mr Malet, February 1881 (vol. 59, p. 11).
107 FOBPP, Mr Malet to Earl Granville, January 1881 (vol. 59, p. 5).
108 The English tradition of appearing in 'Oriental dress' and its relationship to mimicry and empire are discussed in chapter five.
109 FO 84/1472, Mr Vivian to the Earl of Derby, March 1877.
110 FO 84/1618, Mr Malet to Granville, October 1882.
111 FO 84/1642, Malet to Granville, March 1883. He was replaced by Colonel Schaefer Bey shortly afterwards.
112 FO 84/1642, Mr Malet to Chérif Pasha, February 1883.
113 FOBPP, Sir. E. Baring to Earl Granville, February 1884 (vol. 60, p. 4).
114 FOBPP, Lieutenant-Colonel Schaefer to Sir E. Baring, February 1887 (vol. 60, p. 8).
115 FOCP 541/27 and FOBPP, Lieutenant-Colonel Schaefer to Sir E. Baring, February 1887 (vol. 60, pp. 9–10). In 1877 there were seventy-eight slave-dealers and brokers working in Cairo: FOCP 541/47, Vice-Consul Borg to Mr Lascelles, September 1879.
116 This conference was initiated by Queen Victoria as a result of representations by the BFASS.
117 In addition, Ottoman authorities were required to give special attention to the western coast of Arabia, an area of concern for British commanders in the Red Sea.
118 The treaty is printed in *Nouveau Recueil general de traités et autres actes relatifs aux rapports de droit international*, second series, vol. 23, 1898, pp. 166–79; the quotation is of article 5, a measure which made slavery a voluntary condition in the eyes of the law, but even legally manumitted slaves who had not been freed by their masters were not treated as independent people by the Muslim courts, and for this reason, the 1895 treaty did not entirely appease the abolitionists: *ASR* (M-J 1898), 101–2. However, a khedival decree in 1896 made it illegal for anyone to interfere with the liberty of a freed slave, 'de jouir de sa pleine liberté et de disposer de sa personne'. Article 4 of the khedive's decree is printed in the Egyptian *Journal Officiel* for January 1896 and reprinted on p. 177 of *Nouveau Recueil general de traités*. British officials used this law to pressure former slave-owners into giving freed slaves certificates of manumission, so that Muslim courts would recognise them as free subjects: FOCP 541/29, Sir E. Baring to the Marquis of Salisbury, April 1899.
119 FOCP 541/29, Sir E. Baring to the Marquis of Salisbury, April 1889.
120 Beth Baron, 'The Making of the Egyptian Nation', in Ida Blom, Karen Hagemann and Catherine Hall (eds), *Gendered Nations: Nationalisms and Gender Order in the Long Nineteenth Century* (Oxford: Berg, 2000) pp. 137–58, at 148–9.
121 Beth Baron, *The Women's Awakening in Egypt: Culture, Society, and the Press* (New Haven, CT, and London: Yale University Press, 1994), p. 145; also see Soha Abdel Kader, *Egyptian Women in a Changing Society, 1899–1987* (Boulder, CO, and London: Lynne Rienner, 1987); and Margot Badran, *Feminists, Islam, and Nation: Gender and the Making of Modern Egypt* (Princeton, NJ: Princeton University Press, 1995).
122 Cuno, 'Ambiguous Modernization'.
123 'Imad Ahmad Hilal concludes that the abolition of slavery in Egypt would not have been possible without the eventual support of the people and their religious leaders, particularly Muhammad 'Abduh: *al-Raqiq fi Misr fi al-qarn al-tasi' 'ashara* (Cairo, 1999), p. 386.

124 For example, in 1833 the British Parliament recognised 'degrees of unfreedom' and took into consideration the issue of cruelty when defining slavery, allowing forms of bondage to continue in India, while it was opposed in the Caribbean: Madhavi Kale, '"When The Saints Came Marching In": The Anti-Slavery Society and Indian Indentured Migration to the British Caribbean', in Martin Daunton and Rick Halpern (eds), *Empire and Others: British Encounters with Indigenous Peoples, 1600–1850* (London: University College London Press, 1999), pp. 325–44, at 335–6. In addition, from the early to mid nineteenth century, British officials rarely allowed abolitionist concerns to influence their approach to government in India, despite BFASS pressure: Indrani Chatterjee, *Gender, Slavery and Law in Colonial India* (Oxford: Oxford University Press, 1999). It was even acceptable for men associated with the East India Company to have slave concubines, referring to the women, to whose families they paid a fee, as 'housekeepers' or 'prostitutes': Indrani Chatterjee, 'Colouring Subalternity: Slaves, Concubines and Social Orphans in Early Colonial India', in Gautam Bhadra, Gyan Prakash and Susie Tharu (eds), *Subaltern Studies X: Writings on South Asian History and Society* (Oxford: Oxford University Press, 1999), pp. 49–97.

125 Miguel Cabrera's definition of culture as 'society's repertoire of interpretive mechanisms and value systems' is helpful in that we can imagine British officials drawing from such a repertoire in order to create meaning: 'On Language, Culture and Social Action', *History and Theory*, 40 (December 2001), 82–100, at 84.

CHAPTER THREE

Networks of support: English activism and slavery redefined

The activities of British officials in Egypt, described in the previous chapter, represent one aspect of the anti-slavery campaign. Members of the BFASS initiated this movement, volunteered funds and services and provided the link between women and men in England and efforts abroad. While British officials had made a commitment to their Government and accepted responsibility for enforcing its policies, the BFASS assumed the equally challenging task of generating support from private individuals within English society. They succeeded by creating a discourse, or an ideological framework, which appealed to a variety of people for different reasons, but simultaneously united them around a certain conception of English national identity defined in gendered, moral and imperial terms and in contrast to the harem and Islam. In this chapter I examine the creation of this ideological system, a social event in itself, as well as how these ideas functioned politically and were expressed through grassroots activism within the wider British imperial culture.[1]

Central to this framework was a belief that slavery was essentially immoral and that English people were responsible for its eradication. In public meetings and events, and on the pages of its publication the *Anti-Slavery Reporter* (*ASR*), frequent mention was made of England's moral obligation to Egypt. The BFASS called on English people to make sacrifices for the cause and to put aside internal differences and partisan politics in order to unite in the anti-slavery campaign. To neglect this responsibility, it was felt, would be a betrayal: one speaker at a BFASS public meeting stated that General Gordon had given his life to the suppression of the slave trade in Africa, and then asked the audience, 'shall we let his death and those of the hundreds of other martyr heroes whom England has yielded to freedom count for naught? . . . England's answer will be no.'[2]

This type of rhetoric appeared frequently in BFASS speeches and publications. As I show in this chapter, the individuals who involved themselves in this campaign were of diverse background and motivation, and they came from different parts of the British Isles, the British Empire and the world. While most activists were from England, they still represented only a minority in that society. Nevertheless, supporters mobilised themselves around an ideology that associated the cause with the English nation and presented that nation as sufficiently unified or even monolithic that it could be imagined as speaking with one collective voice.

BFASS members drew on beliefs current in English society and culture, expanding on them in significant ways. Even prior to anti-slavery activity in Egypt, a sense of English national identity had developed which was characterised by the belief that slavery was immoral, and that English men and women had an obligation to humankind to spread liberty and fight oppression wherever it occurred, at home or abroad. This assumption existed in England as implicit knowledge. While this type of knowledge, or system of meaning, is regarded as self-evident, and so in need of no explanation or defence, it actually had to be presented repeatedly in order to preserve the illusion of stability.[3]

How the immorality of slavery became implicit knowledge in English society deserves brief discussion, and an examination of this development helps to illustrate the situational and contested nature of English identity. The movement to abolish slavery in the British colonies began in the eighteenth century, early abolitionists drawing inspiration from writers such as Locke and Montesquieu, as well as other Enlightenment figures who asserted the rights of the individual and celebrated the ideals of liberty, equality and universal brotherhood. Certain Christian groups adopted these beliefs as their own: in 1724 the Quakers became the first Christian community in England to take a collective stand on the issue by passing a resolution condemning the slave trade, and Wesleyans, Evangelicals and others soon followed. Some of the most outspoken and active contributors to the cause were similarly members of religious organisations and they understood anti-slavery work as their Christian duty. Both Granville Sharp's legal efforts in the 1760s and the famous Somersett case in 1772 served to publicise slavery as a problem, and as the issue received more attention support for abolition grew in England.[4]

The work of anti-slavery organisations proved crucial to the evolution of public opinion. In 1787 the Society for the Abolition of the Slave Trade was established, and its members helped to publicise the issue through lectures, writings and political agitation. Petitioning efforts were especially successful, and over 500 petitions were presented to Parliament in 1792 alone.[5] Activists continued their work even after the slave trade was abolished in 1807. In 1823 the BFASS, a private humanitarian organisation associated with neither the Government nor the established Church, centralised the movement by linking together smaller groups throughout the country. The eventual abolition of slavery in Britain and its colonies in 1833 was both a great victory for the cause and a high point for the BFASS in terms of recognition and popular support.

After 1833, abolitionists directed their efforts internationally. In 1840 the first anti-slavery world convention was held in London, with representatives from France and the United States, and in 1843 Parliament prohibited British subjects from owning or trading in slaves anywhere in the world. By mid-century the British Government found itself at the centre of an extensive treaty network for the suppression of the slave trade, which would soon include almost every nation with a coastline on the Atlantic or the Indian Ocean.[6] As a strong Anglo-American abolitionist alliance had existed since the early days of anti-slavery activity, the United States became an area of particular concern until the emancipation of slaves in that country in 1863. Thereafter, English abolitionists increasingly turned their attention to female, or harem-oriented, slavery as practised in the Islamic world.[7]

While the abolitionist movement eventually succeeded in convincing the majority of English people that slavery was fundamentally wrong, it is important to understand this change as a historical development as opposed to an attribute of Englishness. For in the eighteenth century the immorality of slavery was not obvious to all, and abolitionists encountered formidable opposition from those who represented the interests of West Indian planters. Their arguments that slaves were not treated cruelly and that slavery was 'countenanced by the law of God' were not unlike those that anti-slavery workers would encounter in late nineteenth-century Egypt. In addition, defenders of slavery maintained that Africans were fortunate to be on plantations where they would be under Christian influence rather than in 'heathen' lands. They also warned that abolition would bring ruin to the West Indian economy, and to the English economy as well, particularly in centres of trade such as London and Liverpool. According to their argument, all property rights would be in danger were planters deprived of their slaves, a serious threat considering the importance of property to the social order.[8]

The transition from a society where such arguments could find acceptance to one in which the immorality of slavery generally was understood as a truth obvious enough to need no explanation had to do with changing social relationships as well as intellectual and political developments; for abolitionism coincided with the emergence of an increasingly influential middle-class that had been inspired by movements such as the American Revolution and Wilkite radicalism to challenge the old social order based on landed property. To these people the privileges of the planter class of the West Indies represented the very inequalities and injustices that they sought to remove from their own society and radicals, 'almost without exception', likened their situation to that of slaves.[9] Anti-slavery had become so much a part of the emerging middle-class value system that when the 1832 Reform Act to enfranchise property-holding males was passed activists celebrated it as a victory for their cause, and within the next year, slavery was in fact abolished.[10]

The association of slavery abroad with inequalities in England began with middle-class agitators and soon spread to the workers. By the 1830s plebeian radicals identified their cause with concern for human rights, which included those of slaves as well as workers. Thomas Hardy, a Paineite and founder of the London Corresponding Society, explained that the rights of man '"are not confined to this small island but are extended to the whole human race, black and white, high or low, rich or poor"'.[11] Members of Chartist and other working-class organisations sometimes even disrupted anti-slavery meetings to demand that middle-class abolitionists recognise the plight of the 'white wage slaves' in their midst as well as that of the plantation slaves in the West Indies.[12]

The belief in the essential immorality of slavery, which became implicit knowledge by the late nineteenth century and was associated with English national identity during this time, had much to do with the social context and class politics in England. As abolitionism was increasingly identified with the rights of ordinary English people and industrialists *vis-à-vis* the aristocracy or the old social order that protected landed interests and privilege, to admit the legitimacy of the practice of slavery anywhere would be to deny the belief system on which both middle-class hegemony and the aspirations of workers rested. The nineteenth century saw the triumph of the middle-class ideal and thus the widespread acceptance of the fundamental wrongness of slavery.[13]

This implicit knowledge or belief in the inherent immorality of slavery was called into question when abolitionists encountered an alternative ideological system, or worldview, in Islam as practised in Egypt and surrounding areas; for slavery was sanctioned in the Qur'an and was considered legitimate by religious authorities in that country until the very end of the nineteenth century. The overwhelming majority of BFASS supporters responded not by attempting to understand this belief system or the different perspectives within it – some of which were compatible with their own agenda, for example the common practice of liberating slaves 'for the sake of God' related in the previous chapter – but instead by increasingly regarding it as the root cause of slavery and oppression and even as an evil that needed to be eliminated.

Understanding Islam in this way served specific political purposes: it generated support for the anti-slavery cause by presenting it as struggle between good and evil; and it also helped to create, or actually recreate in a new context, a sense of English national identity closely associated with liberal Enlightenment ideas. The issue of how slavery in Egypt was represented and understood is not a minor one. It was not inevitable that the anti-slavery movement would be extended to that country; rather it was through representation that individuals were inspired to work to abolish a form of slavery that had hitherto received very little attention.

The anti-slavery workers' portrayal of an evil Islamic world was the result of a conscious effort on the part of BFASS organisers. During the 1870s BFASS members undertook an initiative to educate the English public on the issue of slave-trading, as they understood it, in Muslim countries. In 1873 a BFASS reporter explained that at the public meetings held throughout the country during that year, 'almost without exception the Anti-Slavery Society friends are surprised to find . . . that slavery prevails yet so widely in various forms in Mohammedan countries'.[14] In the years following, slavery as practised in Islam would continue to be on the BFASS agenda for public meetings and events. The BFASS Jubilee pamphlet informed its readers that attention must be turned to the East in order to 'storm' the 'hitherto impenetrable stronghold of Mussulman slavery'.[15] In 1875, a prominent BFASS member published a book in which he criticised the European powers for ignoring slavery in Muslim countries.[16] Lest the people of England become complacent because of the domestic nature of Egyptian slavery, Cardinal Manning warned a crowd at the Manchester Jubilee meeting that 'Mahammedan slavery' was in fact more atrocious, cruel, degrading and brutal than that of the West, and that the Eastern market was much larger than the Western one had been. Therefore, he argued, it was Great Britain's duty to crush it.[17]

Contemporary accounts locate the buying and selling of slaves amid, if not in connection with, religious centres: articles published in the *ASR* contain frequent reports of slave-trading in Mecca and among pilgrims. One of the slides shown at BFASS presentations displays only a single quotation describing the slave market in Mecca:

> The Slave Market in Mecca is on a street leading to one of the gates of the Great Mosque. At certain hours of the day male and female slaves are made to sit on stone benches in front of the houses, so that the passers-by may inspect them . . . the faces of the women are veiled. They lift their veils if requested to do so. Any closer inspection of a slave by a prospective purchaser takes place inside the slave dealer's house. (Mr Eldon Rutter)[18]

The image of the mosque figures prominently in both BFASS illustrations and text: it is recognisable in slides and *ASR* pictures by its dome with a crescent on the top and a minaret, and articles report that slaves were sold 'in the courtyard of the mosque' or 'in view of the mosque'. Certainly, these were statements of fact, though the decision to include them repeatedly served the political purpose of linking Islam with slave-trading in the minds of anti-slavery supporters.

Like British officials in Egypt, BFASS members saw slavery as so intimately linked with Islam that no Muslim society could exist without it, and they frequently expressed the belief that the spread of slavery accompanied the spread of Islam. One journalist remarked that slavery would prevail as long as Islam did;[19] another stated that slavery was 'in practice and theory, the essence and the life-blood of the Mohammedan system'; and Cardinal Lavigerie, the French Roman Catholic primate of Africa who worked with the BFASS and became one of the leaders of an international anti-slavery movement, pronounced at the well-publicised and well-covered anti-slavery congress in Paris that the 'whole framework of Mohammedan society reposes on it [slavery]'.[20]

BFASS supporters expressed doubts that Muslims would obey edicts or honour treaties to suppress slavery both because the Qur'an sanctions it and because the 'Commander of the Faithful', or the Ottoman sultan, was rumoured to have 1,000 women and girls in his seraglio.[21] Often the connection between slave-trading and Islam was communicated through descriptions of slave-hunters who would pray before a capture and then thank God for success or of slave-traders who began human auctions with prayers.[22] Stories like these presented Muslims in the most negative of lights and served to reassure BFASS supporters that even though Islam seemed to challenge their ideas on slavery and morality, this alternative perspective should not bring them to question their own implicit knowledge or assumed beliefs. Instead, they should regard that religion as corrupt, even evil, and interpret its sanctioning of slavery as evidence of its inferiority.

Because of the prominent place of religious leaders in the organisation, BFASS writings often were characterised by a crusading or missionary spirit, promoting Christianity as the alternative to Islam and slavery. Cardinal Lavigerie pronounced Islam to be 'a curse upon Africa' that needed to be eradicated immediately. While Lavigerie was French and so outspoken that he was criticised by the English press for attempting to lead a modern anti-Muslim crusade, his rhetoric was well received by cheering crowds of men and women in England, and similar opinions and attitudes were expressed by others in that country. Frequently, appeals were made in the *ASR* for the countries of Christendom to unite in spreading civilisation in the land of the 'false prophet'. BFASS correspondent, missionary and author Fred Arnot wrote *Garenganze or Seven Years' Pioneer Mission Work in Central Africa* in which he presented Islam as associated not only with slavery but with cannibalism and the worship of Satan. These statements, despite their outrageousness, were accepted by many, and Arnot was awarded two prestigious grants from the Royal Geographical Society.[23]

While Christian leaders acknowledged that the Bible did not prohibit slavery or even polygamy, they still found ways to promote Christianity as the means by which to eliminate slavery in Muslim societies. J. Eastoe Teall, assistant secretary of the BFASS and an author, explained that Christ would have prohibited it had he seen the cruel practices associated with modern slave hunts.[24] The bishop of Manchester pronounced to his large congregation that Christianity was responsible for eradicating slavery from ancient Greece and Rome, and later from the United States as well.[25] Others emphasised Christian teachings about the fellowship of humanity, the value of each individual soul and the sanctity of work. The way to eliminate slavery, such abolitionists argued, was by teaching the Gospel and spreading their faith throughout Africa and the Middle East. For them, Christianisation was the central and most significant aspect of the larger civilising mission. One writer even suggested the establishment of model towns and settlements, accomplished by force, in order to show Africans how to live without slavery or polygamy, a plan that included Christian instruction in order to prevent any relapse into 'barbarism'.[26]

These ideas about Christianity often were conflated with a sense of English national identity in BFASS discourse. One speaker at a BFASS public meeting announced that England had been appointed by God to undertake the anti-slavery mission;[27] another described the cause as a fight for 'Christianity, Liberty and Truth' in which England, with God's help, would put an end to slavery.[28] Even the French Cardinal Lavigerie knew how to appeal to English national pride: at one meeting, he explained to a cheering crowd that slavery was hateful to God and that he was addressing 'Christian England' because he knew of nowhere else where human liberty was as much respected. In these types of writing and speech, liberty was understood as Christian liberty and to spread Christianity was to widen English influence and vice versa.

Many Christian abolitionists, or abolitionists who claimed a Christian perspective or identity, saw Islam with its tolerance of polygamy and slave-trading as both an obstacle to their immediate goals and a threat to Christian people generally. Frequently such articles as 'Missions in Africa: Mohammedan Difficulties' appeared, presenting missionary efforts as thwarted by Islam's appeal as a religion that allows polygamy and slavery.[29] One article related that missionaries found it impossible to convert an African prince to Christianity because he had 1,500 wives and could not be monogamous.[30] Reports of Christian women and children from Russia, Eastern Europe and Abyssinia kidnapped and sold into slavery appeared periodically. One article described a raid in which a church was plundered and five Georgian Christians were captured and enslaved by a *hajji*, who forced them to convert to Islam.[31] Similarly, the *ASR* published a letter, signed by seven Abyssinian Christians who testified that thousands of their brethren had been butchered or sent to Mecca as slaves, which appealed for help, asking: 'Why should born Christians in this nineteenth century be slaves of Mohammedans?'[32] While conflicts between Christians and Muslims had taken place for centuries, with atrocities on both sides, just as there had been periods of peaceful co-existence and cooperation, such writings were presented in a highly-politicised manner with the intention of creating a collective Christian identity in England based on the fear of a common enemy.

Islam sometimes was portrayed as dangerous enough to threaten cherished rights even on English or European soil. For example, one article claimed that Moroccan Muslim men then living in and around Manchester were engaged in trading slave girls who had no knowledge of their rights or of the laws of England.[33] Another account described the abduction from the gutters of London of eleven 'little white Arabs' who had been taken to Istanbul to be sold into slavery, though they were eventually discovered and rescued by an Englishman there.[34] In these writings it seemed that Islam posed a constant danger, and according to some BFASS writers the best defence was one of offence: on at least two occasions the *ASR* reminded its readership that the most recent Muslim slave raid in Western Europe had been on a French peasant village in 1814, but that raids had ceased after the bombardment of Algiers by a British fleet in 1817 and its occupation by France in 1830.[35]

Occupation alone, however, was not enough to check the slave trade, and BFASS supporters argued that the reform or even the elimination of the Muslim legal and judicial system was necessary; articles focusing on this issue appeared periodically. At one point the BFASS memorialised Earl Granville, Her Majesty's principal secretary of state for foreign affairs, regarding the need to establish mixed commission courts which would give the British, or at least Europeans, more power.[36] One writer for the *ASR* stated that slavery existed in the 'barbarous land of Islam' where the 'Koran is the law of the land'.[37] Activists considered Muslim law and the practices it tolerated as an affront to divine law: for example, one article described the human misery of the slave market and noted that it stood near the shrines of Muslim saints despite the fact that slave markets were contrary to 'the laws of God and of man'.[38]

BFASS members drew from a long tradition of anti-Islamic sentiment in England where representations of the religion as evil had existed since the Middle Ages. However, by the late nineteenth century alternative perspectives also could be found in that society, and in England both Muslims who did not own slaves and non-Muslims sympathetic to the religion contributed their different ideas (see chapter five): one writer who helped to create a place for Islam in England was even an active member of the BFASS. However, most BFASS organisers were more interested in creating an image of a monolithic and threatening Islamic world in order to promote a certain ideology and conception of Englishness that would generate support for the campaign in Egypt than they were in engaging with or understanding the religion and its different interpretations.

The creation of an Islamic *other* forged alliances among people with different belief systems and religious backgrounds: for example, a Catholic cardinal, Anglican bishops, Quakers, Jews and Nonconformists of all types gathered at one anti-slavery event.[39] One meeting was 'attended by all the leaders of the humanitarian persuasion', and commentators mentioned the participation of well-known agnostics.[40] The ability of BFASS supporters to create an ideological framework that unified diverse people was crucial to its success, and the organisation attracted support from businessmen, MPs, 'working men', and women from all over England and Great Britain.[41]

This ideological system that provided meaning for so many different people developed through a number of BFASS-initiated activities. Public meetings were especially effective in the 1870s and 1880s, being held throughout Great Britain, from Brighton to Glasgow, in town halls, trade halls and other public facilities. While only rarely do reports of the proceedings include the number in attendance, the success and popularity of such meetings are usually indicated by references to 'densely crowded' or 'well-filled' venues – numbers were most likely in the hundreds. These meetings, the frequency of which could vary from a couple to 40–50 in the course of a year, were publicised both by the press and by BFASS members. Especially important meetings could draw crowds in the thousands, with one attended by nearly 5,000 people.[42]

During the 1890s the BFASS changed its strategy, and the public meeting gave way to the lecture. The organisation employed a 'travelling agent' to give anti-slavery talks, illustrated with slides prepared by the Royal Geographical Society.[43] While most of the lectures were given in and around London, some were presented as far west as Bristol and as far north as Nottingham. In addition to the standard town halls and meeting rooms, lectures took place in schoolhouses, YMCAs and churches, and of the latter it was the Baptists, the Primitive Methodists and the

Unitarians who proved the most supportive. BFASS lectures were as successful as the meetings in terms of drawing crowds and generating interest,[44] and 17 of them were delivered in a 3-month period in 1893.[45]

While public events such as lectures and meetings brought the issue of slavery in Egypt to thousands of people, BFASS printed materials brought it to thousands more. Handbills were distributed to lecture audiences to be circulated among friends, family, colleagues and others who had not attended. BFASS posters and flyers alerted the general public to anti-slavery activities,[46] and the organisation printed and distributed pamphlet-books such as *The Slave Trade in Egypt and the Soudan and Equatorial Africa* written by General Gordon.[47] Finally, contributors who made a donation of 5s or more were entitled to a free subscription of the organisation's publication, the *ASR*.

In addition to producing its own publications, the BFASS enjoyed the cooperation of the press, and articles about slavery, the slave trade and British efforts to suppress it in Egypt and surrounding areas appeared regularly in newspapers throughout England. Sometimes they would focus specifically on BFASS activities;[48] its meetings were featured, and one such, at Princes Hall, was covered by at least twenty-one publications.[49] The BFASS also served as a source of writers and journalists.[50]

It is important to emphasise that the BFASS did not simply transmit information to a passive audience; nor did it devise an ideology and then present it. Rather, certain ideas about English national identity in relation to Islam were developed in the course of its appeals for support, through meetings, lectures and written materials. BFASS organisers learned by trial and error which approaches were more effective than others.

Audience involvement was necessary to generate support for the anti-slavery cause. For example, in 1886 a BFASS representative dressed in Moroccan costume for a speech before parents and children at a local school. His talk included displaying instruments of flagellation and torture from Morocco. The announcement for the event assured prospective attendees that despite his dress, 'his heart is thoroughly English' and the information related 'will make us thankful we live in England'. In this presentation he appeared as or mimicked a Moroccan Muslim. As with any instance of mimicry, slippage occurred: the audience regarded him as really English because of the manner in which he was introduced and what he said. As a result, ideas about the English national character were defined in contrast to the Muslim *other* and affirmed as innate and unchangeable. How this slippage was understood also played a crucial role: members of the audience chose whether to see it as evidence of a slight difference or of an essential and fundamental difference.[51]

Through these various efforts, BFASS leaders succeeded in creating a new ideology of anti-slavery that persuaded individuals and organisations to support the cause. In a typical year 200–300 contributors might be listed, and many donated on behalf of larger groups such as businesses, other anti-slavery societies or the churches.[52] BFASS members also networked with like-minded or sympathetic organisations, for example, religious and missionary groups, temperance clubs and scholarly societies, and by 1890 the BFASS could claim that thirteen other organisations were contributing to the anti-slavery campaign.[53]

From harem slave to domestic servant: the Cairo Home for Freed Women Slaves, gender and anti-slavery ideology

Gender remained central to this new anti-slavery ideology. BFASS members learned, primarily from the Foreign Office correspondence and reports of the Slave Trade Department, that the form of slavery they sought to eliminate in Egypt was female-oriented, the majority of slaves being women or girls. *ASR* articles emphasised this aspect of the slave trade and often included excerpts from the above papers. They described slave dhows filled entirely with women and children, and prices for female slaves were quoted as 2, 3, or even 10 times as much as those for males; one report noted that the highest prices were paid for the pretty young girls 'ornamented with silver bangles' and destined for the harem.[54] Difficulties unique to suppressing the traffic in women were discussed, such as efforts to prevent slave-traders from transporting slaves for sale by obtaining false marriage certificates. For BFASS supporters, such activities were understood to be the result of the 'evils of polygamy' and as 'consistent with the Mohammedan code'.[55]

To win support for anti-slavery efforts in Egypt, BFASS members expanded on the implicit knowledge in nineteenth-century English society regarding the immorality of slavery in order to create a new ethical symbolic framework that specifically condemned the female- or harem-oriented slavery practised there. Descriptions of the slave hunts in Central Africa and the Sudan in which all of the men were killed by raiders or 'women stealers', so that the rest of the village could be captured and sold into slavery served this purpose, and they were related frequently in both the *ASR* and in BFASS speeches and lectures. This particular story served to link familiar images, already a part of anti-slavery culture, with a form of slavery new to the English; it also provided a horrifying and sensationalised narrative which held the attention of large crowds, arousing sympathy and indignation. References to women as victims of 'outrage' or even 'mass outrages' were noted to have caused 'sensation' in the audience. Stories of women separated from their children or forced to watch an infant brutally killed before their eyes appeared periodically. Sometimes speakers would show an actual slave yoke or some other 'instrument of torture' used to keep marching slaves from fleeing.[56] Discussion focused on the death and destruction that resulted both from the rigours of the slave march, which was thought to have been especially difficult for the 'weaker sex', and from the capture, during which, for example, a father and three brothers might be butchered trying to defend an infant.[57]

Slave hunts and slavery in general were blamed on the institution of the harem. One BFASS writer responded to a defence of slavery as practised in the Muslim world by stating that the 'harem system has been the cause of the cruellest massacres' and that nothing could compensate for the 'horrors' of slave-hunting.[58] With reference to Circassian slavery, a speaker at a BFASS meeting told the audience that 'the *sole* purpose of the Egyptian slave trade' (my emphasis) was to fill the harems of the Ottoman Empire. This type of rhetoric, accompanied by calls to crush the slave trade in Egypt and the Sudan, provoked cheers and shouts of support from the audience.[59] Many BFASS activists saw slavery as necessary to the harem and both institutions as integral to Muslim society. One *ASR* article entitled 'Peculiar Character of Egyptian and Soudanese Slavery' described slavery under Islam as radically different from that of the United States and the West Indies, explaining that it is sanctioned by custom and law, 'engrained in the bones of the people' and is even the 'A.B.C. of life'.[60] By abolishing it BFASS organisers hoped to have a profound impact on Muslim domestic life and the entire social structure in Egypt.

BFASS supporters saw the harem as the root of much misery and destruction not only because of the kidnapping and enslavement of women and children but because of the demand for eunuchs to guard it. This issue was addressed in both pamphlets and *ASR* articles, which usually focused on the cruelty of the procedure for making eunuchs and its mortality rate. BFASS estimates ranged from 1 in 2 to 1 in 200 survivors, one article noting that in order to procure the 500 eunuchs living in Cairo itself 100,000 boys would have lost their lives.[61] Much was made of the high prices paid for eunuchs, as compared to ordinary male slaves, and their importance to the harem system. One writer even describes it as a 'vast system of iniquity [which] necessarily involves the degradation of women, the torture of youths, and the massacres and desolation of Central Africa'.[62] The harem was represented as an emasculating institution, both figuratively and literally.

Through such BFASS representations the harem became a token, or signifier, of difference, defining Islam as fundamentally distinct from Englishness and the Anglicisation of Egyptian society, particularly in terms of gender and domestic relationships, as a moral obligation and part of the British civilising mission.[63] This point cannot be overemphasised, for it is not that the institution of the harem was essentially foreign to or incompatible with Englishness: Victorian English women often saw it as similar to the bourgeois home with which they were familiar.[64] Rather, because of certain activities and representations, it became a highly charged idea invested with additional meanings and, therefore, capable of functioning in this new political role. As a result, the widespread belief in the essential immorality of slavery could be extended to include the slave in the harem as well as the slave on the plantation. The familiar narrative of the English fight for liberty received a new addition, and the institution of the harem seemed as oppressive and contrary to freedom as the plantation slave's chains.

Attempts to transgress the boundaries of the harem in the course of anti-slavery activity further reinforced the belief in the illegitimacy of this institution. While the vast majority of BFASS members could not hope themselves to enter the harems, they supported and encouraged policies that would open this space to the scrutiny, and therefore the authority, of British anti-slavery workers in Egypt. They described the 'closed harem' as an obstacle to the necessary reforms in social life that would accompany abolition and advocated policies that would allow them to monitor or regulate its inhabitants.

Despite a statement to the BFASS from Colonel Schaefer of the Slave Trade Department in Egypt stating that in Muslim countries the seclusion of the harem is 'inviolable', as well as Lord Dufferin's words of caution that a system of registering harem slaves would meet with even more resistance than abolition itself, the BFASS repeatedly advocated policies that would allow them to cross the boundaries of the harem and monitor its inhabitants.[65] The Society memorialised and petitioned MPs, Lord Granville, and even Gladstone requesting a census of harem slaves or some sort of system of registration, a strategy that would, in theory, put an end to slave trafficking by monitoring harem populations for any increase in slaves. A physical description of each slave was mentioned as one of the conditions necessary in order for this system to work, and that would require agents not only to enter the harems but actually to unveil the female slaves.[66] BFASS supporters occasionally suggested that women be employed for this purpose, and one *ASR* article provided an example of a situation in which this strategy had worked: in French Tunisia a 'band of ladies' had been formed for the purpose of obtaining information from slaves; as a result of their efforts, the 'impenetrable veil' of the harem had been 'lifted for the purposes of justice'.[67]

In addition to establishing a system of registration, abolitionists advocated entering the harems in order to liberate Christian women and children who had been kidnapped and sold into slavery in Ottoman territories. BFASS supporters argued that these slaves should be considered prisoners of war and, as such, given rights that even the freed Muslim slave did not have because they had been forced to convert to Islam. The most common BFASS strategy was petitioning British government officials to pressure the Sublime Porte to take action regarding this issue. One BFASS document suggested establishing a central commission of Europeans to search the harems specifically for these slaves.

If this approach was not allowed, the author or authors of the document had an even more aggressive and elaborate proposal: a network of 'secret agents', posing as dressmakers, teachers, traders, governesses and servants, would gain access to the harems to search for captives. While these agents would be diplomatic and tactful, they would also have a European 'force within call' in case they encountered non-cooperation from local authorities.[68] Certain women would assist in these efforts. Three suggestions were made: a reverend's wife; the sister of a clergyman; and a 'lady' physician–missionary who had been practising in the harems and who was also the wife of a clergyman. The report emphasises the importance of finding the right women, for it 'is difficult to find women who are upright in intention and yet know Turkish, and Turkish habits'. In fact, one of the three women was considered acceptable but still 'too lenient in her own view of Turkish goodness'. While this proposal was more creative and extreme than most, it reflects the missionary zeal, sense of purpose and desire to transgress the boundaries of the harem typical of BFASS writings and speeches.

Through efforts to penetrate the boundaries of the harem, anti-slavery activists redefined themselves and their conception of justice in contrast to Islamic practices. Like the dungeon, the harem was considered the 'metaphoric opposite' of civilised or enlightened forms of social organisation and control, such as Bentham's panopticon, the effectiveness of which depended on the principle of visibility.[69] For anti-slavery advocates, the secretiveness of the harem violated the ideal of the transparent civil society. Discussion of the harem as an affront to the formal legal system and therefore incompatible with justice appeared frequently in contemporary English discourse, one article, for example, referring to violent murders and tragedies occurring in the harem because life there was 'hidden and concealed' from the law.[70]

Because the harem had come to represent a token of difference, defining Englishness as distinct from Islam, the BFASS could advocate public scrutiny of and government interference in this area without calling in question the value of a private domestic sphere in England, a hallmark of Victorian respectability and also a space apart from this transparent civil society. Thus for the majority of BFASS workers the representations of the harem as a barbaric and oppressive institution obscured the radical implications of anti-slavery activity in Egypt in terms of gender relationships and domestic life in England. However, as I show in chapter four, English feminists did not fail to make the connection between injustices in the harem and those in the English home, and they argued that efforts should be made to put an end to both.

How BFASS activists understood and represented the Muslim harem served to generate support for their cause while at the same time defining *proper* gender relationships both for themselves and for the Egyptians. In the course of working to reform the harem by eliminating female slavery, BFASS supporters promoted certain notions of femininity and female roles, which they associated with English identity and the imperial civilising mission.

Examining the Cairo Home, which operated from 1885 to 1908, helps to illustrate this process. While organisations that provided shelter often had 'home' in the title, the word had special significance for this institution. The harem definitely was not considered a home by most English people involved in anti-slavery activity, and the Cairo Home was meant to help freed female slaves make the transition from the harem to 'respectable' domestic life either as a wife or servant.[71]

Under the auspices of the BFASS and as a result of the Society's fund-raising efforts, the Cairo Home served as a shelter for women who had left their harems and been manumitted but who had nowhere to go; it also helped them to find employment, usually in domestic service.[72] The need for some sort of institution to provide for freed slaves was voiced in the early 1880s: a letter to the BFASS during this period suggested the formation of a separate society to educate and care for them.[73] In 1883 a proposal was made to establish a 'reservation' for freed slaves, complete with farms, schools and programmes to train the inhabitants in skills that would prepare them for paid labour.[74]

The plan to provide this Home was initiated by Clifford Lloyd, British member of the Egyptian Government, and Sarah Amos, the feminist, activist and abolitionist mentioned in chapter two. Amos and Lloyd worked with other British people, both in England and in Egypt, and sought the assistance of the BFASS and the Aborigines' Protection Society.[75] In April of 1884 a BFASS meeting was held in Cairo to create a committee for the Cairo Home.[76] Sir Evelyn Baring became the president of that committee, and he opened the proceedings by explaining that the possibility of manumission was known even in the recesses of the harems, but 'voluntary slavery' still existed because female slaves had nowhere else to go. Baring assured the audience that care would be taken not to transgress the customs of the Egyptians and announced that the queen had already donated £100 to the project and the khedive had promised to contribute as well. The audience responded with enthusiastic cheering.[77]

In May of that year, a similar meeting was held at the Mansion House under the presidency of the Lord Mayor of London for the purpose of generating support for the cause in England and creating a London committee for the Cairo Home. Speakers explained how large numbers of women in Egypt were manumitted while having nowhere to go. One noted that nearly 300 women slaves freed the previous year had been 'driven to a life of misery and degradation' so dreadful that it could not even be described in the meeting. Supporters argued that such a home would strike a blow to the slave trade indirectly by making liberation easier and, therefore, the owning of slaves more difficult and less desirable. As in Cairo, the proposed plan was received with cheers from an enthusiastic crowd, and a total of £1,600 was collected by the newly formed London committee in order to launch the project.[78]

Efforts to establish the Cairo Home were 'strenuously supported in England' particularly by a dedicated few, such as W. E. Forster, an MP who took an interest in the project, convinced friends to donate 'handsomely' to its funds and was instrumental in the success of the overflowing Jubilee meeting, his efforts having secured the presence of the prince of Wales at that event.[79] Initially, the BFASS collected £2,000 for the Cairo Home, and contributions continued throughout the nineteenth and into the twentieth century. Press coverage helped to promote the cause, and one contemporary attributed approximately £1,600 of the initial £2,000 raised to a sympathetic article published in *The Times*.[80]

The Cairo Home was opened in 1885 and was managed by a Mrs Crewe and her assistant. Crewe was an Englishwoman who had lived in Egypt most of her life and spoke Arabic fluently, which made her an ideal matron of the Home; her assistant, whose name was not given by the *ASR* and BFASS materials, was a Sudanese woman and former slave who helped with the housework and went daily to the bureau of the Slave Trade Department, waiting there for hours for newly manumitted female slaves. The building had large gardens and was located in 'a most healthy quarter' close to Miss Whateley's mission schools. It housed Mrs Crewe, and her husband and children as well as her assistant. In January of 1885 the Home received its first freed female slaves, two Circassians who had escaped from the palace of a well-known pasha.

Slaves residing at the Cairo Home were of diverse backgrounds ranging from the harem of the Princess Mansour, sister of the khedive, to the kitchens and washrooms of ordinary Egyptian households; almost all had escaped the confines of the harem. The experiences and life stories of some of them were described as so extraordinary that they could provide any writer of sensationalist novels with ample material. Others, however, had been simply 'domestic drudges' who left after a quarrel or particularly unfair or harsh treatment.[81]

Girls and women alike were admitted to the Home. The majority of the residents were either Sudanese or Abyssinian, although a small percentage of them were white slaves from Circassia, Bulgaria and Georgia.[82] From 1885–95 over 2,000 freed female slaves took refuge therein. Residence was voluntary, and approximately 20 per cent of slaves manumitted by the Cairo police took advantage of this option. Mrs Crewe reported that an average of 15–20 freed slaves lived there at any given time.

The purpose of the Cairo Home was not simply to provide shelter for freed female slaves, but to train them to be like English domestic servants, which would prepare them for waged labour or the role of a wife with no servants of her own.[83] On entering the Home they were given necessities and put to work immediately, caring for the household and doing laundry that was brought to there to help pay for the cost of maintaining the Home. Most had been responsible for domestic chores in their harems prior to escaping, but at the Home they were re-educated; Mrs Crewe commented that none was as good as an English servant and they needed to be instructed in even the most basic tasks. She taught them skills that had more to do with the expectations of English than of Egyptian domestic service: ironing, embroidery and dress-making, and all were taught how to sew their own clothes before being sent out to work – the Cairo committee proudly reported that in one year 600 dresses, in the European or Western style, were made at the Home.[84]

The transition from slave labour to waged labour or marriage was no guarantee of full liberation, and domestic servants and housewives often were trapped in exploitative situations, regardless of whether they lived in England or Egypt: neither were recognised as workers by the Government or trade unions in England and their state was one of legal subordination to their masters or husbands.[85] In Egypt the circumstances for freed female slaves could be so similar to their previous situations that Mrs Crewe sometimes could not be sure that she was not sending them back into slavery;[86] she even periodically visited local harems where children had been placed to remind them that they were no longer slaves.[87]

Despite the disadvantages of domestic labour in the harem or in the home, by re-educating and retraining freed female slaves and publicising their progress, BFASS members communicated the idea that their new role, based on that of the English domestic servant, was liberating and even ideal. Most residents of the Cairo Home found positions in service or were married, and their stories were reported as successes to BFASS supporters in England. One member of the Cairo committee related that former residents often left articles of property or their freedom papers with Mrs Crewe and visited her from time to time to ask for advice, show her their new clothes and communicate their appreciation in general.[88] One group of freed slaves was reported as being as 'happy as the day is long' and so proud of their new status that they would hold their liberation papers in the windows for all to see.[89]

The value of the Home and the roles it promoted were reinforced further by reports of its contribution to the suppression of the slave trade. The Cairo committee's treasurer noted the dramatic reduction of slaves in Egypt during the ten years that the Home had been in operation.[90] Similarly, an *ASR* article commented that the Cairo Home was necessary for the enforcement of emancipation laws. Because this statement followed several paragraphs describing the horrifying slave hunts, the institution appeared as the humane alternative to the brutality and savagery that accompanied the slave trade.[91] In this context, it would have been almost unthinkable to question the benefits of the role of English domestic servant or to consider its limitations.

The Cairo Home, and therefore the ideas about appropriate feminine roles associated with English national identity that it advanced, were publicised by BFASS organisers through open meetings and lectures in order to raise awareness and, ultimately, funds. In one lecture, the speaker addressed the ladies in the audience and called their attention to the good work done by the 'noble institution' that shelters the freed woman slave.[92] Lecturers would present photographs of former female slaves to their audiences. One such picture showed Mrs Crewe surrounded by a group of them in the grounds of the Cairo Home, all of the latter wearing their Western or English-style dresses that they had been taught to make. These images aroused 'the deepest sympathies of the audience', and loud cheers would follow the announcement that the sultan of the Ottoman Empire had arranged for similar homes to be built in his dominions.[93]

Those sympathetic to the cause were educated by the *ASR* about the Cairo Home and its mission. Requests for funds and articles highlighting the Home's successes appeared frequently. One related that Mrs Crewe acted as a foster mother to a group of 'Red Sea waifs', Galla girls who had been liberated by a British cruiser and sent to the Home – she eventually found a permanent place for them at the American mission, and a BFASS deputation to Egypt met them and listened to them sing hymns performed in their own language.[94] In addition to articles, visual images served to connect readers with the Home: the *ASR* printed a sketch of the building and gardens as well as the above-mentioned photograph of Mrs Crewe with a group of slaves, and readers were given instructions on how to purchase their own copies.

BFASS members tried to establish other shelters modelled on the Cairo Home, and met with partial success in doing so. In response to BFASS activism, the British Embassy recommended to the sultan that similar homes be created in Ottoman territories outside of Egypt proper, and in 1891 plans were approved to establish residences for freed slaves, women, girls and boys in Benghazi, Tripoli, Jiddah, Hudaydah, Smyrna and Istanbul, all of them supported by state funds. These institutions trained the women and girls to be domestic servants and prepared the boys for the primary professional schools or service in military bands.[95] While BFASS members saw this as a great success and understood the Cairo Home as the inspiration for this initiative, they had no power, influence or direct connection to any of these institutions. When a BFASS deputation arrived in Tripoli in 1892, the visitors were taken to one such home, but as Christians were not allowed to enter.[96] One prominent BFASS member suggested that an institution similar to the Cairo Home be built in the Sudan, but was told by Lord Cromer that this would not be necessary because, unlike Egypt where 'we deal almost entirely with women', slavery in the Sudan is male-oriented.[97]

The Cairo Home served as a temporary shelter for thousands of women and girls over the years, but by the mid-to-late 1890s demand for its services decreased. Reports reveal the number of residents gradually declining as a result of the almost total suppression of the slave trade by that time. After 1900 the Home saw no more than fifteen slaves each year. In 1908 it finally closed, with the understanding that Mrs Crewe would allow the occasional freed slave to stay with her if needed. The Cairo Home had the support of hundreds of women and men who contributed their time, effort and money to this cause, and it was recognised by thousands more who understood it as a noble and necessary undertaking. The Home's twenty-three year existence is in itself a testimony to the sense of responsibility of certain English people to aid the female slave of the Egyptian harem.

This sense of responsibility was, however, understood in very maternal or paternal terms, female slaves being regarded as 'poor creatures' in need of protection. For example, one anti-slavery activist stated that until a home was established, it would be wrong to encourage either black or white female slaves to escape from their masters, because they would be 'helpless' like 'tame birds set free'.[98] Just as children lack self-discipline and have need of outside structure, freed slaves were given household work in part because it kept them out of the 'proverbial mischief that idleness leads to'.[99] Their morality remained a concern for BFASS supporters, who nevertheless were reassured by the report that of the first sixty women to pass through the Home none of them had '"taken to bad ways"'.¹⁰⁰ Some BFASS members even advocated establishing a system of police surveillance of all unmarried freed female slaves in order to provide 'guarantees of morality'.¹⁰¹

Like the British officials who worked to suppress slavery but did not consider these women to be 'free agents', BFASS members made the female slave of the Muslim harem the object of their concern but did not regard them as subjects in their own right. Except for references to slaves showing their appreciation, their viewpoints or perspectives were ignored. I found no evidence either in the BFASS collections or the *ASR* of any attempt to interview these women and girls. None was brought to the BFASS meetings, not even those held in Cairo regarding the Home. Mrs Crewe's assistant was not mentioned by name, but was referred to simply as the 'freed Sudanese slave woman'.

Through anti-slavery activity in Egypt, BFASS members recreated a class-based understanding of femininity and *proper* female roles. For while abolitionists promoted paid domestic work as a viable and liberating alternative to slave labour, the freed female slave, like the English domestic servant, was not treated as an equal. Thus a certain Victorian bourgeois value system, which celebrated free waged labour but nevertheless relied on class hierarchies, developed in the Egyptian imperial context, reinforcing similar divisions in England.

For BFASS supporters the Cairo Home became a symbol of the importance of the British imperial mission and, therefore, of an understanding of English national identities defined in terms of that mission. For the dramatic resurgence in support for imperialist activity after 1870 was characterised by an aggressive patriotism closely associated with the responsibility to 'civilise' or 'elevate' subject peoples, and the belief that acquiring colonies and spheres of influence abroad was crucial to national prestige.¹⁰² For contributors in England, the Cairo Home helped to justify the British presence in Egypt by allowing them to assume the role of the beneficent imperialist coming to the aid of the female harem slave and 'elevating' her to the 'proper English' roles of domestic servant or sometimes wife.

English women specifically were addressed to assist the anti-slavery cause in Egypt and surrounding areas in part because most slaves were female but also because women were assumed to be more compassionate than men. At one meeting, in Birmingham, they were encouraged as a group to memorialise Lord Vivian, the British ambassador in Brussels.¹⁰³ At the Manchester Jubilee meeting, a speaker told the crowd that the 'fair sex' held a 'position of honour which Englishwomen always take when benevolent and philanthropic objects are to be assisted'.¹⁰⁴ Similarly, Cardinal Lavigerie always mentioned the special mission of English or European women in his speeches. Women were thought to have a unique role because of their understanding of matters of the heart and their capacity for an empathy deeper than that associated with men. However, they were often encouraged to use influence rather than to organise or take action themselves. Lavigerie instructed them to do 'the work of mercy and pity' and to give no peace to the men in their families until they used their authority to stop slave-trading.[105] English mothers were asked to reflect on the 'destruction of child life' and to exercise their 'moral power' to stop it.[106]

Despite instructions that would seem to have encouraged private influence at the expense of a role in the public sphere, a number of English women proved quite capable of becoming actively involved in this campaign, and though it claimed a place for themselves in the imperial nation state. They established female-dominated anti-slavery associations closely connected to the BFASS,[107] and they supported the BFASS by attending meetings and events and by contributing financially. Generous female supporters were recognised by the Society and an *ASR* obituary for two of those women noted the 'real material blow' that their deaths would bring to the organisation.[108] By the mid-1880s and thereafter 30–40 per cent of contributors to the BFASS were women and 35–40 per cent of donations to the Cairo Home were from women.

While most female abolitionists contributed to the cause through donations or other standard methods, some went beyond ordinary expectations. One such woman was Mrs Sarah Amos. Known for her skills as an orator and writer, Amos, like her husband, was a radical, feminist and a social reformer, who involved herself in a number of humanitarian political campaigns both in England and imperial territories. They were interested especially in the emancipation of women through suffrage and access to higher education, as well as through the repeal of the Contagious Diseases Acts and related social purity movements. The couple lived in Egypt during the early 1880s, where Sheldon Amos served as an appeal court judge until his death in 1886; Sarah Amos returned to Egypt towards the end of her life and died in Cairo in 1908.[109]

Sarah Amos worked both in London and Cairo for the anti-slavery cause. She informally monitored the activities of the Slave Trade Department in Egypt. At one point she reported to Baring that Schaefer, the man in charge of the Department, had ordered subordinates to ignore the smuggling of certain female slaves during the hajj; she charged him not only with negligence but with connivance, noting that his social ties were 'among the thick of Pashadom'.[110] Baring eventually dismissed the charge she brought, and while he did not have a high opinion of her his comments are revealing because they testify to her dedication to the cause and willingness to interfere, even when met with resistance. He stated that she gave him 'a good deal of trouble' and quarrelled with everyone, but because she was a crucial link between him and the BFASS he chose to 'temper the often misdirected zeal of the anti-slavery people' by appeasing her.[111]

In her anti-slavery crusade, Amos – the woman discussed in chapter two who attended the proceedings of the Egyptian Muslim courts, or qadi, in an attempt to influence them – was willing to offend the Egyptians as well as the British officials who stood in her way. She was concerned particularly with female slaves and the Cairo Home. Once she had Baring demand to see a slave from the harem of the khedive's sister in order to question her, which brought Baring 'an infinity of trouble' and roused the resentment of the khedive and his family.[112] Amos was well aware of the effects of her activities: in one letter, she explained that the wife of the khedive and other Egyptian women disliked the Cairo Home so much that she had been advised not to call on any 'native lady' as they would be rude to her. She noted that anti-slavery efforts were 'inexpressibly disagreeable to the wives of the Pashas, who see their slaves run away to us and who find it difficult to replenish their households'.[113] Her willingness to offend resulted from her absolute certainty in the rightness of her mission, a common trait among BFASS supporters and one that inspired their work.

BFASS members operated according to a well-defined moral or ideological system in which they believed. The importance of having this type of framework can hardly be overemphasised; for without such cultural patterns the individual would live in a state of intellectual chaos and be unable to function.[114] Through their efforts BFASS supporters, both women and men, created symbolic structures that allowed them to make sense of the world and their place in it, define evil and even combat it with a certain degree of success, albeit at the expense of other perspectives or belief systems they encountered.

The activities of Sarah Amos illustrate a common tension: she held egalitarian political views, yet she promoted them by creating a public role and an identity within an imperial system characterised by class and gender hierarchies. Amos was a well-known radical and feminist who advocated increased opportunities for working-class women, though she and other middle-class activists claimed a place for themselves in the male-dominated imperial nation state on the basis of their connections and positions, and their efforts to liberate the harem slave by socialising her into the role of domestic servant, with all its disadvantages and limitations.[115] Through her work Amos associated with the highest-ranking officers and her activities impacted on British policy in Egypt; indeed, part of the conflict between Baring and Amos can be explained by the fact that she asserted herself in a sphere that British officials tried to preserve as a masculine domain.

International initiatives and English identities

BFASS supporters understood their campaign, and therefore the identities formed through it, as closely linked with the imperial mission. Members encouraged British influence of all kinds in Egypt: economic, political and even military. Almost a decade before the actual occupation, the BFASS petitioned the secretary of state for foreign affairs, stating that extending British rule to that area would advance the anti-slavery cause.[116] Members believed that troops would be necessary to abolish slavery; as General Gordon had warned in 1879: 'If the liberation of slaves takes place in 1884 [in Egypt proper] and the present system of Government goes on, there cannot fail to be a revolt in the whole country.'[117] Frequent references were made to the necessity of using not just influence but 'pressure'. BFASS members treated the actual occupation of Egypt in 1882 as a 'golden opportunity' and immediately sent Prime Minister Gladstone a letter acknowledging that the present conference was limited to the suppression of the military revolt in Egypt, but urging him to introduce the question of the slave trade as well.[118]

The occupation was supported enthusiastically. At one BFASS meeting a speaker announced, amid cheers from the audience, that the nations of Europe could look after the Suez and the bond-holders could take care of themselves, but the *real* reason for the invasion of Egypt was to suppress the slave trade.[119] Concerns raised by those outside of the organisation about overstepping boundaries or offending Egyptian sensibilities were dismissed easily now with the response that Britain had control of the country. BFASS supporters saw occupation as giving both great power and responsibility. At the crowded BFASS Jubilee meeting in London Cardinal Manning announced: 'We are told that slavery exists to this day in the great Mohammedan world. Egypt is the heart of that great Mohammedan world and it is the very heart of this abominable traffic. We are at the heart of Egypt.'[120] At public events and on the pages of the *ASR* the beneficence of British rule was both stated and assumed, and references to successes suppressing the slave trade as well as to the general peace and prosperity as a result of the British presence appeared regularly.

In the process of encouraging British occupation and influence BFASS members promoted a sense of English national identity characterised by difference from the Egyptians and the ability to provide them with good administration which would allow suppression of the slave trade. They frequently argued that Englishmen rather than Egyptians should manage the Slave Trade Department. As the secretary of the BFASS explained in an interview at the Brussels conference, that department would be insignificant without English authority.[121] A BFASS memorandum stated that not only should employees of the Department be English, but that measures should be taken to ensure that they are far removed from the influence of the palace and the local pashas. In addition, the khedive should be prohibited from decorating English men.[122] BFASS members believed that even the adoption of Western ideas or habits could not qualify Muslim Egyptians to rule effectively, at least according to their agenda. As one BFASS correspondent reported, even though the present khedive had been educated in Europe and Europeanised, he was still 'at heart a Mahomedan . . . and Mahomedans dislike free labour'.[123]

One article in the *ASR* claimed that the khedive had the power to stop the trade with a single word, but would not because he profited from it and relied on it to continually increase his 'stock of women'. Corruption in the household or harem signified corruption in the State, as the writer went on to explain how the khedive must continually buy eunuchs to guard his many wives and concubines because even his 'expensive presents of French jewelry' could not ensure their fidelity.[124] The reference to specifically French jewellery is interesting, as the English, and the British more generally, had a tradition of defining themselves, their society and their political system in opposition to the French, often contrasting ideas about their own thrift, industry and liberty with French decadence, luxury and tyranny, traits that they tended to associate also with the rulers in the East or the Islamic world.[125] This statement, then, would have served to link familiar ways of understanding Englishness to the campaign in Egypt.

Coverage of an Egyptian court case provides another example of how BFASS materials communicated the view that British rule was the remedy to corruption in that country. In 1894, an *ASR* article related that 3 pashas had been arrested for buying 6 female Sudanese slaves near Cairo. It included a drawing of the women, and the incident was presented as evidence that despite declining numbers of manumissions the Egyptian elites still could not be trusted and continued vigilance on the part of British officials and the BFASS was therefore necessary.[126] By reporting this particular case in the way that it did, the BFASS presented a narrow view of a situation that created considerable sensation and controversy in Egyptian society. For many Egyptians, the case aroused nationalist sentiment either in the form of hurt national pride and embarrassment because of the actions of the pashas or anger and indignation because of their treatment by the British. While *al-Muqattam* defended the Government, others such as journalists for *al-Ahram* and *al-Mu'ayyad* took the side of the accused.[127]

By criticising not only the elites, but the entire political and social structure in Egypt, BFASS supporters advocated British imperialist influence, while at the same time defining their own society in contrast as more moral, industrious and developed. They portrayed any society in which slavery existed as necessarily backward and corrupt, and therefore in need of foreign intervention. BFASS speakers and writers frequently commented on the general lethargy and lack of industry in slave societies, where work had been devalued. Sheldon Amos, husband of Sarah Amos and a prominent jurist, writer and law professor who was instrumental in the establishment of the Cairo Home, explained in his book *The Science of Politics* that the existence of slavery indicates that the conscience of the State has developed imperfectly.[128] An even stronger condemnation of slave societies appeared in an *ASR* article entitled 'African Slavery an Indigenous Plant'; its author described slavery as having its roots in the 'pagan or Mohammedan social order', which meant that it could be eradicated only through 'complete social reconstruction'.[129] Such writings assumed that the abolitionist agenda involved not just suppressing slavery but reconstituting, on a grand scale, social relationships according to a British or, more specifically, an English model. Such ambitions could have been accomplished only through aggressive imperialistic measures on the part of the British Government.[130]

BFASS writers further defined their own society and the positive influence that occupation and reform would have on Egypt by portraying those Muslim nations where slavery was allowed and the British had very little influence as miserable and degraded. Discussion of Morocco served this purpose. Articles that sometimes sounded like sensationalist exposés about the public slave markets appeared frequently in the *ASR*. One BFASS supporter described Morocco as a 'dark and almost unknown country', noting that only four hours travel separated 'English civilisation' from the 'barbarism of the Middle Ages'.[131] The idea of a sultan who governed both Church and State, remained independent of British influence and allowed open slave markets to exist within his territories was depicted as obscene and tyrannical, an affront to humankind. If the lights of Western civilisation emanated most brightly from England, and Morocco represented the darkest pit of barbarism, then Egypt would have to fall somewhere between those two extremes. According to this logic, continued British occupation and influence could lead only to the eventual improvement and enlightenment of this country.

The improvement of Egypt was understood in *racial* terms. As one petition to the House of Commons stated, freeing the 'subject races' served to elevate the 'character of the British nation'.[132] Given that race is a fluid ideology that changes as circumstances change, it is necessary to ask what it meant for BFASS supporters in the context of the anti-slavery campaign. For them it was defined by religion, culture and physical appearance, with racial inferiority assigned to those who obstructed their efforts, Muslim Arabs.

References to the 'Mohammedans' as a third race appeared in BFASS writings. At one public meeting a speaker claimed that the cry of the 'false prophet' to the Muslims was 'Massacre the whites and sell the blacks', a statement received by the cheering crowd with shouts of 'hear! hear!'[133] Muslim Arabs were depicted as not only degenerate themselves but as corruptors of black peoples. An article entitled 'Decline of the Arab' maintained that Muslim slavery brought absolute ruin, warning the reader not to be fooled by the Arabs' hospitality, courteousness or clean clothes, because they, 'like all Mohammedan peoples', are responsible for preventing black Africans from being exposed to Western ideas and developing their mental capacities.[134] In similar articles, the Muslim was portrayed as teaching black people to hunt other blacks and preventing the whites from rescuing them. In these writings Islam became a signifier of race; in other words, BFASS supporters conflated discourses about race with those about a religion they regarded as inferior and which they sought to undermine.

BFASS members often commented on the absence of a strict colour line in Egypt and surrounding areas. One explained that there was 'no distinction of colour, no nobility of skin', and that white men of the highest ranks married black women and black men often occupied high social stations in Egypt; he went on to note that the 'Sherif of Mecca, a man of the highest authority in the East, is as black as a raven'.[135] Another explained that because of the existence of white as well as black slaves and the equal chances that both had of obtaining their freedom, colour was 'no badge of slavery'.[136] Even descriptions of the society in general remarked on the many shades of skin-colour that existed in between the extremes of black and white.

Contact with racial ideology as practised in Egypt and the surrounding areas helped to define or redefine English conceptions of race. As I have already said, both Egyptian and British officers relied on racial categories, thereby reinforcing them for each other and creating the illusion of their permanence and universality. Yet English anti-slavery activists often interpreted the Egyptian tolerance for interracial unions as proof of the inferiority or backwardness of Egyptian society, believing that such unions would bring degeneration. References to slave-holding 'mongrels' appeared frequently: one article described the brutal slave hunts and blamed not only the Arabs but notably their 'relentless and bloodthirsty followers, the half-caste Negroes'.[137] Racial inferiority was assigned to the enemy, and in this context the enemy became the Egyptian authorities and slave-traders who were considered neither black nor white and with whom members of the BFASS saw themselves engaged in a bitter struggle.

What distinguished the British or the English nation – depending on the views of the BFASS writer concerned – from the subject races in Egypt and the surrounding areas was the former's commitment to a certain moral or ideological system that was characterised by a hatred of slavery, a rejection of Islam and the preservation of racial categories based on physical appearance. Through anti-slavery activity a racial understanding of national identity was created and defined in terms of beliefs and culture as much as physical characteristics.[138] This conception of race and nation united in the cause of anti-slavery a number of people from diverse backgrounds and with different religious or ethical beliefs. At the same time it recreated divisions within English society: as chapter five shows, not everyone living in England, and not even all light-skinned people born there, belonged to the nation as defined in those terms.

While BFASS activists associated their anti-slavery efforts with the English nation and the British imperial mission, this did not prevent them from working with other Europeans. The Society's correspondence is full of references to the tradition of cooperation among European powers and organisations to suppress slavery, for example, those represented at the congress of Vienna in 1815 and the conference at Verona in 1822. The BFASS sometimes worked in concert with foreign anti-slavery societies such as the Société Antiesclavagiste de France, which sought to abolish the slave trade in areas of Northern and Western Africa during the period of British involvement in Egypt. Cardinal Lavigerie, president d'honneur of the French society, helped to link efforts in the two countries, addressing English crowds and holding an anti-slavery congress in 1890 that was attended by BFASS representatives.[139]

A fruitful area for future research would be to consider what Islam and the harem meant for French anti-slavery workers and, for that matter, for other European activists, in terms of their roles and identities within this imperial and international movement. In one contemporary French publication Islam is condemned as corrupt and barbaric, and 'Arab tyrants' are shown hunting for slaves; yet the slavery that the women experience, once they have positions within the harems of the Mediterranean countries of Northern Africa, is described as 'gènēralement doux', meaning gentle, soft, even tender, and the author goes on to say that their environment is a nurturing one in which they remain voluntarily.[140] This representation of the harem differs dramatically from those presented by the BFASS and shows the creative possibilities and the diversity of opinion within the framework of the international anti-slavery cause.

One of the more successful international initiatives on the part of the BFASS stemmed from its request to Lord Salisbury, the secretary of state for foreign affairs, that the British Government call a meeting with concerned world powers to discuss the suppression of the slave trade,[141] a request that eventually led to the Brussels conference of 1889. The Society helped to publicise the conference and advised officials regarding strategy, approach and overall goals.[142] A BFASS delegate was presented to the Belgian king and its representatives remained on hand to provide information and assistance.[143]

That the BFASS worked with other governments and organisations did not compromise but contributed to a sense of national identity, for members still understood anti-slavery as essentially a British project, which required British and, more specifically, English leadership. As one BFASS resolution explained, Britain had distinguished itself from the world's other nations by virtue of its anti-slavery policy,[144] BFASS members having expressed concern that Britain would have to share power with or play 'second or third fiddle' to other nations attending the Brussels conference.[145] Similarly, one journalist maintained that because England had for many years made great sacrifices to combat the slave trade, while other European nations had done nothing but profit from it, British plenipotentiaries should be given 'first voice'.[146]

The BFASS vision appealed to people from all over the British Isles and the world, as Appendix 2 shows. The tendency among BFASS organisers to equate Englishness with the British imperial mission did not prevent non-English Britons from contributing to the cause. As I noted in the Introduction, during the Victorian era people from Ireland, Scotland and Wales had distinct national as well as regional and other identities, and those who reconciled them with membership in this British reforming society chose to do so. Such a choice was not inevitable, for Scots and Irish abolitionists had a history of independent organisation and of forging alternative alliances as well as cooperating with English anti-slavery workers. They were quite capable of rejecting the BFASS agenda and embracing a course of action at odds with an ideology that celebrated the British State and Empire.[147]

Through the BFASS, Scots, Irish, English and other anti-slavery workers found ways to assist officers in Egypt and surrounding areas. A network of informants residing in Africa and the Middle East associated with that organisation would monitor the situation and alert Her

Majesty's officers to particular instances of slave-trading.[148] The Society also contributed to government efforts by printing treaties and proclamations for the Egyptian public. In 1880 it had 200 copies of the 1877 convention and the khedive's corresponding decree printed in Arabic; the documents were posted in public places and some were given to well-known slave-dealers.[149] Similarly, the BFASS printed at 'considerable expense' hundreds of Arabic copies of General Gordon's proclamations regarding the slave trade to be circulated throughout Egypt to serve as a warning to any would-be dealers.[150]

By publicising these types of activity and the efforts of officials stationed in Egypt, BFASS writers and organisers helped to promote identification with the British imperial mission. They used Foreign Office and other government records as well as their network of informants as sources for their writings and lectures. Through them supporters learned of the slave trade and methods to suppress it on the Red Sea, the steamers and the caravan routes. Changes both in the British and the Egyptian leadership were noted. Important treaties, laws and circulars were mentioned, if not reprinted and discussed at length, and success stories such as Count della Sala's exploits were featured regularly.[151] Finally, estimates of the total number of slaves traded and manumitted also appeared in the *ASR* during the years of the campaign. The general tone of these writings was that slave-trading must be eliminated, despite obstacles, and that the British would eventually be able to accomplish this goal with sufficient effort or force.

BFASS members encouraged those interested in the anti-slavery cause to themselves read relevant government documents. Excerpts of Foreign Office materials, including correspondence, were printed in the *ASR*. In addition, the activist and the citizen who wanted even more information were instructed by the publication to purchase additional Foreign Office records, which had been reprinted as parliamentary papers, from *Hansard*. When, in 1890, the slave trade papers regularly presented to Parliament suddenly ceased to be available to the public the BFASS protested, involving itself in endless correspondence until the desired information was obtained via the Belgian minister for foreign affairs at Brussels in 1894.[152] By ensuring the availability of such documents and communicating information from them, BFASS organisers helped to maintain a link between private citizens and government officials or grassroots activism in England and imperialist policies in Egypt.

The organisation also played the role of watchdog, monitoring the progress of the campaign. Any perceived lack of vigilance on the part of British officials was reported by the BFASS either to MPs or to the secretary of state for foreign affairs and often printed in the *ASR* as well.

For example, in 1885 an *ASR* article expressed shock that a man had been allowed to travel to Port Said from Tangier with fifteen slaves, most of whom were women, and that the British officials who questioned him simply accepted his word that all of them were his domestic servants.[153] Another article reported that British authorities had not taken adequate measures to stop slave-trading in the Red Sea, the author complaining that the British warships stationed in the ports did nothing and that their officers were interested primarily in 'shooting parties'.[154] These and other writings implied that neither British nor Egyptian officials could be trusted completely, but through its correspondents, usually missionaries, travellers or residents in the area, the BFASS would 'unravel the dark web of wickedness which has settled like a pall over the territories of the khedive'.[155] In part because BFASS supporters tended to see this issue in such stark moral terms, they had little patience for alternative perspectives or approaches regarding slavery in Egypt, even when they came from their own Government.

BFASS members sometimes would take matters of international diplomacy into their own hands. Its representatives wrote to the king of Italy thanking him for sending ships to assist efforts in the Red Sea and informing him of the need for more stringent international laws regarding the suppression of slavery.[156] They addressed the rulers of Egypt, Tunis, Morocco, the Ottoman Empire and Persia individually at least once.[157] They acted more boldly than most British officials would have dared: for example, in 1873, prior both to the British occupation and the first Anglo-Egyptian convention regarding the slave trade, the BFASS presented a memorial to the khedive stating that slavery must be abolished in Egypt because the 'inalienable right to personal liberty' was endowed by God, a statement that directly challenged the Qur'an as a divine authority and the pronouncements of prominent Muslim religious leaders at that time.[158]

BFASS leaders also put pressure on British authorities in Egypt and appealed to them directly or through the Foreign Office. Letters and memorials to the secretary of state for foreign affairs usually addressed individual incidents of slave-smuggling or the need to abolish the status of slavery in Muslim countries; others outlined specific strategies to suppress slavery such as stationing more British consuls in certain areas, registering slaves or taking control of institutions such as the Slave Trade Department.[159] The BFASS maintained a correspondence with Colonel Schaefer of that Department and Sir Evelyn Baring, Her Britannic Majesty's consul-general and agent in Egypt, as well as other officials in both Cairo and Alexandria. Also, representatives of the Society were sent to Egypt in 1888 and again in 1893 to meet with the khedive, Schaefer, Baring and others.

Members of the BFASS kept British officials accountable for their actions by reading treaties and agreements with a critical eye and reporting their defects to the public. Commentators were quick to catch any ambiguous use of language or a loophole that could function to pacify abolitionists in England without antagonising those who wanted to maintain the status quo Egypt. There was much discussion and controversy surrounding the fugitive slave laws, which stated that slaves who had escaped to British cruisers had to be returned to their masters unless ill-treatment could be proven. BFASS members condemned this policy as an outrageous injustice, and one writer commented that the First Lord might as well deny that the Whitechapel murders took place because '"Jack the Ripper" had not given himself up to be hanged'.[160] They criticised the 1880 treaty with the Ottoman Empire for exempting 'slave seamen' and for the treaty's stipulation to turn over slaves to the Ottoman authorities without any guarantees that they would be freed. Such allowances, they feared, would make the treaty a 'dead letter'.[161] Even circulars were not immune to BFASS scrutiny: when a circular addressed to the Egyptian mudirs and governors stated that no pilgrim could return from Mecca with new servants, the *ASR* responded that such a policy still allowed the pilgrim to enter Egypt with new wives, which left far too much room to those seeking to evade the slave trade laws.[162]

The BFASS used meetings and leaflets as well as the *ASR* to criticise British foreign policy and hold government officials accountable for their decisions to an English public. The BFASS pamphlet entitled 'Scandals in Cairo' sparked discussion at a London meeting, speakers stressing the need to reorganise the anti-slavery administration in Egypt and intensify efforts.[163] The pamphlet itself related stories of known dealers treated mildly by the courts and allowed to continue dealing, and even stated that slaves were taken from dealers and given as presents to Egyptian authorities, including the khedive. The serious accusations and strong statements made about the inadequacy of efforts by the British Government to suppress the slave trade in Cairo are surprising, given that they were expressed in 1885, just a few years after British occupation, when vigilance was at its peak and more slaves were being manumitted than before or after that time.[164]

BFASS criticism of British foreign policy could provoke tension and even open conflict. One British official noted that it hurt morale and actually did more harm than good to anti-slavery efforts.[165] The secretary-general of the Sudan declared that nearly everything published by the BFASS was untrue and that its informants either had no knowledge of the actual situation or were 'dismissed and disgraced government officials' trying to 'mend their shattered reputations by becoming mock apostles of humanity'.[166] The secretary of the BFASS responded to such complaints by explaining that the organisation simply addressed real concerns over slavery and its suppression, and played the important role of helping to satisfy the 'half-awakened conscience of the civilized world'.[167]

Despite conflicts with British officials, BFASS activists continued to see themselves as both the vital link between the English people and anti-slavery activities in Egypt and as true patriots dedicated to English virtues and principles in the face of a Government willing to compromise them. For example, during the controversy surrounding the fugitive slave laws, discussed previously, BFASS members complained that the policy of returning slaves who had sought refuge aboard Her Majesty's ships to their masters was not only a betrayal of the convention but of everything for which England stood. One quoted the oft-repeated lines

> Slaves cannot breathe in England:
> when their lungs reach our air,
> that moment they are free,
> they touch our country,
> and their shackles fall

and stated that the poet, if still alive, would have to rewrite those treasured words as Her Majesty's ships constituted British territory.[168] In these situations, the BFASS acted as part of an extra-parliamentary political culture which sought to maintain and promote a certain conception of Englishness, even when it conflicted with official or governmental policy.[169]

Conclusion

During the late nineteenth century a number of individuals organised themselves through the BFASS to eliminate slavery in Egypt and the surrounding areas and in the process created certain ideas about English identity which they associated with the British imperial mission. The Society was meant to be inclusive, and its title, as well as references to the British people as a whole, encouraged individuals from throughout the British Isles, the Empire and even the world to identify with it. Yet it promoted a certain conception of Englishness, central to which was the belief that English people had the ability to recognise slavery as essentially immoral and, therefore, the responsibility to work to suppress it. While this idea was not new and had developed through abolitionist activities earlier in the century, what was new was that now it would include the form of slavery sanctioned by contemporary Muslim authorites in Egypt and associated with the harem.

Abolitionists had to re-create themselves and their movement in relation to the new situation, which they did through activities such as public meetings, lectures, the production of written materials, most notably the *ASR*, and by networking with sympathetic organisations – humanitarian, religious and commercial. During the late nineteenth century, BFASS writers and organisers made a concerted effort to educate English people about slavery as they understood it to be practised in Islamic countries. As Muslim religious authorities in Egypt and the surrounding areas opposed their agenda, they increasingly regarded this religion as a threat that should be undermined or even eliminated. This approach unified a number of people from different religious or ideological backgrounds around a sense of English national identity that was at once liberal and Christian. Agnostics and humanitarians allied with conservative religious leaders, Catholic, Protestant and Jewish, in opposition to Muslim authorities. Through negative representations of the harem and political advocacy seeking to transgress its boundaries, that institution became a symbol of oppression and a means of defining Englishness as fundamentally distinct and separate from Islam, reinforcing the belief that British imperialist efforts were a moral obligation and part of a civilising mission.

Through activities on behalf of the harem slave, certain class-based definitions of *proper* English as well as Egyptian female roles emerged. The BFASS established and maintained the Cairo Home, which provided temporary shelter for thousands of women and girls for over a twenty-year period. Members held meetings in London and Cairo, worked with representatives of the British and Egyptian Governments, and raised awareness and funds for the project. The English matron who ran the Home trained freed slaves to be like English domestic servants, so that they would either find occupation in this area or apply their new skills once married. Like English domestic servants, however, they were not regarded as equals and their opinions were not consulted. In that respect, the attitude of BFASS activists towards them was similar to that of British officials. Opportunities for freed female slaves were limited, and many found themselves in situations little better than the circumstances they left. Yet compared to slavery and the misery and brutality that accompanied the slave trade, these new roles could be imagined to be liberating, even ideal. For BFASS supporters, the Home testified to the success of their cause and the benefits of British rule in Egypt.

While domestic service was understood as a desirable alternative to harem slavery for some women, middle-class female activists relied on their social position and connections, as well as on what they believed to be their maternal obligation to female slaves in order to extend their own influence beyond the domestic sphere and assert their voices and a place for themselves in the male-dominated imperial nation state. They organised both within the BFASS and in separate female associations in support of the cause and contributed to it financially. Even those with egalitarian beliefs, such as Sarah Amos, a radical and feminist, had to work within an imperial system characterised by hierarchical class and gender relationships. Amos contributed to the establishment of the Cairo Home and, therefore, to the roles it promoted; she also interacted with the highest-ranking British officials, though not without encountering hostility from those who resented her involvement in a sphere that they sought to maintain as a masculine domain.

The British occupation of Egypt provided a 'golden opportunity' as well as a greater sense of responsibility for BFASS members. They assisted British officials by publishing treaties and declarations to be distributed to the Egyptian public, maintaining a network of contacts to report instances of slave-trading and occasionally sending deputations abroad. They also helped supporters in England to identify with the work of their Government by reporting its progress and relating information from Foreign Office records and correspondence, and they even made sure that those documents were available to the public.

In the course of these activities and through their representation, BFASS supporters promoted a version of Englishness that, in contrast to Egyptian society, seemed moral, industrious and developed. This vision of national identity was understood in racial terms, for values and beliefs played as much of a part in defining race as did physical characteristics. For them to be English was not only to be white, but also to abhor slavery, to have little tolerance for Islam and to remain committed to maintaining racial categories by avoiding interracial unions. They assigned racial inferiority to the Egyptians and others who did not share this perspective or obstructed their goals.

While BFASS members identified with imperial expansion and worked with British officials, they did not trust them completely and the two groups did not always see the anti-slavery campaign in the same light. Christian organisations and leaders played a prominent role in the BFASS, and they presented their efforts as part of not just a humanitarian but a religious mission, often conflating ideas about English national identity with Christian values. Because BFASS activists tended to see the anti-slavery movement as a moral crusade, Christian or otherwise, they had no patience with those who seemed less committed or who advocated alternative approaches, even when such views were expressed by representatives of their own Government. Sometimes activists took matters into their own hands and acted independently, for example, in contacting foreign leaders directly. In addition, through their correspondents abroad and their close or critical reading of government papers, they monitored the actions of British officials and were quick to publicise any negligence or lack of dedication on their part.

Through these efforts and the conflicts that arose as a result, BFASS workers developed an image of themselves as true patriots fighting to uphold a certain ideal of Englishness, which they associated with the imperial nation state but which they considered first and foremost a system of values and beliefs that their Government, if not monitored, could compromise for the sake of diplomacy or other interests. Calling attention to areas of disagreement between BFASS members and British officials helps to illustrate the flexibility of English national identity. It shows how through two aspects of the same campaign, slightly different definitions of Englishness were created and circulated within the larger imperial cultural system, contradicting as well as reinforcing each other.

These ideas about English national identity had much to do with existing circumstances, and BFASS workers were influenced by their environment. Most were from a middle-class background during a time in English history marked by middle-class hegemony, a belief in the importance of class hierarchy and waged, not slave, labour. They lived in a predominantly Christian society in which liberal Enlightenment ideas were valued, and Muslims and Muslim voices were few. Most were subjects of Her Majesty when British imperialism was at its height, and the occupation of Egypt seemed to promise reform of the country. Finally, they had inherited a tradition of abolitionist activity which assumed the immorality of slavery and the duty of the English to eliminate it. In these ways anti-slavery efforts seem like a logical outcome of the social context.

It is, however, important to emphasise that people in England did not have to embrace this cause, and only a minority actively involved themselves in it. Abolition had not always been associated with English national identity, and even when New World, or plantation, slavery came under attack during the first half of the nineteenth century the British imperial mission still did not include the suppression of female, or harem-oriented, slavery practised in Islamic countries. In fact, Victorian English women who visited the harems of the Middle East usually identified with the women they met, likened the harem to the English bourgeois home, and compared the slaves not to the slaves of the West Indies but to English domestic servants.[170] Applying previous abolitionist beliefs to the situation in Egypt required effort, initiative and creativity.

Central to this process was the portrayal of the harem as dark and sinister. BFASS organisers and writers ignored positive representations of the institution and instead treated it as the root cause of the death and destruction accompanying the slave trade. Images conveying this idea appeared in the *ASR*, and were expressed in lectures and meetings throughout the course of the campaign. They served to help supporters of the cause associate the harem with oppression, so that they would come to regard it as every bit as confining and opposed to individual liberty as a plantation slave's chains. These representations were crucially important, for if the harem was seen as similar to the English home it would have been difficult to generate support for the cause, and efforts to transgress its boundaries and open it to public scrutiny would have called into question the legitimacy of the private domestic sphere in England.

BFASS organisers and writers drew from existing ideas and belief systems in order to make their case. Certainly, anti-Islamic sentiment was not new to England. They employed arguments associated with Christianity, liberalism and social Darwinism as well. They focused on a specific political goal – the suppression of the slave trade and the eventual abolition of slavery in Egypt – and, as a result, they valued ideas that helped them to achieve this goal and considered perspectives that complicated or interfered with it unimportant.

The system of meaning that oriented a number of people in support of the cause developed in the course of anti-slavery activity. It was not that a few leaders created an ideology and then disseminated it; rather, over time, BFASS writers and lecturers learned which stories and images would provoke a reaction from the crowd and which would generate support and help to raise funds. The response of individuals was part of the process. Organisers tried a variety of methods and approaches through public gatherings, printed materials and networking, and relied on those that proved most effective.

These ideas were created through a network of relationships that crossed national boundaries. BFASS supporters who visited and assisted British officials in Egypt, monitored the situation there and contributed to the Cairo Home in that country formed beliefs about themselves and their mission through experiences in Egypt and encounters with Egyptians which, along with Foreign Office records, were used to educate women and men in England on the subject. As a result, conceptions of English national identity, Islam and the harem, crucial to the ideological framework created by the BFASS, must be understood as the cultural products not of a closed English or Egyptian society but of an imperial system.

This framework and the identities it included were flexible enough for a variety of individuals to find meaning in and particularise their own versions of them, thereby uniting a number of diverse people

THE HAREM, SLAVERY AND BRITISH IMPERIAL CULTURE

around a common goal, including, for example, MPs, religious leaders, businessmen, working-class men and women. The tendency to equate the British imperial mission with a sense of English national identity did not prevent individuals from Scotland, Ireland, Wales and elsewhere from contributing to the campaign. Feminists supported the cause despite the very traditional gender roles it promoted, and at least one man who sympathised with Islam and worked to create a more prominent place for that religion in England also contributed to the BFASS. Some were attracted to the organisation for religious reasons, others out of concern for human rights and still others because of economic issues, patriotism or the opportunity to enter public debate and imperial national life. Perhaps sympathy for or identification with slaves motivated the workers who donated money but did not leave records explaining their reasons. Certainly, others related to the class-based maternal or paternal identities that the movement perpetuated. Most of them probably were motivated by a combination of those factors: just as government officials working for the cause of anti-slavery had different ways of understanding their role in the movement, so did the many people associated with the BFASS.

Notes

1 The idea of a symbolic framework that allows the individual to understand experiences in relation to abstract beliefs, in this case the immorality of slavery, has been discussed by Clifford Geertz's 'Religion as a Cultural System', in *The Interpretation of Cultures* (New York: Basic Books, 1973), pp. 87–125; the reference to the creation of symbolic forms as social events is on p. 91.
2 That BFASS meeting was covered by the *Beverly Recorder* (5 August 1888), MSS Brit. Emp. S. 24, J. 32, BFASS.
3 Mary Douglas, *Implicit Meanings: Essays in Anthropology* (London and Boston, MA: Routledge & Kegan Paul, 1975), p. 4.
4 The Somersett case placed only certain limits on slave-owners in England but did not make slave-holding illegal in that country: J. R. Oldfield, *Popular Politics and British Anti-Slavery: The Mobilisation of Public Opinion Against the Slave Trade 1787–1807* (Manchester: Manchester University Press, 1995), p. 126.
5 *Ibid.*, p. 1.
6 Regarding the convention see John Harris, *A Century of Emancipation* (London: J. M. Dent & Sons, 1933), pp. 94–6; references to legislation and treaties concerning slaves abroad are from David Eltis, *Economic Growth and the Ending of the Transatlantic Slave Trade* (Oxford: Oxford University Press, 1987), pp. 83, 90.
7 Slavery continued to be an abolitionist target in Cuba until 1886 and Brazil until 1888. However, the concern with harem-oriented slavery represents a new phase of activity in the anti-slavery movement, as this chapter illustrates. While this book focuses on the suppression of slavery in Egypt and surrounding areas, primarily the Red Sea, Turkey, the Arabian peninsula, the Mediterranean, and the Sudan, during the mid-to-late nineteenth century, representatives of the British Government negotiated with Islamic leaders in other areas of Africa, particularly South-East Africa, and the Middle East as well. For an in-depth discussion of the various treaty networks and agreements see Suzanne Miers, 'The Attack from the Periphery II: British Treaties with African Rulers and Leaders to 1884', in *Britain and the Ending*

of the Slave Trade (London: Longman, 1975), pp. 40–117. For more about British abolitionism see James Walvin (ed.), *Slavery and British Society, 1776–1846* (Baton Rouge: Louisiana State University Press, 1982); Seymour Drescher, *Capitalism and Antislavery: British Mobilization in Comparative Perspective* (Oxford: Oxford University Press, 1987); David Turley, *The Culture of English Antislavery, 1780–1860* (London and New York: Routledge, 1991); Clare Midgley, *Women Against Slavery: The British Campaigns, 1780–1870* (London and New York: Routledge, 1992); and Leo d'Anjou, *Social Movements and Cultural Change: The First Abolition Campaign Revisited* (New York: Aldine De Gruyter, 1996).

8   Harris, *A Century of Emancipation*, pp. 3–6.
9   Oldfield, *Popular Politics and British Anti-Slavery*, p. 33.
10 William Green notes that the new House of Commons in 1833 was 'virtually divested of West Indian members': *British Slave Emancipation: The Sugar Colonies and the Great Experiment 1830–1865* (Oxford: Clarendon Press, 1976), p. 114.
11 Quoted in Walvin, *Slavery and British Society*, p. 6.
12 Betty Fladeland, '"Our Cause Being One and the Same:" Abolitionists and Chartism', in *ibid.*, pp. 69–99.
13 Walvin accurately describes abolitionism as neither entirely humanitarian nor entirely economic but rather an ideology that combined both concerns and was shared by middle- and working-class people: *Slavery and British Society*, pp. 13–15. For discussion of the triumph of the middle-class or entrepreneurial ideal, which emphasised thrift, hard work and promotion by merit, and its acceptance by workers and aristocrats in Victorian England, see Harold Perkin, *The Origins of Modern English Society 1780–1880* (London: Routledge & Kegan Paul, 1969).
14 *ASR* (April 1873), 149–51.
15 BFASS Jubilee pamphlet, MSS Brit. Emp. S. 24, J. 32, BFASS.
16 Joseph Cooper, *The Lost Continent; or, Slavery and the Slave-Trade in Africa, 1875* (London: Thomas Nelson Printers Ltd, 1875).
17 *ASR* (November 1884), 201.
18 'A Slave Market in Mecca', slide 21 in box 8, BFASS.
19 *Journal of Arts*, 361, MSS Brit. Emp. S. 24, J. 32, BFASS.
20 *ASR* (May 1878), 1–35, at 34, and (July 1872); *Standard* (24 September 1890), MSS Brit. Emp. S. 24, J. 33, BFASS. Similar ideas about the relationship between slavery and Islam were expressed in *Cardinal Lavigerie and the African Slave Trade*, ed. Richard Clarke, SJ, Trinity College, Oxford (London: Longmans, Green, & Co., 1889). It was in response to Lavigerie that Ahmad Shafiq addressed his book *al-Riqq fi al-Islam* (Cairo, 1892).
21 *ASR* (November–December 1890), 296.
22 *Ibid.* (May–June 1894), 182.
23 *Ibid.* (March–April 1889), 109.
24 *Ibid.* (November–December 1887), 184–6; later Teall published *Slavery and the Slave-Trade 1889: Facts and Memoranda Compiled from the Slave Trade Papers, the Statues at Largo and Other Sources* (London: BFASS). As cruelty to slaves is forbidden in the Qur'an, the same argument could be made for Islam.
25 *ASR* (January–February 1890), 17.
26 *Ibid.* (August–October 1897), 210–16.
27 *Ibid.* (July 1872), 58–9.
28 *Ibid.* (August 1883), 192–9.
29 *Ibid.* (March–April 1894), 93.
30 *Ibid.* (September–October 1888), 186.
31 *Ibid.* (January 1879), 136.
32 Letter to the Secretary of the BFASS from seven Abyssinians (20 May 1889), G-23/A (Shoa), BFASS; reprinted in *The Times* and in the *ASR*.
33 'Slave Girls in Manchester', *ASR* (January 1875), 134–5.
34 'White Slaves vrs. Black', letter to the editor of the *Daily News* (1881), MSS Brit. Emp. S. 24, J. 32, BFASS; reprinted in *ASR* (December 1881), 235–6.

35 *ASR* (May 1878), 34–9, and (June 1879), 136.
36 *Ibid.* (November 1881), 200.
37 *Ibid.* (June 1883), 168–9.
38 *Ibid.* (May–June 1887), 92–7.
39 'Cardinal Lavigerie at Prince's Hall', *Globe* (August 1888), MSS Brit. Emp. S. 24, J. 32, BFASS.
40 *St James Gazette* (16 November 1882), MSS Brit. Emp. S. 24, J. 32, BFASS.
41 The mention of support from 'working men' is in *ASR* (November–December 1888), 250; in addition, at least one lecture was presented in association with a 'Young Men's Literary and Mutual Improvement Society', and another with the London City Mission, a religious organisation that ministered to the city's poor: *ibid.* (November–December 1893), 350. Appendix 2 lists the locations of BFASS members.
42 The Jubilee meetings of 1884 in Manchester and London to celebrate the 1834 Act of Emancipation and raise funds were especially popular. The Manchester meeting, held in the Free Trade Hall, was 'densely crowded' with nearly 5,000 people; a simultaneous meeting had to be held in the neighbouring hall of the YMCA for the 1,000–1,500 who could not get inside the other building: *ibid.* (November 1884), 196–221, and (January–February 1889), 1–2.
43 *Ibid.* (January–February 1893), 13.
44 At the Brighton YMCA 4,000–5,000 handbills were distributed to an 'overflowing audience': *ibid.* (January–February 1894), 44; one lecture held in the Stratford YMCA attracted a crowd of 800–1,000 people.
45 *Ibid.* (March–April 1893), 102.
46 Posters, flyers, and announcements are in the BFASS collections.
47 Gordon (London, 1880). This particular one was enough in demand that the BFASS could charge 6d for it. Several other pamphlets relating to slavery in Muslim countries were published by the BFASS during this period, two of which are especially interesting with regard to the female, or harem-oriented, nature of slavery in Egypt. One discusses how women who were sold as slaves could become the wives of their masters; the other described slave raids in which all the men were killed and the women taken to slave markets. At least 1,000 copies of each were ordered; both were printed in 1890 and are in the BFASS collections.
48 For example, in 1894 the *Sussex Daily News* featured an article on the society, praising it for its progress: *ASR* (July–August), 242–3.
49 The BFASS collections contain clippings from 21 different publications which discuss a meeting held in August 1888 at Princes Hall, Piccadilly, London: *Echo, Spectator, The Queen, The Lady's Newspaper, Standard, Globe, Pall Mall Gazette, Morning Advertiser, Variety Fair, Aberdeen Free Press, Bath Gazette, Beverly Recorder, Birmingham Daily Post, Birmingham Gazette, Bradford Observer, Bristol, Bromley Telegraph, Carlisle Journal, The Times* and 2 unidentified newspapers.
50 For example, one reporter working on a series entitled 'Studies in Mohamedanism' for the *Leeds Mercury Weekly Supplement* requested assistance from that organisation: letter from John Pool to the Secretary of the BFASS (7 August 1891), folder G-25 (Egypt), BFASS.
51 Homi Bhabha explains the relationship between mimicry, a difference that is 'almost nothing but not quite', and a menace, a difference that is 'almost total but not quite', in *The Location of Culture* (London and New York: Routledge, 1994), p. 91; 'Entertainment in April', *St Stephen's Magazine* (Hempstead) (April 1886), MSS Brit. Emp. S. 24, J. 32, BFASS.
52 The income of the BFASS could vary so dramatically – from £200 one year to £1,500 the next – that the available records are most likely incomplete. In 1885 after much publicity and activity, the organisation was able to raise over £2,000, and annual contributions totalling over £1,000 were not unusual. The numbers and information regarding donations have been calculated using the lists of contributions found in the BFASS collections and on the pages of the *ASR*.

53 *ASR* (November–December 1890), 269.
54 *Ibid.* (March–April 1892), 93, reprinted from an article in the *Daily Graphic.*
55 'White and Black Slavery in Turkey', *ASR* (April 1876), 44–6.
56 *Pall Mall Gazette* (August 1886), MSS Brit. Emp. S. 24, J. 32, BFASS.
57 James Stevenson, 'The Arabs in Central Africa and at Lake Nyassa' (1889), MSS Brit. Emp. S. 24, J. 33, BFASS.
58 *ASR* (January–February 1889), 32.
59 'Slavery in the Soudan', BFASS meeting covered in *The Times* (16 November 1882), MSS Brit. Emp. S. 24, J. 32, BFASS. The idea that the sole cause of the slave trade in Eastern Africa was the demand for slaves in areas such as Turkey and Egypt is stated in resolution 2 of the document entitled 'Resolutions Passed Unanimously at a Public Meeting of the British and Foreign Anti-Slavery Society held in Exeter Hall' (8 July 1873), folder G-21 (Mozambique and East Coast), BFASS.
60 *ASR* (August–October 1900), 118–19.
61 *Ibid.* (March–April 1889), 54–81, at 67.
62 'Slavery and the Slave Trade in the Ottoman Empire', *ibid.* (January 1877), 169–73, at 170.
63 Aziz Al-Azmeh describes this process, explaining that, 'tokens of a banal nature are taken up and affirmed as tokens – or stigmata – of difference, and differences elevated to Difference based in an absolutization of heritage': *Islams and Modernities* (London: Verso, 1993), p. 6.
64 Billie Melman, *Women's Orients: English Women and the Middle East, 1718–1918, Sexuality, Religion and Work* (London: Macmillan, 1992).
65 Expressed to Charles Allen on his visit to Egypt, *ASR* (March–April 1888), 30 and (May 1883), 131.
66 *Ibid.* (August 1881), 134.
67 *Ibid.* (January–February 1893), 10. The Egyptian Government had taken previous censuses in which women were counted. The above statements, therefore, reflect a certain amount of confusion about the situation in Egypt but, nevertheless, very definite attitudes regarding the harem and the proper approach of British anti-slavery workers towards it.
68 'Considerations as to What Could Most Effectively Be Done at the Present Crisis [of the meeting of a European Conference on Eastern Affairs] to Get Slavery Done Away With in Turkey Once and For All', folder G-96 (Turkey and Bulgaria), BFASS.
69 Inderpal Grewal, *Home and Harem*, p. 26; British officials shared this perspective regarding the harem (see chapter two).
70 M. L. Whateley, 'Women's Condition in Egypt', *Englishwomen's Review* (September 1884), 395–412, at 397.
71 Similarly, for British activists in the earlier part of the century the success of abolition could be measured by the socialisation of freed people into 'appropriate' roles based on the 'patriarchal peasant household': Madhavi Kale, '"When The Saints Came Marching In:" the Anti-Slavery Society and Indian Indentured Migration to the British Caribbean', in Daunton and Halpern, *Empire and Others*, p. 330.
72 There was, in fact, a growing domestic service sector for women in nineteenth-century Egypt: Judith Tucker, *Women in Nineteenth-Century Egypt* (Cambridge: Cambridge University Press, 1985), p. 93.
73 Letter from a Belgian explorer to Charles Allen, reprinted in *The Times* (27 October 1889), MSS Brit. Emp. S. 24, J. 32, BFASS.
74 *ASR* (October 1883), 262–4.
75 The Aborigines' Protection Society was founded in 1837 'to assist in protecting the defenceless and promoting the advancement of uncivilised tribes'. It concerned itself with the welfare of peoples all over the world from Native Americans to Australian Aborigines. Many of its members also belonged to the BFASS, and the two societies eventually merged in 1909: Harris, *A Century of Emancipation*, pp. 80, 89–91.
76 Reports of this meeting list the names only of a few prominent attendees, all of whom were British; no mention is made of any Egyptians present.

77 Summary of the Proceedings, 'Meeting in Cairo', *ASR* (April 1884), 6–7.
78 Summary of the Proceedings in 'Home for Freed Women Slaves, Cairo: Meeting at the Mansion House', *ASR* (May 1884), 108–12, at 110.
79 *ASR* (January 1884), 13, and (July–August 1888), 140–1.
80 *Ibid.* (December 1885), 505, reference to article in *The Times* (23 December 1883).
81 Included in the Treasurer's Report for the Cairo Home, Cairo (18 April 1886) by C. C. Scott Moncrieff, *ASR* (May–June 1886), 57–9, and folder G-26 (Egypt), in BFASS.
82 Reports regarding the Cairo Home often noted the large numbers of Sudanese slaves during a given time period or the arrival of 2–3 Circassian slaves. However, unlike the manumission reports in the Foreign Office records, the surviving documents do not reveal any systematic attempt to identify slaves by race.
83 Some of the 'younger and more intelligent' girls were sent to a nearby mission school where they learned to read and write in Arabic, so that they might become teachers in that school one day, but this was the exception not the rule: *ASR* (March–April 1889), 112.
84 Report of the Cairo Committee for the year 1886 by Mrs Dupont, secretary, *ASR* (March–April 1887), 68.
85 Leonore Davidoff, 'Mastered for Life: Servant and Wife in Victorian and Edwardian England', *Journal of Social History*, 7:4 (1974), 406–23.
86 Crewe tried to prevent this situation: Treasurer's Report for the Cairo Home for Freed Women Slaves, by C. C. Scott Moncrieff, Cairo, folder G-26 (Egypt) BFASS. However, at one point, Sarah Amos wrote to Evelyn Baring that Mrs Crewe had objected strongly to sending her residents to certain local harems but was 'weak' and did so when ordered to by Colonel Schaefer and others. Colonel Schaefer was in charge of the Slave Trade Department, and the 'others' were most likely prominent members of the Cairo committee: FO 84 /1770 Sarah Amos to Sir E. Baring (13 December 1886); the same letter is in FOCP 541/50 1886. Judith Tucker notes the isolation, vulnerability, and powerlessness of female domestic servants in Egypt compared to women in other crafts or professions. *Women in Nineteenth-Century Egypt*, p. 93.
87 FOCP 541/27 Memorandum by Mrs Shakoor, 29 December 1888.
88 Report by C. C. Scott Moncrieff, *ASR* (May–June 1886), 59, and folder G-26 (Egypt), BFASS.
89 'Scandals in Cairo' by an English resident, p. 17.
90 Letter to the BFASS from Colonel Scott Moncrieff (5 April 1894), folder G-26 (Egypt), BFASS.
91 *ASR* (January 1884), 15; a similar article from the *Country Paper* was reprinted in *ASR* (February 1884), 33.
92 *Ibid.* (May–June 1892), 172.
93 *Ibid.* (September–October 1893), 290 and *ASR* (March–April 1893), 102–3.
94 *Ibid.* (March–April 1893), 62–3.
95 'Turkish Home for Freed Slaves', *ASR* (January–February 1891), 44; and 'Slavery in Turkey', *Standard* (10 February 1891), MSS Brit. Emp. S. 24, J. 34, BFASS.
96 *ASR* (January–February 1892), 25–6.
97 Letter from Lord Cromer to Mr Buxton, Secretary of the BFASS, folder G-26 (Egypt) BFASS.
98 Folder G-26 (Egypt: Cairo Home for Freed Women Slaves), BFASS and FOCP 541/29, Memorandum by Mrs Shakoor, 29 December 1888.
99 From the Report of the Cairo Committee for the year 1886 by Mrs Dupont, Secretary, *ASR* (March–April 1887), 68.
100 *ASR* (December 1885), 505.
101 'Slave Trade', in folder G-30 (Suez), BFASS; a similar proposal was also printed in the *ASR* (July 1874), 55–6.
102 Carlton Hayes, 'Bases of a New National Imperialism', in Harrison Wright (ed.), *The 'New Imperialism:' Analysis of Late-Nineteenth-Century Expansion* (Boston, MA: D.C. Heath & Co., 1976), pp. 81–8; also of interest is C. C. Eldridge, *Disraeli and the Rise of a New Imperialism* (Cardiff: University of Wales Press, 1996).

103 'International Conference on the Slave Trade Meeting in Birmingham', *Birmingham Daily Post* (January 1890), MSS Brit. Emp. S. 24, J. 33, BFASS.
104 *ASR* (January–February 1889), 1–2.
105 Lavigerie's speech (July 1888), MSS Brit. Emp, S. 24, J. 33, BFASS.
106 *ASR* (January–February 1894), 44.
107 One was in Bristol, and the other was in Birmingham; by the end of the century both targeted slavery in Muslim countries.
108 *ASR* (January–February 1887), 5.
109 Joseph Baylen and Norbert Gossman (eds), *Biographical Dictionary of Modern British Radicals*, vol. 3: *1870–1914* (New York: Harvester, 1988), pp. 36–8; also see her obituary in *The Times*, 8 February 1908.
110 FOCP 541/50, Sarah Amos to Sir E. Baring, Egypt, 1886; the correspondence of Amos, Baring and other officials regarding this charge can be found throughout both FOCP 541/50 and FO 84/1770.
111 FOCP 541, Baring to Anderson, 15 November 1886.
112 *Ibid.*
113 FOCP 541/50, Mrs Sheldon Amos to the Earl of Iddesleigh, Foreign Secretary, 30 October 1886.
114 As Geertz explains, like a 'formless monster with neither sense of direction nor power of self-control': 'Religion as a Cultural System', p. 99.
115 A similar situation occurred when British feminists claimed a role in the Empire by concerning themselves with the welfare of Indian women even though they did not consider them to be equals: Antoinette Burton, *Burdens of History: British Feminists, Indian Women, and Imperial Culture, 1865–1915* (Chapel Hill and London: University of North Carolina Press, 1994).
116 Memorial to Lord Granville, 1873, folder G-30 (Suez), BFASS.
117 *ASR* (August–October 1900), 118–19.
118 *Ibid.* (August 1882), 231, and (June 1882), 160–2.
119 'Slave Trade in Egypt', *Daily Chronicle* (November 1882), MSS Brit. Emp. S. 24, J. 32, BFASS. This statement has little to do with the actual motivations influencing British foreign policy, but it accurately reflects BFASS zeal for aggressive involvement in Egypt and the association of their mission with occupation.
120 *ASR* (October 1884), 184.
121 Interview with Charles Allen (1889), MSS Brit. Emp. S. 24, J.32, BFASS.
122 Memorandum (undated) from F. Cunliffe Owen, folder G-30 (Suez), BFASS; also printed in *ASR* (August 1885), 446–7.
123 Letter to the Secretary of the Anti-Slavery Society, Alexandria (December 1873), folder G-25 (Egypt), BFASS.
124 *ASR* (May 1876), 59–60; for discussion of a similar attack on the French monarchy prior to the Revolution, in which the idea of morally corrupt women out of control was used to symbolise the illegitimacy of royal power, see Sarah Maza, 'The Diamond Necklace Affair, 1785–1786', *Private Lives and Public Affairs: The Causes Célèbres of Prerevolutionary France* (Berkeley: University of California Press, 1993), pp. 167–211.
125 Linda Colley considers how negative representations of the French served to unify inhabitants of the British Isles during the eighteenth century in *Britons: Forging the Nation 1707–1837* (New Haven, CT: Yale University Press, 1992).
126 *ASR* (July–August 1894), 246; the manumission numbers were declining because anti-slavery efforts had been so successful that by the 1890s Egypt had considerably fewer slaves than earlier in the century.
127 This trial, public opinion in Egypt and the perspectives of Egyptian journalists who wrote for an Arabic-speaking audience are discussed by Muhammad Mukhtar in *Bughyat al-Marid fi Shira' al-Jawari wa Taqlib al-'Abid: al-Awda' al-Ijtima'iyya li al-Raqiq fi Misr 642–1924* (Cairo: Khalid Mukhtar and Muhammad Mukhtar, 1997), pp. 175–9; and by 'Imad Ahmad Hilal, *al-Raqiq fi Misr fi al-qarn al-tasi' 'ashara* (Cairo, 1999), pp. 371–3. Both Mukhtar and Hilal, like a number of Egyptians of the nineteenth century, maintain that the British Government used

this case to embarrass and take revenge on the pashas, particularly 'Ali Pasha Sharif, the head of the Egyptian Legislative Assembly who had, just weeks before his arrest, publicly criticised the British-dominated Egyptian Government and the high salaries of British civil employees, particularly those in the Slave Trade Bureau. Eve Troutt Powell provides interesting analysis and additional insights into this case by considering the slaves and the issue of their guardianship as a 'metaphor for the Sudan question' for nationalists and others in the imperial context: *A Different Shade*, pp. 1–4, 150–5, at 150.
128 *ASR* (March 1884), 67.
129 *Ibid.* (August–October 1897), 210–16.
130 As a way of appealing to commercial interests BFASS supporters frequently contrasted economies based on slavery with 'legitimate' enterprises or 'happy villages and prosperous trade': newspaper clipping covering a BFASS meeting (August 1888), MSS Brit. Emp. S. 24, J. 32, BFASS. Businessmen were active members of and contributors to the organisation, and on several occasions the BFASS sent letters to the chambers of commerce in over fifty cities and towns throughout England urging them to use their influence in the struggle to suppress slavery. In addition, the BFASS sent a memo to the secretary of state for foreign affairs regarding the ways in which the suppression of the slave trade would benefit British commerce: *ASR* (January 1876), 2. The idea of eliminating slavery in Africa by encouraging British or European enterprise on the continent had been a strategy advocated by anti-slavery leaders since at least the mid-nineteenth century: Philip Curtin, *The Image of Africa: British Ideas and Action, 1780–1850* (Madison: University of Wisconsin Press, 1964), pp. 300–1.
131 Folder G-28/A (Morocco), BFASS.
132 Petition to the House of Commons from the BFASS Regarding the Turkish Slave Trade and the Congress of Berlin, signed by Joseph Cooper and Edmund Sturge, honourary secretaries (20 May 1879), folder G-96 (Turkey and Bulgaria), BFASS. The phrase 'British nation' most likely refers to England, Scotland, Ireland and Wales.
133 'Slave Trade in Egypt', *Standard* (November 1882) MSS Brit. Emp. S. 24, J. 32, BFASS.
134 *ASR* (March–April 1896), 83.
135 'Convention', p. 191, BFASS.
136 'Syria', written in Istanbul (4 March 1843), folder G-96 (Turkey), BFASS.
137 *ASR* (March–April 1893), 102–3.
138 This practice was not new, although exactly how the nation would be understood depended on the specific historical circumstances. Kathleen Wilson examines this process in the context of Cook's voyages to the South Pacific and the 'transculture' of the Caribbean during the eighteenth century in *The Island Race: Englishness, Empire and Gender in the Eighteenth Century* (London and New York: Routledge, 2003).
139 *ASR* (September–October 1890), 216–20, and the 'The Anti-Slavery Congress', in *Women's Penny Paper* (27 September 1890), p. 583.
140 Jean Baptiste Gochet, *La Traite des nègres et la croisade africaine* (Paris, 1891), 171.
141 Salisbury became foreign secretary in 1878 and prime minister in 1885.
142 Of particular concern was that the slave trade might be considered piracy, which would allow cruisers belonging to any nation to capture a slave vessel and have traders tried before any available court. Interview with Charles Allen, MSS Brit. Emp. S. 24, J. 33, BFASS.
143 'The Anti-Slavery Conference', *The Times* (23 November 1889), MSS Brit. Emp. S. 24, J. 33, BFASS; Interview with Allen (1889), MSS Brit. Emp. S. 24, J. 33, BFASS; and 'The Anti-Slavery Conference', *Standard*, MSS Brit. Emp. S. 24, J. 34, BFASS.
144 Resolution of a BFASS meeting, signed Mayor, folder G-22 (North Africa – General), BFASS.
145 Frederick Banks, travelling lecturer for the BFASS, 'Slavery and the Slave Trade', letter to the Editor of the *Suffolk Chronicle* (15 April 1891), MSS Brit. Emp. S. 24, J. 34, BFASS.

ENGLISH ACTIVISM

146 'The Anti-Slavery Conference – Brussels, November 21', *The Times* (22 November 1889), MSS Brit. Emp. S. 24, J. 33, BFASS.
147 For example, in the earlier part of the century a number of Scottish and Irish anti-slavery activists preferred the American radicalism of William Lloyd Garrison, whose masthead for the *Liberator* read 'My country is the world, my countrymen all mankind', to the more conservative approach of the BFASS. C. Duncan Rice discusses the traditions of nonconformity and autonomy among Scots abolitionists that played a role in the decision to take an independent course from that of the London committee: Rice, *The Scots Abolitionists 1833–1861* (Baton Rouge and London: Louisiana State University Press, 1981), pp. 4, 35–6, 51–4, 58, 79. He (p. 36), as well as Howard Temperley (*British Antislavery*), notes the support for Garrisonianism in Dublin. Similarly, Scots and Irish female abolitionists during that same period expressed an ability to identify with the plight of the slave because of their experiences both as women and as members of an oppressed nation. Karen Halbersleben describes this tendency among women in Ireland and their sense of a 'dual Irish female mission': *Women's Participation in the British Antislavery Movement 1824–1865* (Lewiston: Edwin Mellen Press, 1993), pp. 123–6; and she explains how Scottish women used anti-slavery activity to assert themselves as both Scots and women, challenging assumptions about male and English superiority (pp. 131–62).
148 For example, an article in the *ASR* informed British officials that vessels shipped slaves to Jiddah in broad daylight with the connivance of Egyptian authorities. Efforts were made promptly to stop these activities: FOBPP, Mr Cookson to the Earl of Derby (with Enclosure to Chérif Pasha), July 1876 (vol. 55, p. 8). Similarly, a BFASS sympathiser teaching at the American missionary school at Assiout, who later volunteered to become an official correspondent and informer for the BFASS, reported that a caravan with 1,000 slaves had been brought to the town. British officials responded immediately: the slaves were freed, the traders were punished, and the local authorities were dismissed or tried by a court-martial. The incident was described as a great success and even as setting an example for others: FOBPP, Mr Malet to the Marquis of Salisbury, April 1880 (vol. 58, p. 51).
149 *ASR* (November 1880), 110 and (September–December 1898), 206–8.
150 *Ibid.* (June 1882), 167–8.
151 *Ibid.* (December 1880), first page.
152 *Ibid.* (July–August 1890), 155; (March–April 1893), 70; (May–June 1893), 172–3; and (January–February 1894), 2.
153 Parliament was scheduled to make inquiries into the matter at the next meeting: *ASR* (January 1885), 268–9.
154 Letter from Donald Mackenzie to Mr Allen (20 May 1895), folder G-95 (Saudi Arabia), BFASS.
155 *ASR* (January 1882), 5.
156 'Lord Granville on Slavery', *Standard* (August 1888), MSS Brit. Emp. S. 24, J. 32, BFASS.
157 Correspondence and memorials are in folders G-25 (Egypt), G 28/A (Morocco), G-94 (Persia); G-31 (Tunisia); G-23/A (Shoa); the Ottoman Government was contacted through British officials, folder G-96 (Turkey and Bulgaria), BFASS.
158 *ASR* (July 1873), 161–2.
159 The last suggestion was made in 1881 just before the occupation: 'Anti-Slavery Society Deputation to the Foreign Office', *The Times* (19 August 1881), MSS Brit. Emp. S. 24, J. 32, BFASS.
160 *ASR* (January–February 1889), 35.
161 *Ibid.* (March 1880), 7; a similar article dealing with this subject appeared in the *Daily News*: clipping from BFASS collection.
162 *Ibid.* (January–February 1887), 34.
163 'Scandals in Cairo in connection with Slavery' by an English resident at Cairo (London: BFASS, 1885).
164 *ASR* (August 1885), 418–35.

[113]

165 FOBPP, Mr Malet to Earl Granville, 2 April 1881 (vol. 59, p. 22).
166 *Ibid.*, Giegler Pasha to Mr Malet, 20 April 1881 (vol. 59, p. 33).
167 *Ibid.*, Mr Allen to Earl Granville, London, 18 May 1881 (vol. 59, p. 41).
168 *ASR* (July–August 1888), 128.
169 For discussion of the development of an extra-parliamentary political culture in England in the eighteenth century see Kathleen Wilson's *The Sense of the People: Politics, Culture and Imperialism in England, 1715–1785* (Cambridge: Cambridge University Press, 1995).
170 Melman, *Women's Orients.*

CHAPTER FOUR

'The British Turk' and the 'Christian harem': imperial ideology in English gender politics

Feminist challenges

The process of defining proper English gender roles in relation to the harem and the position of the Muslim woman had as much to do with domestic gender debates as it did with foreign policy. As a result of increasingly vocal and influential feminist movements, the place that women should occupy in society became a hotly debated and divisive issue in late Victorian England. Both feminists and those who opposed them found meaning in the harem, which they applied to their own circumstances and employed in pursuit of their own political goals. Examining the various ways in which people in that society understood the harem and themselves in relation to it highlights the importance of agency and creativity in the process of identity formation and cultural exchange. For these historical actors did not simply adopt the perspectives of anti-slavery workers and others who had contact with Muslims abroad: they elaborated and expanded on their ideas, considered them in light of new concerns and ultimately contributed original concepts to the imperial cultural system. As this chapter shows, how people in England chose to understand and represent the harem and for what ends could differ dramatically.

By the late nineteenth century the 'woman question' had become a political issue in England, galvanised by an array of contending and complementary feminist movements.[1] Some strands employed the language of republicanism and liberal Enlightenment ideals, as well as beliefs in women's difference from men, their moral superiority and their spiritual influence in the home, in order to claim a role in the public sphere. Others used arguments only about women's unique abilities.[2] Shared convictions in the value of feminine qualities helped to unite women of the middle and working classes in support of feminist causes.[3]

As in the case of the abolitionists, feminists from every part of the British Isles involved themselves in these reforming movements.[4] For example, Irish and Scottish activists associated with the National Union of Women's Suffrage Societies and the Women's Social and Political Union, and they participated in the English campaigns as training for later work at home,[5] and in Ireland the organisers of the Ladies' National Association for Repeal of the Contagious Diseases Acts worked to maintain ties with anti-vice leaders in England.[6] Even those who understood these types of activity in terms of their own separate national identities and resented being described by contemporaries as English nevertheless contributed to the cause.[7]

Feminist agitation concerning issues such as property reform, access to higher education and suffrage all sought to elevate the status of women, give them greater independence and control over their lives, and allow them to play a more active role in society and politics outside of the home. These movements challenged *couverture*, or the idea that females should live under the protection or tutelage of some man, usually a husband or a father. As Sir William Blackstone explained in *Commentaries on the Laws of England*, 'the husband and wife are one person in law: that is, the very being or legal existence of the woman is suspended during the marriage, or at least is incorporated and consolidated into that of the husband: under whose wing, protection, and *cover*, she performs everything'.[8]

The harem similarly was distinguished by its covered, or private, nature and the idea that those within it were under the care, protection and authority of a man. Likening the harem to patriarchal gender relationships in England characterised by *couverture* and the inequalities that resulted from them had a long tradition in feminist thought. In 1792, Mary Wollstonecraft stated in *Vindication of the Rights of Woman* that the institution of marriage as practised in England was no better than the slavery of the Muslim harem.[9] Harriet Taylor, feminist intellectual and later wife of suffragist John Stuart Mill, refuted the claim that affection compensated for inequalities in marriage by remarking that 'such feelings often exist between a Sultan and his favorites'.[10] In *The Subjection of Women*, Mill himself criticised the education available to women in England by likening it to the training given to an odalisque and the Englishwoman's acceptance of her condition to the resignation of the woman trapped in a harem.[11]

One of the most obvious attacks on *couverture* in England was the demand for reform of the property laws. Prior to this movement, the husband had assumed legal possession, or control, of any property that his wife had before marriage or would come to her during marriage. Feminists and reformers first began to challenge this practice in the

1850s by publicising evidence of the hardships it caused as well as by collecting signatures to petition Parliament. As a result, the Married Women's Property Bill appeared before that body in 1857 and 1868. The Bill eventually became law in 1870, but feminists were unsatisfied with its terms, as it guaranteed considerable control to husbands. A Married Women's Property Committee continued the agitation, and through speeches, writings, meetings and petitions it succeeded in its goal to '"press the subject upon public attention"'. Finally in 1882, married women gained the right to own property in their own names and dispose of it as they wished.[12]

That this success took twenty-five years of agitation is remarkable considering that legal reform based on the principle of equity was common practice and had the support of the rising democratic ideologies.[13] Property reform for married women was treated as exceptional because it threatened to give wives a separate identity from their husbands. Its opponents warned of the dangers of allowing women a 'strong-minded and independent position':[14] as one speaker in Parliament stated, the bill would 'disturb the peace of every family, and destroy for ever that identity of interests at present existing between husband and wife'.[15] Women who worked for this cause demanded the right to make financial decisions for themselves and to act in their own best interests.

Those who attempted to deny them property ownership and these rights were, one petition contended, un-English and under the influence of 'Oriental' ideas.[16] Another feminist countered the argument that any further reforms for women would diminish their status by stating that a Turkish father asked to unlock the harem door and allow his daughters to go unveiled would have said the same, but that with 'every fresh instalment of liberty and independence granted to women by advancing civilisation, every step forward from her primitive condition of slavery to her present position of legal subjugation' she has received more kindness and respect.[17] Like imperialist rhetoric, these writings relied on theories concerning the progressive stages of civilisation and hierarchies of peoples and societies that assumed English culture and gender roles to be at the apex.[18] For these feminists, however, truly English gender relationships were not what they experienced in their own society, but rather an ideal they worked to achieve, an ideal that could seem English by contrasting it to the foreign – to the harem.

The movement for women's suffrage had much in common with the demand for property reform: both efforts occurred simultaneously and had many of the same supporters; furthermore, the difficulties encountered in securing the eventual passage of the Married Women's Property Bill served as proof to many of the necessity for female enfranchisement. Feminist writers had advocated women's formal participation in the political system throughout the nineteenth century, and an organised women's suffrage movement emerged in 1866. That was the year when activists in London and Manchester merged to create the organisation that would later be known as the National Union of Women's Suffrage Societies, an event that marked the beginning of sustained and continuous activity. Suffragists held rallies, demonstrations, spoke at public meetings, presented petitions, contacted politicians, published the *Women's Suffrage Journal* from 1870 to 1890, and ensured that the issue was kept before the eyes both of the public and of Parliament. As a result, a woman's suffrage bill was debated in the House of Commons every year except one during the 1870s.[19]

The gender tensions that this movement generated in English society can hardly be overstated. Frustration would eventually escalate into violence, with suffragettes burning buildings, smashing widows and enduring brutal, sometimes fatal, forced feeding in prison because of their hunger strikes.[20] These events had a tremendous impact on the rest of the country, contributing to the demise of the Liberal Party by exposing the hypocrisy of a political organisation which claimed to stand for democratic reform and individual freedom but yet failed to support their cause.[21]

Suffragists used the image of the female confined to the harem to help make their case. They associated the marginalisation of women in politics with Islam and relied on imperialist assumptions regarding the corruption and degradation of Muslim societies to illustrate the disastrous consequences that denying women the vote would have on the people of England.[22] In one article a suffragist claimed that the Egyptian woman who resided in the harem was deprived of all liberty and responsibility, and therefore the entire society suffered, especially the children, who were forced to dwell in filth, misery and disease.[23] The author of another article maintained that a woman should have certain rights, stating that if she is not allowed to freely 'exercise her organizing powers, she becomes a disorganizing influence' like the female slaves of the harem who have enslaved their masters and caused the downfall of some of the greatest 'Oriental' empires.[24] Another suffragist argued that the influence women may exert in political life in no way compensated for their lack of the vote. To emphasise her point, she stated that the harems in Istanbul and Cairo had been influential, yet governments in those cities were corrupt and on the verge of ruin. Using words that evoke the ideal of the transparent civil society in contrast to the closed harem, she concluded that the solution was to allow women to participate in the political system on an 'open field' by giving them the vote.[25]

Ironically, suffragists who used this type of gendered imperialist language did so even when it celebrated the masculine at the expense of the feminine. In one article, a suffragist argued that England would remain a 'masculine nation' only if women were allowed more freedom and power in public life. She went on to warn of the dangers of subjugating women, stating that in Turkey 'men are effeminate because women are practically enslaved'. Neither the individual English man nor the country as a whole could retain the manliness considered necessary to justify authority over national and international affairs unless a women's suffrage bill was passed.[26] Another article appealed on behalf of this cause by considering the advantages that it would have for men, stating that women's enfranchisement would give the English male a companion superior to the Muslim woman of Istanbul.[27] Such approaches, which defer to the masculine or consider the issue of women's suffrage from the male point of view, reflect both the widespread belief that within the parameters of the nation state manliness was the highest of all virtues and the difficulty that even those who worked on behalf of rights for women had challenging this assumption.

Not having the vote kept English women from participating in the political life of the country on an equal level with men, and the grating which separated the Ladies' Gallery from the rest of the House of Commons acted as a visual symbol of their exclusion and marginalisation from the apparatus of government. One critic of this structure complained that when women came to observe the proceedings and were forced to do so from behind the grating, they became like 'caged birds,' a phrase often used in travel narratives, missionary writings and other contemporary sources to refer to the women of the harem.[28] In order to help the reader make the connection, the author then states that this practice approaches 'Eastern barbarism'.[29] A similar article, entitled '"Purdah" in the House of Commons', argued that the grating 'degrades the womanhood of England to the low status of their sex in Oriental countries'.[30] Once again the secluded woman of the harem was used to define the gender inequalities in England as fundamentally un-English.

During this same period, when feminists were demanding a more prominent role in government and the political system, women sought admission to two of the most famous bastions of elite male privilege: the colleges of Oxford and Cambridge. They expected that degrees bestowed by those institutions would improve their status, bring them increased employment opportunities and help to legitimise the power and authority in society that contemporary feminist groups were working to obtain.[31] Female students proved their competence by taking the same examinations as the males: in 1887, much to the surprise of the English public, one of them sat the Cambridge classical tripos examination and she alone was placed in the first class, although at the time women were awarded 'certificates of degrees' rather than actual degrees by that university. Efforts to gain admission for women on an equal basis continued until alumni from all over England met in Cambridge in 1897 and voted against the proposal, by 1,713 to 662. The press covered the event and the festivities that followed, complete with bonfires and fireworks.[32] This movement and its formidable opposition brought the feminist idea of woman as a rational, intellectual being into public debate.

While opponents of higher education for women regarded intellectual endeavours as incompatible with the feminine, feminists challenged their position by maintaining that mental stimulation was necessary for proper female development and that depriving women of educational opportunities was an injustice associated with the harem. For example, one female travel writer stated that the Eastern woman who resided in the harem was denied education and mental improvement and, therefore, experienced a 'slavery of the mind'. Such a situation, she continued, was even worse than her physical confinement, for it deprived her of 'legitimate ambition' and 'mental culture', and 'reduced [her] to the condition of a child'.[33] Another feminist argued similarly that English women should be allowed to earn university degrees, and that the men who opposed this reform exhibited their animal nature by responding to 'the instinct of the harem'.[34] Journal articles, travel narratives and missionary tracts all repeatedly portrayed harem life as unstimulating, dull and discouraging to any type of mental activity. These writings constructed a particular ideal of femininity in opposition to the figure of the Muslim woman, an ideal which required both education and the ambition that education brings.

The belief that the education of women is incompatible with harem life in that the former would necessarily destroy the latter created an alliance between this feminist cause and the imperial anti-slavery agenda in Egypt and the surrounding areas, the supporters of which saw the institution of the harem as an obstacle to their goals. For example, one feminist writer explained that if Turkish women continued to be educated while still confined to the harem 'discontent will assuredly bring about a revolution'.[35] During a time when the educated English woman was depicted by many as an unfeminine misfit at best and a threat to the very survival of the nation and race at worst, statements such as this suggest that her existence should be seen instead as testifying to a society in an advanced state of development and with enlightened institutions.[36] In this context, female education in general appears as an almost patriotic movement that would aid the British imperial project by undermining the harem and helping to Anglicise or Westernise the Islamic world.

The physical abuse of women became another cause of concern for English feminists. As in the movements described above, references to the East, Islam and the harem were used to define the behaviour that they sought to eliminate from their own society as un-English. Because Frances Power Cobbe and others called attention to this problem and worked for legal reform in the 1870s and afterwards, 'wife-beating', a practice formerly called 'physical chastisement' and accepted as a legitimate way for men to control those living in the household, was criminalised, culminating in the Summary Jurisdiction (Married Women) Act of 1895, which allowed wives who were the victims of violence to apply for a legal separation from their husbands.[37] Drawing on familiar ideas about an advancing civilisation and hierarchies of civilisations, Cobbe stated that the male authority within marriage which allowed abuse was inherited from a previous period of 'Western barbarism' as well as the 'lands of Eastern sensuality' where the woman is still the 'slave' of the man.[38]

The poem sub-titled *The British Turk* (see p. 1), published in the *Women's Suffrage Journal*, expresses the idea that this Eastern oppression exists in England:

> I took my paper up to read
> Of wrongs to Servia done,
> When Englishwoman's bitter need
> Made sympathy to groan
>
> How can our Christian voice appeal
> For foreign slaves alone?
> Our gentle sisters, true as steel,
> Fall bruised at Justice's Throne!
>
> Are there no Turks but Mussulmen?
> Have we no monsters here?
> Beneath the eye of Christendom
> Shall not oppression fear!
>
> The cross of wifedom grows amain,
> Dropping with tears and blood!
> Our sad-eyed women scarce complain,
> But die beneath the load.
>
> Let men with men engage in strife,
> Or nations warfare wage;
> But woman, nurse of infant life,
> Spare her from Turkish rage![39]

The second line of the poem, 'Of wrongs to Servia done', connects the international politics of the Ottoman Empire with gender issues. For Ottoman raids in Russia and Eastern Europe had long been associated with the procurement of white female slaves destined for the harem, as the mention of 'foreign slaves' reminds the reader. The poem focuses on the oppression of English women in a general sense, but more specifically on the burdens associated with marriage, or 'the cross of wifedom'. The reference to 'tears and blood' and the statement that 'gentle sisters' fall 'bruised at Justice's Throne' allude to the much debated and publicised issue of 'wife-beating' and the British justice system's inability or unwillingness to stop it. A certain amount of classism informed the presentation of the poem, for its title is *A Cry From The Depths*, and comes from the journal's correspondent in London's east end, associating domestic tyranny with working-class life.[40]

This poem, like a number of contemporary articles, employed imperialist ideology but came very close to challenging it by exposing the reality that conditions for women in England could be as bad as or worse than those abroad.[41] Still, the overall message is that the oppression of women is associated with Muslim practices and gender roles, not those of the English, regardless of where it occurs or who is responsible. While the victim may be the 'Englishwoman', her abuser, in part because of his actions, is not quite English. He is 'British' with 'Turkish' tendencies. Furthermore, he is one of the working poor during a period when, as chapter five discusses, the nation frequently was defined in terms of class. In their effort to criminalise such abuse, feminists treated domestic violence as a foreign and corrupting influence on the English nation.

The institution of marriage often was targeted with this same use of imperialist ideology, associating injustices in England with the harem and female slavery in the Islamic world. One author, who upheld the importance of women in public life, explained that the harem was 'the symbol of female servitude' and, as such, had much in common with marriage laws which perpetuated inequalities in English society.[42] An article explained that while much is said about the degradation and confinement of women of the East, in truth a 'Christian harem' exists in England: for institutions that 'keep grown women in a condition of pupilage' and are as restrictive as the harem thrive in the West.[43] Another advocated the abolition of marriage in favour of free love, stating that woman has been a 'bondslave' in the West as well as the East.[44] Once again, while these types of discourse would seem to challenge imperial ideology by calling into question the superiority of English culture and gender roles, they were intended not so much to inspire international, or cross-cultural, identification as to motivate English people to work for reform at home. The reader was supposed to be shocked and ashamed that the barbaric practices understood to be Islamic existed in her or his own society.

While the image of the harem was used to address the specific feminist issues discussed above, more often it was employed to make general statements about the role of women in public life. For at the heart of the feminist agenda in Victorian England was the effort to create a place for women in politics and the public sphere that would be accepted and considered beneficial to society. It is in this context that hundreds of references to the harem as a prison or a gilded cage appeared. No amount of status or luxury could compensate for confinement to domestic life. As the English governess to an Egyptian princess explained, her pupil had an education, slaves to command and comfortable quarters, but she had nothing to look forward to except 'dreary monotony', and her first day of being 'shut up' in the harem marked her last day of liberty.[45] Others describe women of all ranks resident in the harem as living in a state of 'social slavery'.[46] One calls the harem a prison where the woman has no rights, no liberties, remains dependent on a man and as a result is reduced to 'a mere animal'.[47]

Writings such as these treat the confinement of women to the domestic sphere as an oppressive Eastern practice with no legitimate place in England. In contrast, the reader is supposed to imagine a society in which both sexes do not 'deteriorate' from lack of stimulation but rather interact with each other freely and progress as a result: for, 'like flint and steel, the brilliant spark only comes forth when the necessary amount of friction has been applied'.[48]

Through a number of related movements, feminists of the late nineteenth century promoted a certain ideal of English femininity that was characterised by independence of male authority and equality of opportunity to participate in the political, economic and intellectual life of the country. They considered those who opposed their efforts to be backwards and barbaric. To help make this point they evoked imperial images of the harem and the Muslim woman to describe gender inequalities in English society. If injustices on the basis of gender that existed in England had more in common with the practices and beliefs of those at the peripheries of empire than they did with true Englishness, as feminists argued, then by this logic they were not making radical demands. Rather they were pursuing an agenda not unlike that of British officials and BFASS supporters: they were trying to improve society by Anglicising it and eliminating practices associated with Islam and the East.[49] Feminists drew from the words of anti-slavery workers and the power of that campaign, yet rejected the belief that the Egyptian slave would be liberated by accepting English as opposed to Muslim forms of male authority.

Conservative reactions

It is in this context of contemporary feminist movements that efforts to suppress slavery in Egypt and surrounding areas are to be understood. While feminists and reformers were demanding that English women be liberated from a patriarchal system that denied them certain rights and freedoms, using the image of the Muslim woman to make their case, this particular anti-slavery campaign promoted conservative understandings of traditional English gender roles as the ideal. The activities of an overwhelming majority of the movement's supporters, from government officials to members of the BFASS, reinforced the assumption that patriarchal English gender relationships elevated the women of that country and would do the same for those of Egypt. Regardless of the inherent limitations of these roles, they were portrayed as the remedy to what was understood as truly oppressive: the Muslim man and Islamic law. Gender inequalities in England could be dismissed as insignificant compared to the plight of the female slave of the Muslim harem. Because this perspective was based on beliefs about English superiority and the association of national identity with certain gender roles, a policy that was radical in terms of its approach to Egyptian society acted as a conservative, even reactionary, force in England itself.

Discourses which drew on the imperialistic ideology associated with anti-slavery efforts in Egypt and the surrounding areas in order to present monogamous marriage and a conservative version of English, or Christian English, gender roles as desirable were used and appropriated by a variety of people. Advocates of this position included public figures such as Sir Evelyn Baring, missionaries, religious leaders, and supporters of the BFASS, as well as travel writers, journalists and others who appealed to a general audience.[50] These historical actors were not so much a unified group cooperating to promote a defined political agenda as much as they were individuals who accepted and defended a dominant belief system that was being challenged.

The belief that according to Christian teachings the woman's proper place is as a helpmate to her husband would seem elevating when contrasted to the idea that the Egyptian woman could never be more than a 'slave' or a 'toy' to her husband.[51] Mary Whateley, who ran a children's school and was known by Mrs Crewe and others involved with the BFASS and the Cairo Home, expressed the hope that her school and others like it would transform the girls of Egypt, so that one day they would be able to rise to their divinely ordained station as helpmates of man as opposed to sinking 'into the barbarism of their mothers'.[52] Similarly, one of the teachers at her school expressed fear that without it the girls would be sent to 'their ignorant homes or rather closed harems'.[53]

At a time when marriage itself was under attack in England, certain representations of the polygynous harem served to promote a version of Christian–English monogamy. Travel writers, missionaries and scholars often would describe the harem as dark with intrigue, jealousy and hatred, assuming that the wives were bitter rivals who longed for a monogamous relationship with the husband. One female travel writer referred to a Muslim woman who stated that she was made '"nearly mad by troubles"' and who expressed envy for women who did not have to share their husbands. The writer concluded from this statement that a new young wife had become the favoured female of the harem or else that a divorce was impending.[54] According to this author polygyny was the outcome when women failed to reach a certain ideal of femininity: wives who were 'ugly or bad-tempered' and did not take care of the household properly made men polygynous.[55] Such writings not only reinforced ideas about the superiority of the monogamous marriage, but served as a subtle warning to English women who questioned or deviated from the prescribed role of angel in the house celebrated by the Victorians.

Whatever the limitations of this role and of Victorian bourgeois domesticity, they would have seemed less important after reading works which presented the English home as the preferred alternative to the supposed sorrows of the polygynous secluded harem. One clergyman wrote of the harem destroying family ties, especially between mother and child, and stated that Muslims lacked the 'purity, affection, self denials, and mutual helpings for love's sake implied in the sacred individuality of the English home!'[56] Similarly, another writer stated that polygyny and its accompanying laws of succession created a situation in which men could feel little or no love for their children:[57] the perceived absence of parental bonding seemed to preclude any sort of a family life. One Englishwoman claimed that Persian Muslims have no word for home because they lack the 'associations or tender memories which that word awakens in us'.[58]

Such writings communicated to English people, particularly women, the idea that they did not realise how lucky they were to have the gender roles and family relationships that they did. Rather than taking them for granted or agitating for reform, they should be thankful: after all, according to them, the Muslim woman longs for the kind of life that the English woman has. For example, the well-known traveller Lady Duff Gordon wrote that on a visit to a harem, she was told: '"If I had a husband and children like thee, I would die a hundred times rather than leave them for an hour."'[59] Similarly, BFASS members depicted the very traditional and somewhat restrictive status of 'lady' as the most liberating and empowering role to which a woman could aspire when they translated the words of pride voiced by newly freed slave women as '"I'm not a slave; I'm a Lady."'[60]

Missionaries and other Christian writers who were as concerned about retaining the faithful at home in the face of declining numbers as they were about saving souls abroad repeatedly stressed that the status of women is low in Islam as compared to Christianity. Books published by the Society for Promoting Christian Knowledge and the Church Missionary Society, or articles that appeared in *Looking East: The Journal of the Church of England Zenana Missionary Society*, also titled *India's Woman*, would give descriptions of women enslaved in harems, portraying Muslim women as being so accustomed to poor treatment that they were shocked to learn that Christ and his followers cared for them. In the book *Missionary Heroines*, the author stated that the recent activities of Miss Whateley in Cairo were no doubt the first efforts made on behalf of Muslim females since 'the rise of the False Prophet'.[61] A similar book maintains that Islam actually instructs its followers to 'oppress the widow', and depicts Muslim women confiding to English missionaries that their religion brings only misery, unlike Christianity which brings joy.[62] Articles with shocking titles, such as 'Women for Goats', or those that described the brutalities experienced by female slaves served to illustrate the debased status of women where slavery existed.[63]

In the light of these sensationalised narratives, issues such as the vote or property reform would have seemed almost trivial complaints against a Government engaged in combating what was portrayed as the real threat to the status and dignity of women: Islamic laws and customs. If English or English–Christian gender roles liberated women and protected them from exploitation and oppression, then wouldn't it be dangerous to challenge them? Didn't feminists and others who criticised them threaten to dismantle women's only protection against brutality and barbarism? These questions and concerns were never far from discussions of the harem, slavery and women in the Islamic world.

One of the harshest critics of Islam and the harem was a former Muslim woman, Melek Hanum, who had spent much of her life in a harem. Hanum escaped with her daughter from her husband and the authorities, established residence in Europe and converted to Christianity. She published two books about her life for an English readership entitled *Thirty Years in the Harem* and *Six Years in Europe*[64] in which she detailed her escape to the West as well as her criticisms of every aspect of harem life, from veiling and seclusion to polygamy, and the entire Islamic social and legal system.

Melek Hanum was the exception rather than the rule. Her narrative is interesting not so much because it is representative of the experiences of women in the Islamic world, but rather because it testifies to the possibility of manipulating the fictive border between East and West that existed within the imperial cultural system. The secluded, veiled woman of the harem recreated herself to become the anti-Muslim Christian who entered the English public sphere by adopting and contributing to a type of dominant discourse. One person lived two roles often understood in opposition to each other. Yet her books do not reflect any attempt to reconcile the two: she reproduces the same dichotomy between Islam and the West seen elsewhere, and in fact her tone resembles that of Christian missionaries and writers.

This dichotomy between the Eastern–Islamic, on the one hand, and the Western or, more specifically, English, on the other, often was symbolised by the veil, which served as a signifier of difference. British reformers hoped that as Egypt became more Anglicised–Westernised, this practice gradually would fall out of favour. Lord Cromer believed that seclusion and the veiling that accompanied it had a 'baneful' effect on Egyptian society,[65] and a British girls' school in Cairo required all of its pupils to dress in frocks and pinafores with hair 'in Western fashion'.[66] The association of Englishness with an unveiled face is described perhaps most dramatically in a scene of Alexander Kinglake's *Eōthen*, where Lady Hester Stanhope withdraws her *yashmak* before a group of hundreds of armed Bedouin horsemen, transforming their threatening cries into 'shouts of joy and admiration at the bravery of the stately Englishwoman'.[67] On a lighter note, a contemporary musical comedy about reforming Moroccan society by establishing English music-halls contained numerous references to veiling. At one point the *vizier* forces his harem to unveil by threatening them with divorce, because 'To-night we're English.'[68]

While some discussions of the Islamic world communicated a conservative message by focusing on differences such as the veil, others did the same by reinforcing beliefs about women in general, particularly the idea that they are naturally weak and helpless, and are therefore in need of male, preferably English male, protection. These assumptions appeared frequently in coverage of British efforts to rescue the female slave otherwise condemned to a life of misery. They are portrayed visually in the *Slave Market in Constantinople* by Sir William Allan (see figure 1), kept among the BFASS slides and no doubt shown at the Society's many public meetings and lectures. It depicts two women who are the epitome of helpless Victorian femininity: one swoons while the other assumes the position of suppliant. This type of image was shown to suggest the need for British or, more specifically, English chivalry, for the men in the picture appear to be unmoved by the plight of the slave women, and one contemporary writer declared that Muslim

THE HAREM, SLAVERY AND BRITISH IMPERIAL CULTURE

1 *Slave Market in Constantinople*, Sir William Allan.

men had none of the chivalry which made life 'pure and honourable'.[69] This representation complemented the discourse of BFASS meetings in which chivalry was discussed as a motive for anti-slavery activity. During a time when arguments about women's inherent weakness and need for protection were being used to justify denying them a voice in the public sphere, this emphasis on female vulnerability had domestic as well as foreign political implications.

Imperialist assumptions regarding Muslim gender relationships were used to bolster the claim that women did not belong in positions of power or authority, particularly where affairs of the State were involved. For example, one writer referred to the female slaves of the imperial harem as the elite of the Ottoman Empire, which was ruled by, using an oft-quoted phrase, a '"monstrous regiment of women"'. Corruption flourished as a result, and civil offices were awarded to humour a new wife.[70] Similarly, the mother of the sultan often was portrayed as an especially dangerous figure who had illegitimate influence. One author describes her as a libertine hungry for power, inviting the reader to imagine what would be the consequences of her actions for the administration of the country.[71]

The harem, 'the cradle in which Eastern manhood is reared', often was depicted as the root of the Ottoman Empire's problems.[72] A writer

[128]

for *The Times* stated that the sultan was unable to work because of his 'effeminate bringing up', and that the harem had thoroughly coddled him and left him unfit for rule, a mere 'pampered and cloyed voluptuary' who lived in 'a fools paradise' of obsequious eunuchs and slaves.[73] The male, once he had been emasculated by the harem, could not exercise power legitimately or govern effectively. An English commentator feared that if the imperial harem's eunuch guards acted as advisors to the sultan, then the great questions determining the future of Europe would be decided 'by the caprice of one of these women'.[74]

This type of commentary presented Islamic countries as feeble and in need of strong British rule, while lending credence to the belief that the feminine was destructive of the body politic.[75] It warned an English readership that even in patriarchal societies, illegitimate female influence still posed a constant threat, for the feminine out of place could jeopardise the welfare of the nation. According to this perspective, the success of the nation state depended on maintaining proper gender roles defined in narrow terms. Such ideas buttressed the arguments of the increasingly vocal anti-suffragists who claimed that giving women the vote would debilitate the British Government, rendering it incapable of participating in the competitive arena of international politics or ruling its Empire.[76]

Perhaps the most obvious example of the compatibility that existed between promoting a conservative version of proper gender roles in England and the campaign in Egypt can be seen in the person and actions of Sir Evelyn Baring, later Lord Cromer. Baring worked to suppress female slavery in Egypt and expressed the desirability of eliminating seclusion and the veil. While his beliefs and goals would seem to have much in common with liberal feminism, he was not a feminist. A form of English patriarchy, not individual freedom or independence for women, was his goal and he advocated this ideal both at home and abroad. He even became president of the Men's League for Opposing Women's Suffrage and was so active in this movement that it was sometimes called the '"Curzon–Cromer combine"' after its two most dynamic leaders, Earl Curzon and Lord Cromer.[77]

Like Cromer, most of the anti-slavery workers had connections with England. Many either lived there or looked forward to returning from abroad. The decisions that they made regarding female slaves in Egypt had as much to do with their own identities and concerns in a society fraught with gender tensions and conflict as it did with foreign policy. For example, both British officials and BFASS workers made extra efforts to prevent giving a large number of female slaves complete independence, and as a result sometimes even risked sending them back into slavery. This approach was not their only option; it was their choice. They rejected liberal feminist perspectives, and the ideas regarding proper gender roles that they promoted through their words and actions meant that they entered the ongoing debates in English society on the conservative side. Anti-slavery ideology, however, was flexible enough to appeal to a number of people with different points of view: feminists such as Sarah Amos were drawn to the movement as well, and women who participated in it helped to counter its more conservative elements by claiming a place for themselves in the public sphere through their activities.

'White slavery' and the anti-vice movement

The relationship between foreign policy and domestic gender debates is especially manifest when considering the widespread concern with prostitution, or 'white slavery'. English women and men first began to involve themselves with this issue publicly in 1869 with the movement to repeal the Contagious Diseases Acts (henceforth CD Acts). The Acts allowed police officers to arrest any woman even suspected of being a prostitute; the woman then would be forced to undergo a physical examination, the result of which could be her detention for up to three months in a lock hospital. The Acts generated opposition in part because of the power they gave police over women and in working-class neighbourhoods and in part because they seemed to sanction vice. Two national associations were established: the National Association for the Repeal of the Contagious Diseases Acts, dominated by working-class men, and a *ladies'* organisation, with the same name, in which middle-class women played the more prominent roles. The two supported hundreds of branch associations throughout the country with thousands of members and sympathisers. Repealers pressured MPs, publicising the issue through large public meetings and demonstrations as well as the written word. As a result of these activities, the CD Acts were repealed in 1886.[78]

The initial efforts to repeal the CD Acts mark the beginning of public activism on the issue of prostitution, which reached its peak in 1885 in response to W. T. Stead's sensationalist and wildly popular exposé 'The Maiden Tribute of Modern Babylon', published as a four-part series in the *Pall Mall Gazette*.[79] These articles described how 'daughters of the people' regularly were captured and sold as prostitutes to aristocratic rakes for £5 each. His stories, which resembled the melodrama and the gothic fairytale, distorting and misrepresenting London's underworld, succeeded in rallying widespread support for the movement to eliminate prostitution and vice. As a result of public outcry and indignation, the Criminal Law Amendment Act of 1885 raised the age of consent for girls and gave the police greater power to combat prostitution and brothel-keeping. Grass-roots purity groups and vigilance committees were organised throughout Britain to ensure that these new laws were enforced.[80]

Organisations such as the National Vigilance Association (NVA) sought to eradicate prostitution and vice in England and prevent English girls from being lured into brothels abroad. Not surprisingly, anti-vice activists understood the trade to be linked to the East, which included Ottoman territories such as Egypt. Articles entitled 'The White Slave Trade' appeared in the *Vigilance Record* and focused on how young women from Europe were promised jobs as servants or governesses in cities such as Istanbul, Port Said and Alexandria, but once there found themselves 'prisoners in houses of ill-fame'.[81] In these articles the East poses a constant danger to and a corrupting influence on the West; females were not safe even in England. One writer relates that a woman was almost kidnapped in Wellington Square by dealers in 'white slaves' who planned to take her to Bombay or Calcutta.[82] In 1889 The NVA of England communicated with the Anti-Slavery Conference in Brussels, urging the plenipotentiaries not to focus on African slavery at the expense of the traffic of girls in Turkey, as such corruption 'can not be permitted to remain in any corner of Europe'.[83]

The anti-vice movement set a precedent in that women as well as men took a public stand on issues regarding sexuality and sought to remove laws oppressive to them. They even experienced considerable success. However, the eventual result was, in certain respects, more restrictive than had been the previous situation: the activities of working-class women could still be monitored and regulated according to the new legislation. Also the entire campaign reinforced very conservative and patriarchal ideas regarding English gender roles. For example, crowds of approximately 250,000 people demonstrated in Hyde Park to demand enforcement of the new laws carrying banners with phrases such as 'Protection of Young Girls' and 'Innocents Will They Be Slaughtered?' Such statements, as well as images created by Stead and others of prostitutes as 'simple', 'weak' and like 'frightened lambs', encouraged a protective or custodial attitude towards these women, fostering dependence and hierarchical relationships, as opposed to the feminist ideal of individual liberty.[84] Anti-vice activists promoted a reformed English patriarchy, but a patriarchy nonetheless.

It might seem that efforts to eliminate prostitution and vice indigenous to English society would have nothing to do with British foreign policy; in fact, however, certain of the words, phrases and beliefs which served to generate support for the campaign in Egypt were also at the heart of anti-vice activism. Like the feminists discussed earlier in the chapter, these reformers promised to Anglicise England and rid it of an element that was essentially foreign, Islamic, or Eastern. When the issue first emerged as a matter of public concern, they called it 'white slavery', the very same phrase used to describe the trafficking in Circassian women in Egypt and surrounding areas that British officials and BFASS members were working to suppress. Similarly, prostitutes were, in their words, not simply solicited on the streets, but rather 'sold' at 'the London slave market'; sometimes prostitutes were even referred to as 'white odalisques'.[85]

Readers of the 'Maiden Tribute' would not have had difficulty in making the connection between foreign policy and domestic agitation, as the *Pall Mall Gazette* regularly ran stories about the slave trade in Egypt during the period when it published Stead's four-part exposé. In fact, in one issue the articles 'French Views of Modern Babylon' and 'How to Check the Slave Trade in Egypt' shared the same column.[86] Stead encouraged this association with the East when he explained that 'the head of a great London emporium regards the women in his employ in much the same aspect as the Sultan of Turkey regards the inmates of his seraglio'.[87]

Opponents of this movement adopted the same terms and allusions to the East: for example, Stead's critics called him and his supporters 'howling dervishes'.[88] There is no apparent connection between English anti-vice activists and Muslim mystics, and the only logical explanation for the use of this phrase is that it plays on the Eastern imagery and associations with the Islamic world which had already become so much a part of the way that this issue was represented and understood in England.

Those who tried to rescue and reform the English prostitute associated her with the female slave of the Muslim harem. They communicated this idea when appealing for assistance on her behalf: notices for the London Female Preventive and Reformatory Institution appeared frequently in the *ASR*, and its section requesting donations, entitled 'Friendless and Fallen: Young Women and Girls', often was printed on the page opposite a report on the Cairo Home for Freed Women Slaves. Similarly, the well-known suffragist Millicent Garrett Fawcett assumed an affinity between slavery and polygamy, on the one hand, and English prostitution, on the other, when she referred to the former as contrary to the spirit of equality in her article condemning practices of the underworld exposed by Stead.[89] For Sarah and Sheldon Amos combating 'white slavery' and helping exploited females at home and abroad belonged to the same overall mission. The couple contributed to the establishment of the Cairo Home and campaigned to repeal the CD Acts. Sarah assisted Sheldon with what many regarded as the authoritative argument for the cause, *A Comparative Survey of Laws in Force for the Prohibition, Regulation, and Licensing of Vice in England and Other Countries.*[90]

There is no apparent rationale for treating English prostitution as something foreign or Islamic. Such a strategy begins to make sense only in the light of the many contemporary discourses which depicted the East, or the Islamic world, as a place of licentiousness and moral depravity. In this respect the BFASS and the NVA seemed to work in concert. While anti-vice activists represented 'white slavery' as a foreign influence, BFASS members portrayed Egypt and surrounding areas as hotbeds of vice. They referred to white female slaves as 'fancy girls' who contributed to the corruption and decay of the ruling classes in the Ottoman Empire.[91] One BFASS supporter claimed that the slave trade in that part of the world was sustained simply to feed 'the passion of lust', which is even stronger than desire for gold.[92]

In addition to BFASS members, other English writers contributed to the belief that Islam encourages vice. For example, one clergyman concluded that because beautiful *houris* await the faithful in heaven 'indulgence of the senses is the chief good' in Islam.[93] Similarly, while discussing the treatment of women, the scholar and popular author Lane-Poole referred to the 'cruel indulgence' which, he stated, 'left its mark on the Muslim character'.[94] One scholar claimed that Muhammad had more than one wife because of his weakness for beautiful women. He dismissed the argument that those women would have been condemned to poverty had Muhammad rejected them by posing the question: why then did he not establish almshouses? His words provide an example of the way in which English institutions, despite their well-publicised shortcomings, were presented as the obvious solution to social ills both at home and abroad.[95]

The association of English prostitution and vice with harem-oriented slavery in Egypt and the surrounding areas served several ideological functions. It helped social purity activists win support for their cause by labelling practices in their own country that they hoped to eradicate as essentially un-English. It made a movement that in many ways promised radical changes in the relationship between the State and the individual appear an almost conservative patriotic response to an illegitimate foreign influence. In addition, these writings simultaneously reinforced the belief that the Eastern or Islamic world was degenerate and barbaric, and that the British presence and influence in Egypt and surrounding areas, particularly with regard to the suppression of the trade in slaves, therefore would have to be noble and worthy of support. Finally, the mere fact that English people were engaged in ridding their society of 'white slavery', while others supposedly let it thrive and corrupt their institutions and ruling classes, would seem to prove English superiority and the legitimacy of the British Empire.[96] The notion of 'white slavery', then, was redefined through these related movements' linking of foreign affairs and domestic politics.

One issue that must be addressed regarding the term 'white slavery' is its implications concerning race. While this phrase was used by Egyptians as well as throughout the Middle East, it had certain connotations in English society, particularly when describing practices there such as prostitution; the word *white* in the phrase 'white slavery' referred to a way of understanding English national identity as well as a physical characteristic. For many, to be English was to be racially white. If the English understood themselves not only as white but as lovers of freedom and defenders of liberty against tyranny and slavery, as maintained throughout the book, then the idea of a white, English slave living in England would have been shocking. The use of 'white slavery' served to mobilise support for anti-vice legislation while reinforcing certain racialist notions of English national identity: in this context to be English meant to be white, free and to have no tolerance for slavery.

If the image of the white slave fused ideas about race and nation conflating Englishness with whiteness and freedom, then the practice of slave-holding served as a marker of racial difference defining the English in contrast to Muslims. Physical traits are only one, and often not the most important, signifier of race: as I have said, language, religion and cultural practices were treated as indicators that helped to define racial categories. The rhetoric of 'white slavery' and the concepts associated with the term communicated the idea that their abhorrence of slavery distinguished English people in a fundamental, even a racial, way from the Muslims who allowed it.

While the idea that English society was racially homogeneous was problematical, given its divisions, conflicts and multiple influences, it could have seemed to be so after reading articles that described and, in the process of describing, emphasised and dramatised the different physical characteristics of female slaves destined for the harem. For example, one observer in a Moroccan slave market remarked that all the slaves were 'females of varied degrees of colour. One alone is white.'[97] Another wrote of an Egyptian slave market:

> In colour they varied from the very blackest Negro shade to those who were sufficiently fair to compare favourably with the finest complexioned lady in London. I was astonished to see such white skins where their eyes were so very black, as was also the hair.[98]

Here hair, eye and skin colour become signifiers of difference. Masters of slaves could be just as diverse, and the offspring of masters and their slaves would, with each new generation, challenge and undermine existing racial categories based on physical traits as quickly as the categories were recreated and redefined.[99]

These writings are to be considered in the light of contemporary ideas about 'race science', for while in the late eighteenth and early nineteenth century the English public generally accepted the idea of monogenesis – that all human beings had the same origin and that physical differences were simply the result of climate or environment – the mid-to-late nineteenth century saw a 'hardening of attitudes', with universality giving way to imperial hierarchies.[100] Miscegenation was thought to cause degeneration, harming the individual and society as a whole. Discussions of slave-trading reproduced the idea of a white race while presenting a society in which procreative practices jeopardised it. Descriptions of diversity in relation to female, or harem-oriented, slavery combined with the new race science helped to create, in contrast, a model of Englishness characterised by patriarchal family and gender relationships that discouraged unions between people with different backgrounds and beliefs, and as a result maintained a homogeneous, and therefore according to this logic, superior country capable of imperial rule.[101]

It is not so much that this ideal accurately described English society as that it oriented men and women – working-class men and middle-class women in the case of the movement to eliminate 'white slavery' – around a certain conception of national identity that gave meaning to their particular political positions and defined behaviour normatively. For anti-vice activists, 'the English nation' described a place where men protected white women from exploitation and prostitution, which they associated with corrupting foreign influences and Eastern, Islamic practices. Such an approach excluded from the nation a number of people living in England, an issue that will be explored in chapter five.

The harem and genteel femininity

Thus far this chapter has focused on the ways in which ideas about the harem and slavery entered English gender debates and helped to create versions of English national identity in opposition to Islam understood in negative terms. However, some English people identified with the Muslim woman and used positive representations of her in order to present alternative beliefs about femininity generally and English womanhood specifically. While the harem may have symbolised oppression to a number of abolitionists, defenders of English patriarchy, liberal feminists and anti-vice activists, it represented a place of power, prestige and opportunity for cultural feminists who focused on women's unique qualities and placed great value on the preservation of separate feminine spaces.¹⁰² These writers saw the harem as a pre-Enlightenment institution, but only in the sense that is was aristocratic, or refined, not backward or uncivilised. Celebrating genteel femininity could reinforce certain classist assumptions: for example, one English traveller notes that the ladies of the harem had better lives than the Turkish peasant woman who had to work 'like an ox', and that they were less likely to be victims of abusive husbands than were females of the English 'lower classes'.¹⁰³ Similarly, a writer for the magazine *Woman's World* explained that while the Turkish wife addressed her husband as *effendi*, or 'sir', she was not abasing herself but was simply showing respect for him just as 'people of quality in England' used to do 'some generations ago'.¹⁰⁴ The reader is supposed to identify with a class-based version of Englishness.

In these writings much is made of the respect and deference shown to the lady of the harem. She is described as mistress of her domain whose word is obeyed without question. She buys her own slaves over whom she has complete control. Her adult sons are not allowed to sit in her presence without permission, and even her husband is barred from the harem when she places a pair of shoes at the door.¹⁰⁵ One Turkish lady referred to her husband as 'my henpecked one'.¹⁰⁶

Contrary to BFASS rhetoric, the relationship between the lady of the harem and her slaves was depicted as beneficial to all and as similar to that between the English lady and her domestic servants. One English governess remarked that she had seen fewer cases of ill-treatment of 'servants' (actually slaves) in her ten years of residence with Turkish families than she had in the same amount of time spent with English families: not only did the slaves live as comfortably as European servants, but after a certain amount of time their mistress found husbands for them and even bought them wedding dresses.¹⁰⁷ In the female networks of the harem, loyalty and respect were reciprocated with patronage and gifts. This report is not unusual, and more often than not in these writings, female slaves residing in the harem are likened to English domestic servants rather than to plantation slaves.¹⁰⁸

The harem frequently was described as a place of opportunity and upward mobility for women of all backgrounds. As one writer explains, in the imperial seraglio, slaves, 'no matter how low their origin', developed skills and social graces such as 'the elegance of deportment, the graceful formalities of Turkish etiquette . . . dancing, singing, and playing on the lute or viol'.¹⁰⁹ It was possible for a female slave to become a sultana. In addition, brilliant Turkish 'poetesses' had been recognised by Eastern and Western men of letters since the seventeenth century.¹¹⁰ The fact that the polygynous harem provided more opportunities for marriage and motherhood than the English system did not go unnoticed, and more than one contemporary commented on the relative absence of 'old maids' in the Islamic world. As trivial or lighthearted as such a remark might seem, it had to have had resonance in a society where the question of what to do with the high number of unmarried or 'redundant' middle-class women was seen as such a serious social and even moral problem that agencies were established in the late nineteenth century to help them emigrate from England to the colonies where they could gain respectable occupation.[111] A later article in the *Islamic Review* presented the argument that Islam, not emigration, was the solution, because in Islam 'every woman is entitled to a husband and to have children' and through 'polygamy alone can the English race be replenished; in no other way can England's otherwise certain decay be arrested'.[112]

The harem was praised as a private feminine space in the most positive sense. Any man other than the husband who attempts to violate it 'would run the risk of being torn to pieces by an enraged populace', and when a woman entertains visitors from another harem, even the husband does not dare enter.[113] One writer describes the seclusion of the harem as a manifestation of a lady's modesty that shields her 'womanly purity' from the outside world.[114] It could be seen also as a place of feminine solidarity where wives lived 'in perfect amity... like affectionate sisters'.[115] One English traveller remarked that in a harem she had visited the women showed care and concern for each other's children, and she even contrasted their kindness and understanding with the rivalries and bickering she had known among sisters in Christian families.[116] In such writings the harem, and even the polygamy associated with it, are empowering, encouraging of sisterly bonding and protective of female privacy, just as the home was supposed to be in Victorian English society.

Writers also celebrated the feminine sphere of the harem by focusing on its splendours and beauty. They would dwell on such delights as the rich, luxurious fabrics of the women's clothing, the sumptuous decor, the intricate latticework and the dishes of gold inlaid with precious stones and filled with compotes and sweetmeats. The slaves looked magnificent when dressed in silks, velvet and glittering jewels, and the thin muslin veils were 'piquancy to the beauty of a pretty woman'.[117] The most important feature, however, was the hospitality shown by the hostess, whose 'natural good breeding and untaught courtesy' were considered the mark of all civilised peoples.[118] The genteel and charmed life led by these ladies of leisure called to mind the great matriarchs of London and Parisian society. One traveller emphasised this similarity by using the term *grande dame* to describe the Turkish woman who orchestrated the ceremonies of entertainment with calmness and

THE HAREM, SLAVERY AND BRITISH IMPERIAL CULTURE

2   *The Harem*, John Frederick Lewis.

grace.[119] These descriptions of the dazzling but elegant harem reminded readers of scenes from well-known Orientalist literature such as William Beckford's *Vathek* (1786), Thomas Moore's *Lalla Rookh: An Oriental Romance* (1817), and Edward Lane's and later Sir Richard Burton's translation of *The Book of the Thousand Nights and a Night* (1840 and 1885–88, respectively), the latter work sometimes being mentioned by name.

These descriptions of harem life, whether in imaginative literature or in travel narratives, complemented contemporary Orientalist paintings such as John Frederick Lewis's *The Hhareem* (1850; also known as *The Harem*) and *In the Bey's Garden, Asia Minor* (1865). Lewis experienced remarkable critical and popular acclaim in his lifetime,[120] and *The Harem* (figure 2) was one of his most appreciated works.[121] In this painting, as well as in others, he effectively communicated the idea that the abode of the Muslim woman could be lovely and inspiring. As John Ruskin commented, Lewis knew how to present accurately the Eastern 'races' as people who possessed the 'refinements of civilization' if not its 'laws and energies'.[122] An especially interesting painting in terms of gender politics is Lewis's *The Reception* (1873), in which he depicts an Egyptian lady meeting visitors in the male area of the household. This painting presents the idea that women in Egypt had more power and freedom than the architecture of the house acknowledged and English people realised, and it therefore challenged Victorian assumptions about Egyptian society, subtlety criticising imperialist efforts to reform domestic life in that country.[123] The work also makes a general statement about the woman who remains in the private sphere: she occupies a prominent position and is able even to manipulate gender, crossing boundaries and entering 'male' spaces.

Paintings, imaginative literature and travel narratives that portrayed the harem in a positive light can be understood as supporting the separate spheres' ideology popular among the Victorians: they show women to be empowered or fulfilled not by concerning themselves with public affairs or matters of state but by remaining in the private sphere and engaging in domestic pursuits. Because these images present a certain version of femininity transcending the created boundaries of nation, culture and religion, they communicate the idea that it is innate or natural.[124] It could even be argued that these representations reinforced patriarchal beliefs because a male presence is often stated or implied: for example, the painting *In the Bey's Garden* focuses on a woman, but the title reminds the viewer that this seemingly feminine space is in fact the property of a man.[125]

However, there is another, equally possible but less conservative, way to read these images. In them the male is of marginal significance; technically he may have authority, but the woman is the focus. She is the important one.[126] The viewer must put aside petty mundane concerns and political squabbles and enter her world where creating beauty and nurturing infant life are the very noblest of pursuits. Such an interpretation bolstered the contemporary feminist argument that the moral superiority of women and their ability to make the home a haven or spiritual refuge not only qualified them to play but demanded that they play a role in a public sphere in dire need of reform. To some degree these discourses and images represented a fantasy, an escape to a world where conflicts disappeared and the feminine reigned supreme. However, fantasy or not, any celebration of the feminine in a society which so often valued the masculine as superior had a certain subversive potential.

These depictions of the elegant harems of the East had as much to do with defining proper English gender roles and thus Englishness itself as did the words and actions of the individuals discussed earlier in the chapter. For the practical effect of such representations would not have been to inspire English women to convert to Islam and travel abroad in search of a pasha or bey, but rather to generate support for separate spheres' ideology in English society. Likening the mistress of the harem to an English lady of generations past served to define this role as part of an English tradition. In addition, given the increasing prosperity, the rise of the middle- and to a lesser extent the working-class, and the widespread admiration for the lady or for ladylike behaviour in late Victorian England, genteel femininity more likely would have been seen as an ideal, or a desirable goal, by women from a cross-section of society than as an elite privilege.

Conclusion

Chapters two and three examined how workers in the cause of anti-slavery eradicated this institution in Egypt and surrounding areas and through these efforts developed their own gendered national and imperial identities in relation to the harem. This chapter has elaborated on those two by showing that this process of identity formation was not limited to concerns in Egypt, but was transnational and could be found at the heart of nineteenth-century English gender politics. Feminists, conservatives, anti-vice activists and others considered the circumstances of the Muslim woman and believed that they had relevance with respect to their own situations and political agendas. The image of the harem helped them to understand and communicate competing versions of Englishness and proper English gender roles within that society, the very roles that were central to the conflicts, campaigns and movements surrounding the 'woman question' during the late Victorian period.

Liberal feminists were motivated by an ideal of English womanhood based on beliefs about individual liberty, justice and equality, which they created through organisation and agitation for reform. They worked to promote causes such as property rights, suffrage and access to higher education for women, and they had a considerable impact. One way of defining this ideal for themselves and generating support for it and their efforts was by contrasting it to the Muslim harem. If the existing obstacles and limitations imposed on women in England were in the spirit of that institution, then they could be treated as illegitimate foreign influences. This approach created an alliance between English feminism and the imperial project abroad: for, like British officials and BFASS supporters who tried to reform Egyptian society, feminists attempted to elevate the English by Anglicising the gender relationships in their own country, ridding it of influences depicted as Eastern or Islamic.

Similarly, anti-vice activists mobilised themselves around the belief that prostitution and vice had no legitimate place in English society. This conviction informed their activities, from their public demonstrations to the establishment of watchdog committees to ensure that new legislation was enforced. Its acceptance was central to the ultimate success of the movement. Yet the logic of this belief was not as obvious as it may seem in hindsight. These practices had existed in England for centuries, so that defining them as essentially un-English required some effort. By calling English prostitution 'white slavery' and associating it with the traffic of females in Egypt and surrounding areas, activists succeeded in convincing the public that slavery and vice in general had more in common with 'Eastern barbarism' than they did with the goals and ideals of the true English nation.

It is in the context of these controversial feminist movements that the conservative views of anti-slavery workers, missionaries and others, who understood themselves in contrast to Muslims and evoked images of the harem to promote versions of English domesticity and a male-dominated public sphere, are to be considered. They reacted as much to the many voices challenging these more traditional beliefs in their own society as they responded to circumstances abroad. The policies that they advocated in Egypt, such as taking extra measures to prevent the independence of a large number of female slaves, even if that required compromising the goals of the campaign, meant that through their words and actions, they participated in contemporary English gender debates by defending roles that they saw as under attack.

Even the cultural feminist interpretations of the harem represent a political position. By celebrating a version of genteel femininity that transcends national and religious boundaries, they helped to make the case for separate spheres' ideology in English society. At the same time, they encouraged the audience to identify with and appreciate aspects of femininity in a way that supported contemporary arguments to expand this sphere.

Each of these perspectives, or systems of meaning, should be considered as having been in conversation and, therefore, incomplete in isolation. They reinforced each other in some respects, yet were created in opposition to each other. For example, feminists who argued against the 'harem in England' drew power from conservative discourses portraying that institution as dark and oppressive, but they did so to promote an agenda fundamentally at odds with that position in regard to the role of women in society and the family. By engaging with alternative viewpoints in this way, ideas were recreated and exchanged within the imperial cultural system. For only a small minority of those involved in the English gender debates had any direct contact with the harems of Egypt; most obtained information from other sources, even from their opponents, and reproduced images of the harem in the light of their own concerns and political goals.

Conservative interpretations were influenced also by feminist ideas; in fact the two were so intertwined that it is often difficult to tell which one had a greater impact on the other. One reason why advocates of patriarchal views presented such a formidable opposition to feminism is that they appropriated feminist arguments and addressed feminist concerns. They did not pose their position in terms of male superiority and boundless male licence and privilege; rather they maintained that only by preserving certain gender roles characterised by male authority would women be protected from injustice and abuse. This contention informed the words and actions of British officials in Egypt and a number of BFASS supporters and anti-vice activists.

The approach described above helped to create an uneasy but at times successful alliance between conservatives and feminists. Feminists could appreciate conservatives who agreed that under present conditions women were exploited, understood that this exploitation was wrong and were willing to take measures to correct the situation. For a number of traditionalist males, on the other hand, efforts to improve conditions for females allowed them to promote their own patriarchal agendas in the face of increasing feminist criticism by contrasting abuses at home and abroad with their efforts to protect women. These two beliefs or political perspectives were tied closely together, both practically and intellectually, yet they were at odds over the question of female authority and independence. The ability of advocates of both sides to work in concert and their motivations for doing so had as much to do with their competition for public acceptance and support as they did with actual points of agreement. As with national and imperial identities in general, identification is forged though perceptions of difference.

Historical actors borrowed from each other and other ideologies and belief systems available within British imperial culture in order to contribute new ways of understanding Englishness, demonstrating agency and creativity. Feminism, liberalism, the Enlightenment, Christianity and social Darwinism all proved to be influential in this respect. Certainly, advocating separate spheres for the masculine and the feminine, patriarchal gender relationships and middle-class domesticity in general had resonance in that society well before the development of the movements discussed. Finally, familiar conceits about the British imperial mission and Englishness as characterised by justice and liberty, and alternatively Islam as backward and uncivilised, symbolised by the oppressive harem, all informed new political perspectives. Variations of these ideas were reinterpreted and invested with additional meanings that reflected specific political concerns and individual circumstances. For example, anti-vice activists furthered their cause by drawing from racial ideology, 'race science' and representations of the East as a place of moral depravity and licentiousness in order to reinvent 'white slavery' in a way that obscured the more mundane aspects of prostitution in England and the slave traffic in Egypt, while conceptualising the English nation as white and racially homogenous.

One way of illustrating the importance of agency in this process of identity formation would be to consider the cultural feminist voices in contrast to the others. Their approach went against the grain of how English womanhood was being defined in relation to the harem at that time. Cultural feminists chose to ignore the words of anti-slavery and anti-vice workers, as well as much of the dominant imperialist rhetoric. Instead they embraced an alternative tradition in respect of the East and Orientalism, finding inspiration in Orientalist art and literature.[127] Unlike others who employed arguments based on liberal or Enlightenment thought and modern conceptions of the nation state, they evoked images of the aristocratic English lady and her sphere of influence.

These representations remind us that Orientalism was alive and well during the Victorian period. The decision of anti-slavery activists to ignore it was a deliberate choice. In fact, one of the more important aspects of identity formation involves weighing the various possibilities, and then engaging with and elaborating on some ideas while dismissing others. When activists portrayed the harem as barbaric and even evil, they did not simply misperceive or misunderstand the institution; rather they tried to create images that would counter the Orientalist tradition – popular among both men and women – of imagining it as a beautiful, desirable place. If the harem protected and empowered women, than how could anti-slavery workers justify attempts to transgress its boundaries? If slaves were treated better than the servants in English households, then why should they be manumitted and trained in domestic service? Even though the words of abolitionists with regard to the harem may seem to have little in common, and therefore no obvious connection with the cultural feminist and Orientalist discourse, the former should be considered a bold and aggressive reaction to the latter, an attempt to overshadow it.

When I speak of anti-slavery workers or cultural feminists, or any of the positions discussed in this chapter, I am referring not to a category of person or a social type, but rather to perspectives and strategies for participating in late nineteenth-century political life that appealed to a variety of people, women and men with different backgrounds and beliefs. It is not that individuals existed as, for example, liberal feminists or conservatives, and then at certain points in time asserted themselves, making their voices heard. Nor were they predisposed by their social situations to think or act in one way or another. Rather it was that historical actors oriented themselves around those concepts, finding meaning in them and applying them to their own lives and actions, and in doing so contributed to the further development of the ideas. Class and other divisions informed the process, but they did not prevent cooperation in the campaigns discussed; even the images of the refined and genteel harem were produced for the general public. Because people came to these ideological positions with different concerns and viewpoints, their motivations for identification were not the same, and as the circumstances changed so too did their politics.

These political identities were highly unpredictable, situational and temporary. For example, BFASS materials show that at least some members had been exposed to Orientalist art and literature. It was possible that a supporter of this movement could contribute to anti-slavery efforts and feel motivated by the rhetoric at meetings, yet in another setting enjoy Lewis's paintings or stories from *The Book of the Thousand Nights and a Night*. Similarly, women like Sarah Amos could dedicate themselves to liberal feminist causes that advocated equality and independence for women, such as access to higher education or suffrage, and still identify with the agenda of the BFASS or anti-vice organisations, despite the patriarchal gender roles they promoted. The unpredictable and situational nature of identity formation is perhaps most evident in the case of Melek Hanum, a traditional, secluded, Muslim woman who adopted a new persona and outlook by becoming a vocal anti-Muslim Christian, condemning the harem, and participating in English political and intellectual life.

In English gender debates, the harem and the slavery associated with it usually, although not always, served as a signifier of difference distinguishing between what was English and therefore considered the model, on one hand, and what was Islamic and believed to be in need of reform, on the other. For anti-slavery workers, Christian missionaries and others, the Muslims in want of guidance existed at the peripheries of the British imperial system in places such as occupied Egypt. For the feminists and anti-vice activists, foreign or Islamic influences could be found in England itself in the form of domestic tyranny, prostitution, and a patriarchal political and legal system that denied certain rights and opportunities to women.

Does this mean that English people thought that the pimps and 'wife beaters' among them were Muslims? Of course not. Rather they imagined the true English nation to be based less on geographical borders than on ideas about a shared culture and a value system characterised by legitimate hierarchies. It was the belief in this just, fair and responsible rule that justified imperialism in Egypt and throughout the British Empire. Abuse and exploitation, sexual and otherwise, simply did not fall within the pale of true Englishness regardless of the physical place where they occurred; according to the imperialist ideology through which the nation was defined, these were characteristics associated with colonised peoples whose systems of government were less advanced. In this context, associating certain practices with Islam had less to do with religion than it did with labelling them as backward, oppressive and in need of reform, if not elimination. Thus examining the use of the harem and 'white slavery' in English domestic debates in relation to anti-slavery efforts abroad sheds light on how imperial identity politics functioned in English life, and served to construct and maintain boundaries defining the nation within the metropole of the British Empire.

Notes

1 I use the term 'feminist' as Jane Rendall does, describing women 'who claimed for themselves the right to define their own place in society', as well as the men who sympathised with them. 'Feminist' therefore includes women of the late eighteenth and nineteenth centuries prior to the first use of the term in English in 1894: J. Rendall, *The Origins of Modern Feminism: Women in Britain, France and the United States, 1780–1860* (London: Macmillan, 1985), p. 1.

2 Linda Colley discusses the ways in which ideas about separate spheres were used by women in the late eighteenth century to justify their role in politics and public life in chapter 6, 'Womanpower', of *Britons: Forging the Nation 1707–1837* (New Haven, CT, and London: Yale University Press, 1992), pp. 237–81. In addition, Anna Clark shows that the popular response to the Queen Caroline affair in the early nineteenth century, particularly among her female supporters, set an important precedent by asserting the importance of women's concerns in the public sphere without challenging the idea of essential differences between women and men: L. Colley, 'Queen Caroline and the Sexual Politics of Popular Culture in London, 1820', *Representations*, 31 (summer 1990), 47–68. Finally, Philippa Levine explores the many ways which nineteenth-century feminists challenged patriarchal power, noting that they 'consistently and determinedly yoked public to private and private to public', in *Feminist Lives in Victorian England: Private Roles and Public Commitment* (Oxford: Blackwell, 1990), p. 179.

3 Suffrage was one such cause which mobilised both middle- and working-class women. The important contributions made by the female textile workers in northern England to a movement which was in many ways predominantly bourgeois has been documented by Jill Liddington and Jill Norris, *One Hand Tied Behind Us: The Rise of the Women's Suffrage Movement* (London: Virago, 1978). In addition, the relationship between working- and middle-class suffragists is explored by Sandra Stanley Holton in *Feminism and Democracy: Women's Suffrage and Reform Politics in Britain, 1900–1918* (Cambridge: Cambridge University Press, 1986).

4 Antoinette Burton notes that feminists 'of all persuasions' from different areas of Great Britain saw British political traditions and culture as an 'irresistible justification for their claims on the State': *Burdens*, p. 5.

5 See Leah Leneman, *The Scottish Suffragettes* (Edinburgh: NMS Publishing Ltd, 2000), pp. 11, 28, 45, 47; and Cliona Murphy, *The Women's Suffrage Movement and*

Irish Society in the Early Twentieth Century (New York: Harvester, 1989), pp. 68–9. As Leneman notes, both the first suffragette hunger-striker to serve time in Holloway prison and the suffragette who spent the longest time in that institution were Scots: *Scottish Suffragettes*, pp. 45, 47. One Irish suffragette described experiences in England as a '"helpful apprenticeship" for the campaign in Ireland': quoted in Murphy, *Women's Suffrage Movement and Irish Society*, p. 69. For more on the women's suffrage movement in Ireland see Rosemary Cullen Owens, *Smashing Times: A History of the Irish Women's Suffrage Movement 1889–1922* (Dublin: Attic Press, 1984).

6 Margaret Ward, 'The Ladies' Land League and the Irish Land War 1881/1882: Defining the Relationship Between Women and Nation', in Ida Blom, Karen Hagemann and Catherine Hall (eds), *Gendered Nations: Nationalisms and Gender Order in the Long Nineteenth Century* (Oxford: Berg, 2000), pp. 229–47, at 231–2.

7 Both Leneman and Murphy discuss this tension experienced by Scottish and Irish feminists respectively. Irish suffragists took care to counter the perception in Ireland that they involved themselves in an English movement, as this would brand them unpatriotic: Murphy, *Women's Suffrage Movement*, pp. 74, 82. The first suffragette hunger-striker in Holloway prison mentioned previously described herself as '"a direct descendant of the mother of William Wallace"': Leneman, *Scottish Suffragettes*, p. 47. Certainly, not all feminists in the British Isles reconciled their sense of national loyalty with activities in England. Many worked within their own counties and had as little to do with the English as possible. The members of the Ladies' Land League in Ireland, for example, challenged patriarchy within the framework of activism for Irish rights and rejected the Ladies' National Association because of its support of the British State and its repressive policies: Ward, 'The Ladies' Land League'.

8 William Blackstone, *Commentaries on the Laws of England (1765–1969)*, Book 1: 'Of the Rights of Persons', in a facsimile of the first edition (Chicago, IL: University of Chicago Press, 1979), p. 430.

9 Both Malcolm Kelsall and Joyce Zonana discuss Wollstonecraft's use of the slave of the Muslim harem in her feminist writings: Kelsall, 'The Slave–Woman in the Harem', *Studies in Romanticism*, 31 (fall 1992), 315–31; and Zonana, 'The Sultan and the Slave: Feminist Orientalism and the Structure of *Jane Eyre*', *Signs*, 18 (1993), 592–617.

10 Harriet Taylor, 'Enfranchisement of Women', *Westminster Review*, 55 (July 1851), 289–310.

11 John Stuart Mill, *The Subjection of Women* (London: Longmans, Green, Reader & Dyer, 1869), pp. 9, 144.

12 Lee Holcombe, 'Victorian Wives and Property: Reform of the Married Women's Property Law, 1857–1882', in Martha Vicinus (ed.), *A Widening Sphere: Changing Roles of Victorian Women* (Bloomington: Indiana University Press, 1977), pp. 3–28, at 22.

13 Holcombe discusses the issue of equity, *ibid.*

14 *Hansard's Parliamentary Debates*, vol. 145, 14 May 1857, col. 275.

15 *Ibid.*, vol. 201, 18 May 1870, col. 889.

16 'The Ladies' Petition'was presented to the House of Commons by John Stuart Mill in June of 1866: *Westminster Review*, 87 (January1867), 29–36. Despite the confusion of this particular writer, the fact that Muslim women could own property when English women could not did not go unnoticed by contemporaries, and is discussed in Billie Melman, *Women's Orients: English Women and the Middle East, 1718–1918: Sexuality, Religion and Work* (London: Macmillan, 1992).

17 'The Emancipation of Women', *Westminster Review*, 102 (July 1874), 63–80, at 71.

18 For example, the following writers and scholars commented on the supposed backwardness of Muslims and related it to the treatment of women: Major Milligan, *Slavery in Turkey: The Sultan's Harem (A Paper Read Before the Anthropological Society of London)* (London: Stanford, 1870), pp. 1–23; J. W. H. Stobart, *Islam and its Founder* (London: SPCK, c.1876); and Isabella L. Bird, *Journeys in Persia and*

Kurdistan, vols 1 and 2 (London: John Murray, 1891). Along the same lines, Sir William Muir understood Islamic societies as less civilised because 'the cankerworm of polygamy, divorce, servile concubinage and the veil, lay at the root': *Annals of the Early Caliphate from Original Sources* (London: Smith, Elder & Co., 1883), p. 458. The practice of using the status of women to evaluate and compare different societies and cultures had a long tradition in England: see, e.g., William Alexander, *The History of Women, from the Earliest Antiquity, to the Present Time: Giving Some Account of Almost Every Interesting Particular Concerning that Sex, Among All Nations, Ancient and Modern*, 2 vols (London: C. Dilly, 1782). For an in-depth discussion of the process of defining and ranking peoples and civilisations see George Stocking, *Victorian Anthropology* (New York: Free Press, 1987).

19 Roger Fulford, *Votes for Women: The Story of a Struggle* (London: Faber & Faber Ltd, 1957), p. 82.

20 The word 'suffragist' refers to advocates of women's suffrage, while 'suffragette' is used to refer only to those involved in the militant wing of this movement.

21 George Dangerfield makes this argument in *The Strange Death of Liberal England* (New York: Capricorn Books, 1935). The tensions and conflicts that had begun during the nineteenth century escalated to militancy in 1905; Dangerfield's book focuses on the period 1910–14.

22 Women's suffrage in the context of imperialism and the transnational circulation of ideas has been explored at length in Ian Christopher Fletcher, Laura Nym Mayhall and Philippa Levine (eds): *Women's Suffrage in the British Empire: Citizenship, Nation and Race* (London: Routledge, 2000).

23 'The Women's Suffrage Bill 1: The Enfranchisement of Women', *Fortnightly Review*, 268 (April 1889), 555–78, at 557–8.

24 'Woman's Place in Modern Life', *ibid.*, 304 (April 1892), 522–9, at 523–4.

25 Emily Pfeiffer, 'The Suffrage for Women', *Contemporary Review*, 47 (March 1885), 418–35, at 423. By contrasting the harem with the 'open field' of universal suffrage, Pfeiffer plays on the idea of this institution as opaque and therefore illegitimate in order to reinforce the connection between her cause and Enlightenment ideas. The political significance of the opaque harem for the English is discussed in chapters two and three.

26 'The Women's Suffrage Bill 1', 559.

27 'The Political Enfranchisement of Women', *Fortnightly Review*, 62 (February 1872), 204–14, at 208.

28 For example, Amelia Edwards uses the phrase 'a bird in a cage' in *A Thousand Miles Up the Nile* (London: George Routledge & Sons, 1890) and M. L. Whateley uses 'caged birds of women' in *Scenes from Life in Cairo: A Glimpse Behind the Curtain* (London: Seeley, Jackson and Halliday, 1883), p. 56.

29 *Women and Work*, 40 (March 1875), col. 2.

30 Mabel Shannan Crawford, '"Purdah" in the House of Commons', *Women's Penny Paper* (May 1890), 363. Purdah (Urdu and Persian) means curtain and may be used to refer to the seclusion of women in the East in general; the Victorians often associated it with Muslim women: for example, an article written by Mrs Meer Ali entitled 'Mussalmans in India' (*Observer* 1832) calls Muslim women 'purdahed dames'.

31 Drawing from Enlightenment thought, generations of feminists have employed ideas about reason and the intellect to bolster their position. Mary Wollstonecraft argued that because women, as human beings, had both reason and conscience, they deserved nothing less than complete equality with men: *A Vindication of the Rights of Woman: With Strictures on Political and Moral Subjects* (1792), reprinted in *A Critical Edition of Mary Wollstonecraft's* A Vindication of the Rights of Woman, ed. Ulrich Hardt (Troy, NY: Whitston Publishing Co., 1982). Other scholars have noted the connection between Wollstonecraft's ideas and the women's suffrage movement: Holton, *Feminism and Democracy*, p. 9; and David Morgan, *Suffragists and Liberals: The Politics of Woman Suffrage in England* (Oxford: Blackwell, 1975), p. 9.

32 For a complete discussion of women's efforts to attend Cambridge on equal terms

THE HAREM, SLAVERY AND BRITISH IMPERIAL CULTURE

with men see Rita McWilliams-Tullberg, 'Women and Degrees at Cambridge University, 1862–1897', in M. Vicinus (ed.), *A Widening Sphere: Changing Roles of Victorian Women* (Bloomington and London: Indiana University Press, 1977), pp. 117–45.

33 Mrs Harvey, *Turkish Harems and Circassian Homes* (London: Hurst & Blackett, 1871), pp. 90–1.
34 'Should University Degrees Be Given to Women?' *Westminster and Foreign Quarterly Review*, 59 (April 1881), 493–505, at 497.
35 Mrs Brassey, *Sunshine and Storm in the East or Cruises to Cyprus and Constantinople* (London and New York: Henry Holt & Co., 1890), p. 100. The idea that reading novels encourages the emancipation of secluded females, allowing the Turkish woman of the harem to step 'from darkness into light', is also presented in 'Turkish Slavery', *Women's Penny Paper* (August 1890), p. 523.
36 The theory that education interferes with a woman's ability to produce healthy offspring, therefore posing a threat to the prosperity and even survival of the nation and race, was presented by T. S. Clouston, MD, in 'Female Education from a Medical Point of View', *Popular Science Monthly*, 24 (1883), 214–28.
37 For an analysis of this movement and the legislation regarding violence against women see Judith Travers, Cultural Meanings and Representations of Violence Against Women, London 1790–1895, PhD thesis, SUNY at Stony Brook, 1997, pp. 37–67.
38 Frances Power Cobbe, 'Celibacy v. Marriage', *Fraser's Magazine*, 65 (February 1862), 228–35, at 235; in this article Cobbe argues for the benefits of celibacy over the inequalities of marriage. For discussion of Cobbe see Barbara Caine, *Victorian Feminists* (Oxford: Oxford University Press, 1992), pp. 103–49.
39 *A Cry From The Depths: The British Turk*, Women's Suffrage Journal, 9 (October 1878), 173.
40 As 'wife-beating', or domestic violence, became criminalised, it began to be associated exclusively with the working class. This was a strategy used to counter the increasing political and economic influence of working-class men: Travers, Cultural Meanings and Representations of Violence Against Women, section entitled 'Violence, Class and "Primitive"' Man', pp. 29–36.
41 Similarly, Clare Midgley notes that English women sometimes identified their oppression with that of the black female slave in her discussion of the ways in which their anti-slavery efforts, particularly in the first half of the century, contributed to the development of feminism both ideologically and practically. 'Anti-Slavery and the Roots of "Imperial Feminism"', in C.Midgley (ed.), *Gender and Imperialism* (Manchester: Manchester University Press, 1998), pp. 161–79.
42 Elizabeth Martyn, 'Women in Public Life', *Westminster Review*, 132 (1890), 228–85, at 279–80.
43 'The Christian Harem', *Westminster Review*, 122 (July 1884), 105–15.
44 Annabella Dennehy, 'The Woman of the Future', *Westminster Review*, 152 (July 1899), 99–100, at 100.
45 Ellen Chennells, *Recollections of an Egyptian Princess by Her English Governess, Being a Record of Five Years' Residence at the Court of Ismael Pasha, Khédive* (Edinburgh and London: William Blackwood & Sons, 1893), pp. 114, 133.
46 For example, certain BFASS supporters maintained that freeing female slaves would liberate the wives and daughters of the men who owned them from their state of 'social slavery'. 'Considerations as to what could most effectually be done at the present crisis (of the meeting of a European conference on Eastern affairs) to get slavery done away with in Turkey once and for all', folder G-96 (Turkey and Bulgaria), BFASS.
47 *ASR* (March 1881), 42–4
48 Mrs Harvey, *Turkish Harems*, pp. 12–13.
49 Similarly, Joyce Zonana describes how feminists likened the oppression of women in England to the oppression of women in the East in presenting their agenda as a conservative attempt to 'make the West more like itself': 'The Sultan and the

Slave', p. 594. Other scholars also have explored how British women, including feminists, viewed Muslim females as necessarily oppressed and understood that oppression as a signifier of difference defining the English as superior and more civilised: see Frédérique Apffel-Marglin and Suzanne Simon, 'Feminist Orientalism and Development', in Wendy Harcourt (ed.), *Feminist Perspectives on Sustainable Development* (London: Zen Books, 1994), pp. 26–45; Inderpal Grewal, *Home and Harem: Nation, Gender, Empire, and the Cultures of Travel* (Durham, NC, and London: Duke University Press, 1996), pp. 57–84; Mervat Hatem, 'Through Each Other's Eyes: The Impact on the Colonial Encounter of the Images of Egyptian, Levantine–Egyptian, and European Women, 1862–1920', in Nupur Chaudhuri and Margaret Strobel (eds), *Western Women and Imperialism: Complicity and Resistance* (Bloomington: Indiana University Press, 1992); and Kelsall, 'The Slave–Woman in the Harem'.

50 Lord Cromer, previously known as Sir Evelyn Baring, acted as Her Britannic Majesty's consul-general and agent in Egypt, and his activities in Egypt regarding slavery are discussed at length in chapter two.
51 M. L. Whateley, 'Women's Condition in Egypt', *Englishwoman's Review* (September 1884), 411–12.
52 'An Egyptian Girls' School', *Journal of the Women's Educational Union*, 3 (June 1875), 92–4, at 94.
53 Letter by Mrs Alice Leider, teacher at Mrs Whateley's school, O 48/113, Cairo, 25 August 1860, CMS Archive. Publications which advertised the demand for women missionaries or educators in the East also helped to promote the idea that the English woman could bring light into the 'closed harems'. For example, one article in *The Year Book of Women's Work*, available at the Fawcett Library, London, relates such a need in the Levant and Turkey (1875), 71–2.
54 Isabella Bird, *Journeys in Persia and Kurdistan*, vol. 2, p. 179.
55 Ibid., vol. 1, pp. 214–15.
56 Reverend George Townsend, *A Cruise in the Bosphorus, and in the Marmora, and Aegean Seas* (London: SPCK, c.1890), p. 77. The term 'sacred individuality' is a perfect example of how liberal Enlightenment concepts of the independent individual subject were fused with Christian ideas.
57 Mrs Harvey, *Turkish Harems*, p. 13.
58 Mary Bird, *Persian Women and Their Creed* (London: Church Missionary Society, 1899), p. 22.
59 Lady Duff Gordon, *Last Letters from Egypt to Which Are Added Letters from the Cape*, 2nd edn (London: Macmillan & Co., 1876), p. 56.
60 *ASR* (January–February 1892), 50.
61 Mrs Emma Raymond Pitman, *Missionary Heroines in Eastern Lands: Woman's Work in Mission Fields* (London: S. W. Partridge & Co., 1884), p. 139.
62 Bird, *Persian Women*, p. 14; an example of a story of conversion and persecution is given on p. 82.
63 *ASR* (March–April 1894), 98. Similar articles were published in *Southampton* and the *Echo*. Another shocking story complete with illustration, and not surprisingly with a crescent in the background, told of a woman who had been sold along with her infant son in order to pay her husband's debts: *ASR* (May 1877), 227. However, legally, any slave who became pregnant with her master's child could not be re-sold and became free on the death of her master. In addition, her child was free at birth: Ehud Toledano, *Slavery and Abolition in the Ottoman Middle East* (Seattle and London: University of Washington Press, 1998), p. 13.
64 Melek-Hanum, *Thirty Years in the Harem; or the Autobiography of Melek-Hanum, Wife of H. H Kibrizli Mehemit-Pasha* (London: Chapman & Hall, 1872) and *Six Years in Europe: Sequel to Thirty Years in the Harem* (London: Chapman & Hall, 1873).
65 Earl of Cromer, *Modern Egypt* (New York: Macmillan, 1908), vol. 2, p. 155.
66 'Girls' Education in Egypt', *Englishwoman's Review*, 5 (1874), 219. A similar article discusses two girls' schools in Cairo, one run by Miss Whateley and the other by a

group of nuns with an English mother superior: 'Education in Egypt', *Journal of the Women's Education Union*, 2 (April 1874), 63–4.
67 Alexander Kinglake, *Eōthen; or, Traces of Travel Brought Home from the East* (London: Routledge, originally published in 1844), p. 90.
68 Adrian Ross and Arthur Branscombe, *Morocco Bound: A Farcical Comedy in Two Acts*, p. 91, British Library, Manuscripts Collection.
69 Stanley Lane-Poole, *Studies in a Mosque* (London: W. H. Allen & Co., 1883), p. 109.
70 *ASR* (December 1879), 283–5; see also *ASR* (January 1877), unnumbered first page.
71 Melek-Hanum, *Thirty Years in the Harem*, p. 42.
72 'The Harem', *Saturday Review*, 63 (June 1887), 914–15.
73 'Turkey', *The Times* (April 1876), p. 8 B.
74 'The Turks of the Day (By a Recent Visitor). Some Domestic Institutions: The Harem', *Leeds Mercury*, reprinted in *ASR* (March 1881), 42–4.
75 Similarly, in British India both English women and Bengali men were disqualified from public roles in politics because of their 'feminine' characteristics: Mrinalini Sinha, *Colonial Masculinity: The 'Manly Englishman' and the 'Effeminate Bengali' in the Late Nineteenth Century* (Manchester: Manchester University Press, 1995), p. 35.
76 For discussion of anti-suffrage arguments see Brian Harrison, *Separate Spheres: The Opposition to Women's Suffrage in Britain* (London: Croom Helm, 1978), especially pp. 75–8.
77 Constance Rover, *Women's Suffrage and Party Politics in Britain, 1866–1914* (London: Routledge, 1967), pp. 171–2; also see chapter 7 of Harrison, *Separate Spheres*, 'Cromer Takes Control', pp. 126–46.
78 Judith Walkowitz, *Prostitution and Victorian Society: Women, Class and the State* (Cambridge and New York: Cambridge University Press, 1980), especially part 2.
79 'The Maiden Tribute of Modern Babylon', *Pall Mall Gazette*, four-part series (July 6, 7, 8, 10 1885). This exposé is discussed at length by Judith Walkowitz, *City of Dreadful Delight: Narratives of Sexual Danger in Late-Victorian London* (Chicago, IL: University of Chicago Press, 1992).
80 Walkowitz, *City of Dreadful Delight*, pp. 81–102.
81 'The White Slave Trade', *Vigilance Record*, 6 (January 1893), 99; The other articles are in the same publication: 3 (August 1889), 83; 6 (November 1892), 78–9; 7 (February 1893), 15; and 7 (March 1893), 21.
82 W. M. Johnstone, 'The White Slave Traffic', *Vigilance Record*, 6 (August 1892), 54.
83 'To the Anti-Slavery Conference at Brussels: The Memorial of the National Vigilance Association', printed in *Vigilance Record*, 3 (December 1889), 131. The BFASS recognised this movement. The Congress at the Hague for the British, Continental and General Federation for the Abolition of State Regulation of Vice (September 1883) had its 'warmest sympathies': *ASR* (July 1883), 185.
84 The terms 'simple' and 'weak' were used in the pamphlet *The White Slavery of Europe from the French of Pastor T. Borel of Geneva with Supplement Relating to the Foreign Traffic in English, Scotch, and Irish Girls*, ed. Joseph Edmondson 2nd edn (London: Dyer Brothers, 1880), p. 51. The use of the term 'frightened lamb' is noted by Walkowitz, *City of Dreadful Delight*, p. 102.
85 Horace Victor, 'Eastern Women', *Fortnightly Review* (October 1889), p. 514.
86 *Pall Mall Gazette*, 42 (21 July 1885), 11.
87 Ibid., 4.
88 Walkowitz, *City of Dreadful Delight*, p. 123.
89 Millicent Garrett Fawcett, 'The Protection of Girls 1: Speech or Silence', *Contemporary Review*, 48 (September 1885), 326–31.
90 Published in London, 1877. The relationship between these two movements in England and Egypt and their representation contributes to Philippa Levine's discussion of the malleability of the late 19th-century white slave trade narrative in different settings. It also necessarily complicates the idea that the narratives, popular in English-speaking countries and the metropoles of Europe, depicting the 'white woman sexually enslaved against her will could not and did not work in the

colonial context'. 'White Slave Narratives', *Prostitution, Race, and Politics* (New York: Routledge, 2003), pp. 245–50, at 247.
91 *ASR* (November 1876), 149. The idea that white slavery and the influence of concubines brought corruption to the State has been expressed also by writers for an Arabic-speaking audience sympathetic to Islam: e.g. 'Abd al-Salam al-Tirmanini, *al-Riqq Madihu wa Hadiruhu* (Kuwait: al-Majlis al-Watani al-Thaqafa wa al-Funun wa al-Adab, 1979), pp. 137–43.
92 *ASR* (August 1878), 62.
93 Reverend Charles Bell, *A Winter on the Nile, in Egypt, and in Nubia*, 2nd edn (London: Hodder & Stroughton, 1889), p. 270.
94 Lane-Poole, *Studies in a Mosque*, p. 105.
95 J. D. Bate Allahabad, 'The Wives of Muhammad', *Indian Antiquary, A Journal of Oriental Research in Archaeology, History, Literature, Languages, Philosophy, Religion, Folklore*, 7 (April 1878), 93–101, at 98 (published by Tribner & Co., London).
96 The importance of English moral superiority to imperial rule and the necessity of maintaining this belief, despite the tensions surrounding prostitution and efforts to regulate it during the late nineteenth century, are explored by Philippa Levine in 'Rereading the 1890s: Venereal Disease as "Constitutional Crisis"' in Britain and British India', *Journal of Asian Studies*, 55 (August 1996), 585–612.
97 *ASR* (March–April 1886), 43–5.
98 *ASR* (April 1874), 28–9.
99 As discussed in the Introduction, racial categories had meaning in the Middle East and Turkey just as they did in England. One article, entitled 'The Removal of Racial Traces', presents the idea that the Turkish people's race has changed over the centuries because of the importation of white slaves from Eastern Europe, as well as slaves from other parts of the world: *ASR* (November–December 1890), 295.
100 Robert Young, *Colonial Desire: Hybridity in Theory, Culture and Race* (London and New York: Routledge, 1995), pp. 118–19; see also Nancy Stepan, *The Idea of Race in Science: Great Britain 1800–1960* (London: MacMillan, 1982).
101 In fact, Stead's exposé led to prohibitions against liaisons with 'native' women: Walkowitz, *City of Dreadful Delight*, p. 83. Fears of degeneration were widespread in late Victorian England and intimately linked with class and gender anxiety. For degeneracy was neither specific to European nor colonial society, but was rather a '"mobile" discourse of empire': Ann Laura Stoler, *Race and the Education of Desire: Foucault's History of Sexuality and the Colonial Order of Things* (Durham, NC, and London: Duke University Press, 1995), p. 32. Daniel Pick and Gareth Stedman Jones have discussed English concerns regarding degeneration, particularly the role of this concept in class politics and representations of the urban poor, and Anne McClintock has examined the importance of gender in the process noting how control of female sexuality served to preserve 'racial, economic and political power': D. Pick, *Faces of Degeneration: A European Disorder, c.1848–c.1918* (Cambridge: Cambridge University Press, 1989); G. Stedman Jones, *Outcast London: A Study in the Relationship between Classes in Victorian Society* (Oxford: Clarendon Press, 1971); and Anne McClintock, *Imperial Leather. Race, Gender and Sexuality in the Colonial Contest* (New York: Routledge, 1995), p. 47.
102 Both Billie Melman and Reina Lewis focus on the perspectives of English women who identified with the women of the harem. Melman shows how their writings challenged male, Orientalist discourses by de-eroticising this institution and presenting it as similar to the bourgeois home. Lewis adds to Melman's work by explaining that the 'feminine' understanding of the Orient was culturally-constructed and defined difference as well as sameness, although not in the ways that the male and liberal-feminist writings did. Billie Melman, 'Desexualizing the Orient: The Harem in English Travel Writing by Women, 1763–1914', *Mediterranean Historical Review*, 4 (December 1989), 301–39; and see her *Women's Orients*; Reina Lewis, 'Women Orientalist Artists: Diversity,

Ethnography, Interpretation', *Women: A Cultural Review*, 6 (Summer 1995), 91–106; and *Gendering Orientalism: Race, Femininity and Representation* (London and New York: Routledge, 1996).
103 Mrs W. M. Ramsay, *Everyday Life in Turkey* (London: Hodder & Stoughton, 1897), pp. 106–8.
104 Lucy Garnett, 'The Mohammedan Women of Turkey,' *Woman's World*, 3 (1890), 4.
105 Mrs Ramsay, *Everyday Life in Turkey*, p. 105.
106 *Ibid.*, p. 5.
107 'The Present Condition of Muhammedan Women in Turkey', *Fortnightly Review*, 343 (July 1895), 53–66, at 62, 66.
108 Melman also has made this point. One contemporary female writer even went so far as to say that among Arabs, slaves are really more like 'spoiled children' than slaves or even servants: Lady Anne Blunt, *A Pilgrimage to Nejd, The Cradle of the Arab Race: A Visit to the Court of the Arab Emir, and 'Our Persian Campaign'* (London: John Murray, 1881), vol. 2, p. 47.
109 Lucy Garnett, 'The Ladies of the Imperial Seraglio', *Woman's World*, 3 (1890), 233.
110 Garnett, 'The Mohammedan Women of Turkey', p. 3.
111 Millicent Garrett Fawcett made the statement that as long as women outnumbered men and polygamy did not exist in England, the country would have a considerable number of single women: 'The Future of Englishwomen: A Reply', *Nineteenth Century*, 4 (1878), 347–57.
112 'Polygamy to Save England', *Islamic Review* (published in Woking, England, by the Woking Muslim Mission and Literary Trust and edited by Khwaja Kamal-ud-din) 9 (September 1921), 307–8.
113 'Eastern Women,' *Fortnightly Review*; Emily Beaufort, *Egyptian Sepulchres and Syrian Shrines Including Some Stay in the Lebanon, at Palmyra, and in Western Turkey* (London: Longman, 1861), vol. 2, p. 415.
114 'Eastern Women', *Fortnightly Review*.
115 Chennells, *Recollections of an Egyptian Princess*, p. 6.
116 Mrs Baille, *A Sail to Smyrna: or, An Englishwoman's Journal; Including Impressions of Constantinople, a Visit to a Turkish Harem, and a Railway Journey to Ephesus* (London: Longmans, 1873), p. 169.
117 Townsend, *A Cruise in the Bosphorus*, p. 74.
118 Mrs Baille, *Smyrna*, p. 167.
119 Mrs Harvey, *Turkish Harems*, p. 61.
120 He regularly exhibited at both the Academy and the British Institution and easily found buyers for his new works: 'British Artists: Their Style and Character, with Engraved Illustrations: No. XXXIL, John Frederick Lewis', *Art Journal*, 20 (1858), 42. His obituarist noted that 'Eastern Lewis', so named for his 'Oriental' subject matter, was regarded with 'universal admiration', and that his paintings 'arrested public attention and fixed it'. Obituary, 'John Frederick Lewis', *Art Journal*, 38 (1876), 329.
121 It was displayed in the gallery of the Society of Water-Colour Painters in 1850. One London critic stated that it 'took everyone by surprise . . . and few came away from it without acknowledging that *The Hhareem* was the most extraordinary production ever executed in water colours': *ibid.*, 43.
122 Ruskin is quoted in 'British Artists: Their Style and Character', p. 42. The idea of the harem as a beautiful, private, feminine space is also communicated in *A New Light in the Harem* by Frederick Goodall (1884), an artist who had achieved success and recognition during the 1860s; was elected Royal Academician in 1864; and afterwards began to focus on Egyptian subjects: Jane Turner (ed.), *The Dictionary of Art* (New York: Macmillan, 1996), pp. 925–6.
123 Emily Weeks, 'Imperial Peripheries: John Frederick Lewis (1805–76) Inside and Out', paper presented at the Interdisciplinary Nineteenth-Century Studies Conference, Yale University, Spring 2000.
124 For a discussion of the process of creating and maintaining these unstable boundaries in the face of a much more complicated and fluid reality see Robert John

Ackermann, *Heterogeneities: Race, Gender, Class, Nation, and State* (Amherst: University of Massachusetts Press, 1996).

125 Grosrichard's thesis supports such a reading: Alain Grosrichard, *Structure du sérail: la fiction du despotisme asiatique dans l'occident classique* (Paris: Seuil, 1979).

126 As Emily Apter has argued, Orientalist representations of the harem could be seen as 'antiphallic' 'feminocentric' dreams: 'Female Trouble in the Colonial Harem', *Differences*, 4 (Spring 1992), 205–24.

127 Their approach was, nevertheless, complicit with the imperial project. English women who praised the Muslim harem as a place of female empowerment still participated in the male imperial tradition of Orientalism. For example, according to Meyda Yeğenoğlu, Lady Mary Wortley Montagu assumed a position of masculinity when she completed the Orientalist narrative by contributing what male writers lacked, an accurate description of the inside of a harem: see chapter 3, 'Supplementing the Orientalist Lack: European Ladies in the Harem', in *Colonial Fantasies: Towards a Feminist Reading of Orientalism* (Cambridge: Cambridge University Press, 1998), pp. 68–94. Similarly, Felicity Nussbaum maintains that women like Montagu impersonated males when they gazed upon women of the harem with fascination: chapter 6, 'Feminotopias: The Seraglio, the Homoerotic, and the Pleasures of "Deformity"', in *Torrid Zones: Maternity, Sexuality, and Empire in Eighteenth-Century English Narratives* (Baltimore, MD, and London: Johns Hopkins University Press, 1995), pp. 135–66. In chapter five I discuss ways in which Orientalism functioned within the British Empire with regard to Anglo-Muslim relationships.

CHAPTER FIVE

Islam in England

Introduction

While the perspectives presented by the various historical actors in the first three chapters were far from unified, they had certain characteristics in common. Almost all understood Englishness as an ideal and as fundamentally different from and more advanced than Islam and the values, customs and traditions they associated with Muslim societies. This basic assumption remained at the root of the dominant imperialist discourse as well as the British campaign to suppress slave traffic in Egypt and surrounding areas. It was reinforced by the actions of British officials, BFASS supporters and even those involved in English gender debates. In this chapter, however, I focus on ways in which this ideology, or understanding of English national identity, was challenged by Muslim immigration and the creation of Muslim communities in England, as well as by those who produced sympathetic writings about the faith for an English audience. Through these historical developments Islam was presented as if not actually English at least compatible enough with English society–culture to exist comfortably within it, and in some cases as even elevating to it.

Examining these individuals and discourses adds a critical dimension to the discussion of how ideas about Islam and Englishness functioned in the context of the British Empire during the late nineteenth century. They show how unpopular and minority perspectives could operate within and contribute to the larger imperial cultural system, as well as how such perspectives were limited by it. This approach also helps to illustrate the shifting nature and the political role of the border between the metropole and the periphery. For even though a religion usually associated with the colonies or occupied territories existed within England, the boundary between the English nation and the rest of the Empire did not disappear but rather was drawn and re-drawn within that country through individual relationships so that, despite similarities and mutual influences, beliefs about essential difference were maintained.

Like the people discussed in the previous chapters, those who were sympathetic to Islam engaged with ideas already culturally available in English society and the Empire, but expanded on them in order to create unique perspectives. For example, they sometimes drew inspiration from Orientalist art and literature; at other times they formulated arguments directly in response to those presented by feminists or anti-slavery advocates. These alternative ways of understanding the relationship between Islam and Englishness reflect the unprecedented political circumstances during the late nineteenth century, which provided opportunities for the creation of a place for that religion in England.[1]

Immigration, ethnicity, and identity: lascars *and* ayahs

The first significant influx of Muslims to England resulted from trade associated with the Empire and began during the late eighteenth century. Lascars, a general term for African and Asian seamen, worked on East India Company ships.[2] So many were employed that the Government actually required the company to hire at least one British seaman for every three lascars.[3] Between 1794 and 1814, 2,500 lascar sailors had visited England,[4] and by the late nineteenth century between 10,000 and 12,000 came to the country annually,[5] the overwhelming majority of them Muslims.[6] They came primarily from India, especially the areas of Bengal, Gujarat, Punjab and Sind, but also from the Middle East, especially Aden and the Yemen, and Northern Africa as well.

The welfare of lascar immigrants was both a domestic and an imperial concern, and in 1857 a number of individuals and organisations from England and elsewhere established the Strangers' Home for Asiatics, Africans and South Sea Islanders, so that these sailors would not be condemned to impoverishment when work was unavailable.[7] The Home could accommodate roughly 200 people at a time, and 5,709 individuals passed through it during 1857–77.[8] One lascar described the institution as 'a Home for Mohammedans in the Christian capital'.[9] Unlike the Cairo Home for Freed Women Slaves where proselytism was forbidden, members of the London City Mission (LCM) regularly visited the Home. A missionary's house stood just across the yard, and the Home's library had the Bible and Christian writings in several languages. However, the religious needs of Muslims, who comprised the majority of residents, were not neglected, and a copy of the Qur'an as well as sketches of Mecca and Medina were kept there.[10]

The LCM established a similar residence for women, the Ayah's Home, which for over 40 years sheltered nearly 100 female immigrants annually. Ayahs were nannies who had worked for English families living abroad, usually because the husband or father was affiliated with the East India Company or the Government of the British Empire, and were primarily Muslims and Hindus from 'all parts of the East'. Those who came to the LCM did so because they had been dismissed by the families who had brought them to England; they could not pay for a return ticket home and had nowhere else to go.[11]

The border separating Islam and Englishness maintained through the dominant imperialist ideologies meant little to Muslim immigrants, who saw their faith as universal and made it conspicuous in English society. As early as 1805, the *Gentleman's Magazine* reported a 'Mahommedan Jubilee' in which 'the Lascars of the Mahommedan persuasion at the East end of town had a grand religious festival'. They marched through the streets with drums and tambourines; some performed pantomimic dances, and at every turn of the street a group would lift their heads and hands 'to the canopy of Heaven' and chant passages from the Qur'an. The procession was repeated for three days and was conducted with 'great propriety, although a multitude of people followed them'. The 'Jubilee' was said to have been held in honour of Muhammad's ascension into Paradise.[12] The *London City Mission Magazine* (*LCMM*) gives more detailed, although less sympathetic, descriptions of the *Muharram* commemorating the martyrdom of Husayn ibn Ali. In one account the author notes that about 400 men took part in the activities.[13] Burials could also command attention: one lascar burial procession attracted 'an immense concourse of persons', despite bad weather.[14] A sketch of another shows a crowd in attendance.[15]

The significance of these public events should not be underestimated, for previous generations had seen processions that communicated a radically different understanding of the relationship between Islam and Englishness. During the eighteenth century, freed Barbary captives, dressed in clothing acquired during time spent in Northern Africa, attracted the attention of crowds on their way to St Paul's Cathedral, where they were congratulated on their return to '"English air, and English liberty"', and reminded of the importance of their allegiance to the Government. They even saluted the king during the final stage of the ceremony.[16] A service conducted in the 'Christian capital of a godly nation' was meant to exorcise recent Islamic influences and re-establish previous loyalties.[17] These ceremonies left little room for interpretation, and the ordinary observer would have left them assured that Islam did not belong in England. In the nineteenth century, however, individuals wearing clothing that would have appeared to be as foreign to onlookers as would those of the Barbary captives a generation or two earlier, walked, marched and danced through the streets making known their Islamic faith. They did not go through a process of transformation; English air did not change their beliefs. They presented their religion as universal, belonging in England as much as anywhere else in the world.

Some lascars tried to teach people in England about their faith and convert them to Islam. Christian missionaries describe listening to Muslim prayers and beliefs, and engaging in Muslim–Christian theological discussions. One LCM missionary referred to the man who taught him Hindustani, or Urdu, and had written a book sympathetic to Islam as one of the many 'pseudo-reformers' from the East who attempted to convert English people. He called their doctrine 'Islamo-Christianity' presumably because Muslim missionaries appealed to English Christians by stressing the similarities between the two religions or the idea that Islam is an extension of Christianity, with Muhammad as the last of the prophets bringing divine revelation to mankind.[18]

This increasing Muslim presence in England was a part of the larger trend of immigration in the nineteenth century. During this period the composition of English society and the landscape of its urban areas changed dramatically.[19] The English, especially English liberals, took pride in the idea that they lived in a land of tolerance, and from the mid-nineteenth century until the passing of the Aliens Act of 1905 no law existed to keep immigrants or refugees out of the country.[20]

While the lascars and ayahs may have been tolerated, the missionaries and other middle-class Victorians who came into contact with them did not consider them to be English, not only because they had been born outside of the country, but ironically because their circumstances and lifestyles resembled those of other English people who seemed to threaten the social order and were therefore considered outsiders existing beyond the pale of the true English nation. Ayahs and lascars were a part of the urban, migratory, labouring poor who had not embraced Christianity. For contemporary reformers these people were an 'alien nation' living in the heart of the city in areas that were 'unexplored', 'uncivilised' and even 'colonial'. Similarly, home missionaries described a 'heathenism' in their midst '"as dense as any in Polynesia or Central Africa"'. Like a tent community of Arabs, to which John Ruskin likened them, the urban poor presented the 'threat of nomadism', a disruptive element that undermined the stability of society.[21]

Like the underclass in general, lascars were thought to inhabit spaces that existed in England physically but were removed from it culturally. LCM missionaries described 'Oriental' enclaves of poverty and despair where vice of various forms provided the only relief or temporary escape. For example, one contemporary book, entitled *The East in the West*, by Joseph Salter, an LCM missionary, includes chapter titles such as 'Plague Spots of Oriental Vice', 'Chinese Opium Dens', and 'Heathenism in the Inner Radius'; he even refers to 'colonies' within London and other cities. Thus while the presence of Muslim immigrants in England could, in theory, offer a challenge to the idea of an English culture that did not include Islam, they instead came to symbolise the *alterity* imposed on the urban poor.

How lascars and ayahs were perceived in England had much to do with class tensions and conflict. By labelling the un-Christainised poor as no better, and often as even worse, than the 'uncivilised heathens' of the Empire, middle-class reformers and missionaries avoided the possibility of a cross-class alliance. They divested charity work of its radical potential and instead turned it into a means of reinforcing social divisions and the status quo. Working-class radicals, on the other hand, rejected this discourse sometimes by advocating universal equality, but often by expressing outrage that they, as English people, were being compared to foreign races.[22] They promoted a definition of Englishness which included labourers of all kinds but excluded those from elsewhere in the Empire on the basis of race. This political strategy did not challenge the importance of hierarchy and English superiority, ideas central to the British imperial system both in England and abroad, but shifted the dividing line which separated the nation from the rest of the world.

Lascars and ayahs often found themselves caught between reformers who wanted to change their lifestyles and beliefs and English workers who considered them outsiders and feared that associating with them would undermine their own claims to Englishness and their position within the nation state. Because competing class-based constructions of the nation which informed individual identities and aspirations were defined through or in contrast to imperial subjects and spaces, they rested on the assumption that these immigrants could not be a part of it. Lascars and ayahs, then, were understood in terms of empire not only because of their origins, but also, and perhaps more importantly, because of the role of imperial politics within the metropole. As a result of their precarious circumstances, any given situation, even a verbal exchange on the street, could define them through signifiers of difference, so that similarities and common interests between these Muslims and non-Muslims would seem less important than ideas about what separated them. Thus to be a Muslim lascar or ayah in England during the late nineteenth century was to occupy the uncertain position of sometimes being regarded as a part of society and other times being excluded from it and encountering hostility.[23]

Because the concept of English national identity created through these competing class interests was intimately linked with contemporary gender politics, a lascar could not become English by living with or even marrying an English woman.[24] For the women with whom they associated were already a part of the social fabric in the *uncivilised* or poor areas of the city and were, therefore, considered by the majority not to be truly English. In addition, it was assumed generally that a female's position in society was determined by the men in her life, so that while the women could be Orientalised by lascars, lascars could not be Anglicised by their new companions. Their names reflect this idea: for example, Sarah Graham became 'Lascar Sally' because of her association with lascars 'whose language and habits she had acquired'. Similarly, others were given names such as 'Canton Kitty', 'Chinese Emma' and 'Calcutta Louisa'.[25]

Because Muslims found themselves excluded from the English nation, their position can best be understood through the concept of *ethnicity*. I use this term to refer not to a unified, self-conscious, political position,[26] but rather in this case, to the marginalisation experienced by diverse individuals with unique histories and distinct identities. Such was the situation for Muslims living in England during this period when their area of origin, their language and even their particular version or understanding of Islam all divided them. For example, *Ahmadi* Muslims, such as Kwaja Kamel-ud-Din, a missionary who established a base outside of London in the early twentieth century, were rejected by many Sunni Muslims because of the formers' belief in prophets after Muhammad.[27] Ethnicity is, therefore, necessarily multi-faceted and multidimensional, and is to be understood in a way that engages with rather than suppresses difference. For the myth of a unified immigrant population only reinforces the equally erroneous belief in a unified English nation, and a central purpose of this book is to examine the ways in which these types of collective identity developed not only despite but through internal conflicts and tensions, as well as how they were created by the actions of individuals with various perspectives, backgrounds and circumstances.

Given their shared experiences of exclusion and marginalisation, it is not surprising that Muslims who may have had little in common before arriving in England soon formed bonds and associations with one another. They established communities that revolved around the *zawiya*, run by a local sheikh, which provided a place for the *salat*, or daily prayer, *'eīd* celebrations and care of the sick, as well as facilities for marriage and burial ceremonies.[28] The sheikhs taught the principles of Islam to the English wives and children of Muslim men; and as they had the trust of these immigrants, they also became their bankers and were able to provide for the unemployed with zawiya funds.[29]

Some Muslim immigrants did not remain in any one city or town but rather travelled throughout Britain following opportunities for temporary work as they became available. Those who had to leave their new families in order to find seasonal employment tended to confine their trips to the summer months, sending cash home periodically.[30] One missionary called them the 'Bedouins of England', explaining that 'these disciples of the prophet of Mecca' would 'wander from Plymouth to Ben Lomond, and from Aberdeen to Hastings' and 'thread their way among the mountains of Wales'. Provincial towns and autumn retreats were also favourite spots. Even the most seemingly isolated immigrants were connected to a larger community: as one LCM missionary stated, the 'Asiatics' of London and the provincial towns were like the 'links of a long chain; if one link is found, the others soon come in view'.[31]

As this discussion has shown, the Muslim lascar and ayah immigrants of the late nineteenth century were not so much a foreign element, suddenly appearing in an otherwise unified English society, as they were part of a British imperial culture which existed within England as well as in the colonies or occupied territories. Because competing class-based English identities were already defined in relation to the Empire, new immigrants found themselves in the awkward position of being both symbolically in the middle of domestic political conflict yet simultaneously marginalised by opposing class interests. While they were able to represent themselves, their faith and their place in English society via public ceremony, individual relationships and the formation of new communities, they still had to operate within an imperial system characterised by as many constraints as there were opportunities.

William Henry Quilliam and his community of Muslim converts in Liverpool

Not all Muslims living in England during the late nineteenth century came from abroad. William Henry Quilliam, a solicitor and 'a genuine DickySam', or native of Liverpool, led a group of recently converted English Muslims in that city. Before focusing on Quilliam and his followers, however, I wish to discuss briefly Liverpool itself. For Muslim communities in late nineteenth-century England tended to exist either in or in close proximity to urban and commercial areas, and certain characteristics which were especially pronounced in Liverpool during this period, such as rapid growth, immigration and contact with the Empire, created an environment which allowed a small number of people to identify with a religion that usually was seen as foreign to the nation. Liverpool was a centre of commerce, its famous docks forming a continuous line of sea wall for 6 miles.[32] It surpassed all other English ports in terms of foreign trade, particularly with Africa and the East in general.[33] In fact, by mid-century, by any criteria, Liverpool was England's 'first port of the empire'.[34]

The commercial connections that linked Egypt and India to Liverpool were especially important. Indian goods via Egypt and Egyptian staples such as cotton entered England through that port.[35] The town received Egyptian visitors, notably Ibrahim Pasha, known by the 'familiar appellation' or the Anglicised version of his name, Abraham Parker. In 1845 he travelled to Liverpool, where he was popular for his 'sagacious appreciation of English commerce', being met by cheering crowds and received with 'all due honour'. Similarly in 1862 Muhammad Said, the viceroy of Egypt, spent three days in Liverpool, where he was entertained by the mayor and addressed by 'commercial bodies'. Not only distinguished Egyptian travellers, but even the welfare of ordinary people living in India could arouse concern among Liverpudlians, and in 1860 a public meeting was held in the town hall by the mayor to raise funds for victims of famine in India's north-west provinces.[36] For many residents of Liverpool, a relationship with the people of India and Egypt was seen as positive, mutually beneficial, and a source of wealth and prosperity. For a small group, however, respect for and appreciation of Muslims living in the East went beyond practical and economic interests, and included adopting their religious traditions and beliefs.

In addition to trade, immigration – a trend that had an especially profound impact on the Liverpool area – exposed residents to foreign influences. The town grew rapidly during the nineteenth century, with its boundaries continually expanding in order to accommodate increasing numbers of people from the English countryside and throughout the Empire, eventually becoming a city in 1881. Irish and Chinese immigrants contributed to the city's distinctive ethnic makeup, and Liverpool had a higher concentration of people from those parts of the world than any other city or town in the country.[37] As a result of these changes, Liverpudlians had become used to encountering a certain amount of difference in their society, either because they were immigrants from elsewhere and themselves had to adapt to new circumstances or because frequently they came into contact with newcomers whose appearance, values, religion or behaviour seemed different from their own.

Because of immigration and trade, and the phenomenal growth that resulted from both, Liverpool was a city in constant motion – motion of people, products and ideas. Even the architecture of the city, from the dockyards to the railroads, served as a continual reminder of the new capacity to 'distribute with great rapidity an ever-increasing quantity of bodies and goods, and to redistribute the very spaces of the city itself: to imperialise the city, and to urbanise the countryside'.[38] In this imperial *entrepôt* characterised by incessant flux, W. H. Quilliam succeeded in manipulating the already unstable boundaries that divided the English nation from the rest of the world in order to lead a community of newly converted English Muslims.

William Henry Quilliam was a direct descendent of Captain John Quilliam, RN, an officer who distinguished himself in the battle of Trafalgar and was one of the pallbearers at the funeral of Lord Horatio Nelson.[39] W. H. Quilliam was educated in Liverpool and King William's College, Isle of Man.[40] He began working as a solicitor in 1878 and eventually had the largest advocacy practice in the north of England one article noting that his 'extensive legal practice' was well known.[41] He had associated with Wesleyans, Unitarians and Deists before visiting Morocco and Algeria in 1882 and embracing Islam.[42]

Figure 3 shows Quilliam in what was known as Eastern, or Islamic, dress; he also wore the 'distinguishing Fez of the Mahommedan Races' at consular gatherings in order to make his faith conspicuous.[43] This behaviour was tolerated by non-Muslims in England in part because of the Orientalist tradition of appearing as a Muslim from the East: English diplomats, travellers, journalists, businessmen and others who had reason to travel or live in any part of the East, from the Ottoman Empire to India, often would have their portraits painted in the clothing of the area where they had stayed.[44]

The significance of this practice changed over time. From the Renaissance through the seventeenth century, Islam's appeal for the English had much to do with the power of the Ottomans: it was the 'allure of an empire' that led the Englishman to change his 'hat into a turban – with all the symbolism of strength associated with the Islamic headdress'.[45] With the decline of Ottoman power in the eighteenth and nineteenth centuries, to assume a Muslim appearance became fashionable or eccentric. Lady Mary Wortley Montagu made harem attire *chic* in England after her return from Turkey. Similarly, during his days as a London dandy Benjamin Disraeli was fond both of dressing extravagantly and of prefacing his remarks at social gatherings with the statement 'Allah is great', in part to remind guests that recently he had taken a grand tour which included Turkey and Egypt.[46] Imitating the Muslim from the East had the effect of domesticating the foreign so that it would seem less threatening.[47]

Because of his attire, Quilliam appeared more like an eccentric English Orientalist gentleman than an outsider, and even his background

3 Photograph of William Henry Quilliam in 'Eastern Dress' from a nineteenth-century newspaper clipping.

fitted this role: he was a middle- or upper-middle-class English man who had travelled to the East and studied Arabic. Ironically, the mimics who did the work of empire by appropriating and neutralising the power of those with different customs and traditions also helped to make Quilliam's behaviour acceptable, and in doing so unintentionally contributed to the establishment of Islam in England.

Quilliam's status as a British subject, a Muslim and a man of influence in England allowed him to establish various connections abroad. In 1889, the sultan of the Ottoman Empire invited him to visit Istanbul and made him the 'sheikh-ul-Islam of the British Isles' and the 'Ottoman consul for the Isle of Man', and his sons too received honours. In 1893, the sultan of Morocco gave him the respected title of *'alim*, along with appropriate vestments. The *amir* of Afghanistan donated £2,500 to him and his community. Finally, the *shah* of Persia visited Quilliam in Liverpool, where he presented him with a diamond and pearl ornament and bestowed on him the title of 'Persian Consul for Liverpool'.[48] Through his newfound faith, Quilliam created a network of political alliances for himself and his followers which transcended the commonly accepted boundaries meant to distinguish the English nation from the Islamic world.

Quilliam used the money donated by the amir of Afghanistan to improve the Liverpool Muslim Institute and make plans for additional building work. The Institute included a newly constructed lecture hall and a mosque on the ground floor, where the community would gather for prayers on Fridays.[49] Meetings were held on Sundays for those who had converted to Islam from Christianity and were used to Sunday services, but care was taken to ensure that the proceedings were 'purely Islamic in word and spirit'.[50] By 1896, plans to construct an elaborate mosque that would accommodate approximately 1,500 worshippers were progressing. This 'Moslem Cathedral' would attract 'holy shrine votaries from the far East', and for that reason a *khan*, or caravansary, would be built as well. Included in the plan were a library, a small museum and a printing office for the publication and dissemination of Muslim materials.[51] Despite preparations made by the architect and the community in general, no such mosque was built. Perhaps after Quilliam's mysterious disappearance in 1908, his followers lacked the connections and resources to continue the project.[52]

The creation of a community of Muslim converts in the Liverpool area resulted primarily from the efforts of Quilliam himself. After embracing Islam, he converted his family to the faith and established the weekly publication the *Crescent*, the organ of the newly founded British Muslim Association. In addition to speaking at the Institute and elsewhere in Liverpool, Quilliam travelled to major cities throughout

Britain to deliver lectures on Islam;[53] he also published pamphlets on the topic and worked to establish a Medina Home for Outcast Children to provide care and a Muslim education to orphans and children in need.[54] Finally, he used his connections with Manx societies, temperance organisations and the Liverpool Geological Society, of which he was vice-president, to further the cause.

Quilliam and the members of his community had to find ways of reconciling their new faith with English culture and a sense of national identity. One approach was to focus on common values and beliefs. Because Islam forbids the consumption of alcohol, temperance societies proved to be an especially effective source for Quilliam's converts. During his lectures on total abstinence from alcohol he would refer to Islam, drawing 'public attention to the matter' and initiating 'inquiry upon the subject'. He lectured on temperance at the Vernon Temperance Hall and the Liverpool Muslim Institute, and he won his first as well as his one hundred and seventy-first convert to Islam through this method.[55]

In his pamphlet *Fanatics and Fanaticism* Quilliam maintains that temperance advocates should be proud to be called 'fanatics' because great reformers before them, both abolitionists and the followers of Muhammad, had been called the same. While British Government officials and members of the BFASS may have understood and depicted the spread of Islam and the abolition of slavery as necessarily in conflict, Quilliam argued that these movements are perfectly compatible moral crusades, with much in common. He countered the dominant imperialist discourse by explaining that Islam 'almost abolished slavery' by allowing it only as an alternative to killing prisoners of war, requiring the fair treatment of slaves and rewarding those who free them. He went on to argue that Islam is the most liberating system because it prohibits intoxicants and the 'drink curse is a worse slavery than that which Clarkson and Wilberforce abolished. It is a slavery of the passions – of the soul; the drunkard is a greater slave than the poor Negro.'[56] According to Quilliam, Islam is noble and elevating, and no more foreign to England than indigenous reform movements, which, while initially opposed by most, eventually triumphed, won popular support and ultimately contributed to the advancement of civilisation. Such was the case for abolition, and the temperance audience to whom the pamphlet is addressed hoped that their movement would yield the same results.

Quilliam was not alone in drawing attention to the Muslim prohibition of alcohol or associating it with the goals of English temperance reformers. Even Christian writers and missionaries commented on this issue. One explained that because of Islam, Egyptian society did not have 'drunkenness' for a 'national vice' as England did. She went on to say that while missionaries try to encourage sobriety among their converts, they regret that total abstinence is not a tenet of Christianity.[57] Similarly in 1887, in a Church of England Temperance Society meeting, supporters raised the concern that British Christians were corrupting the Muslims and Hindus of India by bringing them alcohol when they had been sober beforehand.[58] The temperance reformer James Buckingham, who collaborated with Thomas Cook to arrange trips to the Middle East for English people, promoted the cause in northern England by praising the sobriety of Muslim countries where '"on nothing stronger than milk and sherbet, the athletes of Persia and wrestlers of upper Hindoostan excelled"'. Cook, whose tours were responsible for bringing thousands of middle-class English people to Egypt, Palestine and Jerusalem during the late nineteenth century, began work in the tourism industry by arranging trips to Liverpool and London for Midlands' labourers so that they could attend temperance society meetings and find entertainment that did not involve drinking.[59]

The temperance movement became both a vehicle through which converts found Islam as well as a way to legitimise or justify this religion in terms culturally available to the English. Temperance had begun in the 1830s with clergymen and middle-class reformers, but grew to include members and leaders from the working classes as well. By the end of the nineteenth century, it had become well known, with thousands of supporters throughout England. Temperance workers presented memorials, established vigilance committees, agitated for stricter licensing laws and publicised the issue generally. Their efforts were associated with other reforming causes of the time such as the campaign for the improvement of working conditions or public education.[60] While historical actors discussed in previous chapters regarded the Islamic world as in dire need of reform, through the temperance movement English Muslims presented their faith as a solution to England's problems and societal ills and as compatible with the Victorian impulse to improve.

Quilliam's Liverpool was a centre of temperance activity, in part because the conditions that inspired agitation were especially pronounced in that city:[61] for temperance was meant to transform the misery and dependence of the urban poor into self-help and respectability, and this area had a disproportionate share of poverty.[62] Those attracted to the cause sought to alleviate the physical and psychological dislocation that accompanied immigration and industrialisation.[63] The supporters of temperance in Liverpool who converted to Islam found in this religion many of the same qualities that drew them to the movement in the first place: a community or supportive environment;

a vision of a reformed society; and the avoidance of strong drink. Islam's complete prohibition on alcohol must have been especially attractive to teetotallers, or those who called for total abstinence from alcohol.

In addition to temperance organisations, Quilliam was involved in the Liverpool Manx Society, a group that encouraged interest in the Isle of Man, where both of his parents were born. Through his activities he created a Manx–British–Muslim identity, and he understood these three aspects of himself as entirely compatible. For example, when speaking about temperance and Islam, he might include a Manx legend or proverb;[64] also, he had 'A Sample of Manx Folklore' printed in the *Islamic World*, and the *Crescent* published one of his articles on the Isle of Man. In a lecture given to the Liverpool Manx Society, Quilliam explained that while Manxmen should be proud of their island and seek to understand its history and legends, this interest should not threaten loyalty to the imperial State since Manx people always have had respect for their sovereigns. The meeting was concluded with the British national anthem. Because Quilliam refused to separate his Manx from his Muslim identity, he succeeded in presenting Islam to those interested in Manx culture and did so without challenging an allegiance to Great Britain.

Despite Quilliam's involvement in Manx organisations, his words and actions had much to do with contemporary understandings of Englishness. He lived and worked in England, as did most of his followers and the thousands more he tried to convert. He presented his faith in ways that would help English people reconcile Islam with the society and culture in which they lived, as well as with whatever additional ethnic identities they had. Furthermore, he received honours and gifts from foreign leaders because he was regarded as a respectable Englishman and, as such, an individual assumed to have considerable influence in that country – neither Muslim immigrants nor the British–Muslim statesmen from elsewhere in the Empire who also lived in England during that time received the same attention.

Quilliam's ability to win converts also resulted from his presentation of Islam as a reasonable religion. As in his appeals to temperance workers, he focused on a value that already existed in English society to bridge what many saw as a great cultural divide between the English nation and that religious and social system, repeatedly stressing the reasonable nature of Islam in his writings and speeches. Quilliam delivered a series of lectures for 'the consideration of all thoughtful persons', one of them entitled 'The Reasonableness of a Belief in Immortality'.[65] He often compared Islam favourably with Christianity in this respect, at one point calling the crucifixion of Christ a 'pathetic story' not based on evidence but used solely to appeal to the emotions.[66] He believed that the influence of Buddhism contributed to the mystical, or what he considered illogical, nature of Christianity.[67] Finally, he used the findings of contemporary archaeologists, anthropologists, geologists and historians to argue that, unlike those of other faiths, Islamic beliefs about human history and past civilisations were supported by scientific evidence.[68]

Quilliam's strategy of presenting Islam as a reasonable religion was employed later by other Muslims in England. As one writer for the *Islamic Review* states: 'We have no missions, no "revivals", no pomp or splendour or beautiful music to play on your emotions ... we appeal to your logic – your reason'.[69] Quilliam and others adopted an approach that seemed to provide an alternative to those disillusioned with the established Church but also uncomfortable with the open expression of spirituality that could be found in evangelical or Methodist services. They also tried to associate their faith with the scientific method and the increasing respect enjoyed by men of science in England during and after the Victorian period.

Quilliam sought to educate the English public about the basic tenets of the faith and its social virtues, many of which also were valued by English Christians and English people in general. In one article, written for the *Liverpool Review* in order to counter the 'bigotry' and 'ignorance' of the 'British mind' on the subject of Islam, Quilliam relates Muslim beliefs regarding the prophets and the compassion and justice of God, also discussing the emphasis that Islam places on charity, justice and control of the passions.[70]

In addition to certain values, belief systems – particularly Unitarianism and Deism – could serve to foster sympathy for Islam in England. Unitarianism proclaimed the unity of God and the humanity of Christ, a doctrine which challenged Trinitarianism, or the belief in the holy trinity. Similarly, the oneness of God is a fundamental tenet of Islam. The Muslim who testifies to the unity of God performs *tawhid*, while anyone who attributes partners to God is called *mushrik* and considered no better than an idolater or a polytheist. In addition, both Unitarianism and Deism place a high value on human reason, and when reason is elevated to the degree that it becomes a legitimate authority superior to that of the established Church and even of scripture which is examined critically, the individual becomes free to explore a variety of belief systems, weighing the pros and cons of each. Quilliam had associated with both Unitarians and Deists before becoming a Muslim and, as I have said, used arguments about the reasonableness of Islam in order to convince others to convert.[71]

Deism and Unitarianism, like rapid immigration, increased contact with the Empire, and the rise of the temperance movement provided cultural windows or opportunities for people living in England to sympathise with Islam and understand it as consistent with their culture and values, whether they identified strongly with Englishness or were involved in the process of assimilating another ethnic identity – Manx in Quilliam's case – with their roles in English society.[72] The ability to do so crossed both class and gender boundaries: while Quilliam came from a middle- or upper-middle-class background, other Muslims in the community were described as 'working men', and his mother Harriet, along with 'a number of spinsters and widows', converted to the faith.[73] The fact that a relatively small number of Liverpudlians were able to find ways of reconciling their national identities and previous beliefs with conversion to Islam, while most English people did not even make the attempt, testifies to the importance of agency and affirms that culture, or systems of meaning, are actively constructed by individuals as opposed to passively accepted. Certainly, the members of Quilliam's community could have chosen to regard people whose practices and religious traditions differed from their own with suspicion or even hatred, as did many in Liverpool during the nineteenth century.[74]

Quilliam maintained that Islam not only had a place in English society but would even improve it, and while he was criticised by some his conversion was accepted generally. He continued to be treated with respect as long as he lived in the Liverpool area. At least four Liverpool publications presented Quilliam's religious activities in a positive or a neutral light.[75] Article titles such as 'Men Who Are Talked About' and 'Men You Know' suggest his status as a public figure; another article similarly refers to his role in the 'Islamic movement in England' as 'too well-known to need any comment'.[76] He was even praised by one contemporary who referred to him by the affectionate title of '"our Mahomedan solicitor"' and included him in *Liverpool's Legion of Honour*.[77]

Despite his successes in creating a place for Islam in England and presenting the faith as elevating to that society, imperial politics both at home and abroad as well as the situational nature of identity prevented him from reconciling Islam and Englishness in all circumstances. Whenever he perceived a conflict, his religious identity took primacy over his loyalty to the British Empire: for example, in 1896 he issued a proclamation asking the Egyptian soldiers who were preparing for the re-conquest of the Sudan to refuse to take up arms against their Muslim brethren.[78] He also promoted the idea that he and his followers were superior to English people who had not converted to Islam. He criticised English missionaries abroad and Christianity in general. Furthermore, even though he tried to spread his religion to the smaller towns and the countryside, he succeeded only in establishing a Muslim community in a city considered by many contemporaries to be more a part of the Empire than a part of England due to poverty, immigration, rapid growth and extensive commercial connections.

Sayyid Amir Ali and the British Muslims of the Raj

In addition to recent converts, lascars and ayahs, Islam was practised in England during the late nineteenth century by men who journeyed there for the purpose of furthering their education or careers. Muslim students, men of business and other professionals had visited London since the beginning of British rule in the East. Many would return to their homelands eventually, but some stayed to practise law or medicine or to involve themselves in the politics of the Raj.[79] As one contemporary LCM missionary explained, England's 'unique position' in the world as a result of imperialism was attracting more visitors from Africa and the East than ever before, including not only lascars and noblemen but 'Mahommedan gentlemen' who hoped to 'improve themselves in their positions or professions'. He later noted the arrival of 'wealthy merchants . . . the expositors of Mohammedan law and faith' and young men from the East who studied for the Civil Service, at the Inns of Court, or at the medical schools, and who 'form an attractive element in London life'.[80]

One of the best-known Muslim gentlemen from the East who resided in England during the late nineteenth century was the writer and statesman Sayyid Amir Ali. Born in India and educated in England, Amir Ali served as a barrister, professor of Islamic law, and judge in the Bengal High Court. He was the first Indian to be appointed a member of the Privy Council and its judicial committee. Amir Ali dedicated his life to representing Muslim interests in the British Empire, organising the Central National Mohammedan Association in 1877 with branches throughout India; the London branch of the All-India Muslim League, founded in 1908; and the British Red Crescent Society, the Muslim counterpart to the Red Cross. His support contributed to the establishment of a mosque in Woking, England, and he worked to erect one in London as well. Through his career and activities, he self-consciously promoted a British–Muslim identity, perhaps best symbolised by swearing on the Qur'an the oath required to become privy councillor. Eventually England became his home, and after retirement he and his wife lived on an estate outside of London.[81]

Amir Ali was a prolific writer who sought to educate the English public about Islam and present it in a positive light as a system of central importance to the British Empire which was compatible with English values. Thus, he began his book *Islamic History and Culture* by noting that Muhammad 'is regarded with veneration by forty millions of Her Majesty's subjects in the East'.[82] He defended the faith in 'Islam and its Critics' in which he addresses slavery, an issue of no small importance in the creation of English national identities in relation to Islam and imperial politics. He noted that Christian leaders had not opposed slavery until recently, and that Muhammad required masters to provide for their slaves and refrain from treating them cruelly; moreover, Islam does not allow the separation of mother and child, husband and wife or brother and brother. He continued by relating that the prophet repeatedly encouraged the liberation of slaves and even declared the emancipation of a slave to be 'the greatest act of virtue'. From this evidence Amir Ali argued that Islam not only discouraged but actually condemned slavery.[83]

In a similar writing Amir Ali adopts the language of the Enlightenment and associates it with his own religion, as did English Christian abolitionists before him. After stating the importance of liberty, equality and universal brotherhood, he explained that Muslims must now 'show the falseness of the aspersions cast on the memory of the great and noble Prophet, by proclaiming in explicit terms that slavery is reprobated by their faith and discountenanced by their code'. He called on humanity to condemn servitude in general regardless of 'the shape or under whatever denomination it may be disguised'.[84] He felt that the belief in the essential immorality of slavery, which existed as implicit knowledge in English society and played an integral role in the shaping of English national identities during the nineteenth century, was not unique to the English, but was in the true spirit of Islam itself. Thus the very ideas so often used to distinguish English people from Muslims should instead serve as a common bond, promoting mutual identification and collaboration.

Amir Ali also challenged an idea that remained at the heart of the imperialist ideology informing anti-slavery activity in Egypt, that Muslim gender roles oppress women, while those of the English liberate them. In 'The Real Status of Women in Islam' he discusses the rights of the Muslim woman. She may, for example, demand a separation from her husband on the grounds of 'ill usage' or 'want of proper maintenance'; and he maintained that Muhammad practically forbade polygamy by requiring that a man treat his wives equally, noting that 95–8 per cent of Muslim men were monogamous. As for the seclusion of women, Amir Ali explains that while the prophet recommended that their privacy be protected, he never intended to inhibit their freedom: for Muhammad's wife 'Aisha commanded troops at the battle of Camel, and his daughter Fatima gave sermons and took part in discussions regarding the succession of the caliphate. His overall argument is that historically the status of women in the Islamic world had been higher than in Christendom, and to further support this contention he gave examples of unjust treatment of women in Europe, from the early Church fathers who portrayed them as evil temptresses to the daily reports of brutalities inflicted on them by 'professed Christians'.[85]

In England, Amir Ali was considered an authority on Islam and was read by both scholars and a general audience. He published over 15 books in English on the religion and contemporary political issues relating to areas of the Islamic world, and at least 9 of his letters to the editor appeared in *The Times*. Even those who did not share his views would cite him.[86] Discussion of Amir Ali's writings regarding polygamy and slavery in Islam can be found among BFASS papers; in fact, one BFASS supporter suggested using Amir Ali's arguments to persuade Muslim authorities in Egypt to consent to the abolition of the legal status of slavery.[87] Even British officials in Egypt read his work: Sir Evelyn Baring, Her Britannic Majesty's consul-general and agent in Egypt (discussed at length in chapter two of this book) refers to him as '"a well-known Indian Mahommedan lawyer"' and quotes from his *The Personal Law of the Muhammadans*, published in London in 1880, in his dispatch to Earl Granville, the Foreign Secretary.[88]

Amir Ali appealed to English people by trading on the cachet of Britain as the premier imperial power in order to claim a place for his religion and for Muslims in English society. For example, he promoted efforts to establish a mosque in London by explaining that it was necessary to have one 'worthy of the position of Islam as a world religion in the metropolis of Great Britain'.[89] He adopted the dominant imperialist discourse and used it as a source of power. However, the political potential of this strategy was limited in that it in no way challenged English hegemony within the British imperial system or the exclusion of Muslims from the English nation. For he claimed a British–Muslim, not an English–Muslim, identity. His vision of empire did not address directly the role and status of other Britons such as the Irish, Welsh and Scots, but it assumed that the London area remained the core, with a vast periphery comprised of many nations and peoples from the British Isles to the Far East.

Sayyid Amir Ali successfully integrated his identity as a Muslim with his loyalty to the British Empire and his activities in England. He organised Muslim groups in both that country and India, and in his daily life practices such as regular prayer and work for the British Government, for example, went hand in hand. His unique position in the imperial political system as well as his own creative and intellectual resources allowed him to present a persona that crossed commonly accepted cultural boundaries. British Muslims like Amir Ali who claimed a place for themselves and their faith in England called into question assumptions about essential differences between that country and the rest of the Empire

Like Amir Ali, others from the Indian subcontinent had been involved in efforts to foster Anglo-Muslim unity in that part of the world.[90] A key figure in this movement was Sayyid Ahmad Khan, whose writings sought to convince a Muslim readership that Western thought was not anti-Islamic and that the teachings of Islam had much in common with Victorian liberal ideas about progress. Sayyid Ahmad Khan founded a translation society in order to introduce European sciences to educated Muslims. In addition, with the assistance of the British administration and local Muslim princes, he worked to establish the Muhammadan Anglo-Oriental College in the district town of Aligarh, near Delhi, in 1875 in order to produce a class of leaders who would have a solid understanding of both Western and Islamic traditions, feel comfortable in England and India, and consider themselves leaders in the Raj as their predecessors had been in the courts of the Mughal Empire.[91]

There were others who attempted to bridge this gap, such as 'Abd al-Latif, who founded the Muhammadan Literary and Scientific Society of Calcutta in 1863 which encouraged the study of Western sciences, and Chiragh Ali, who proclaimed British India to be neither the abode of Islam, *dar al-Islam*, nor that of war, *dar al-harb*, but rather a place of security or protection, *dar al-aman* or *dar al-dhimma*.[92] Muslims who supported the Raj understood it as a government that would allow them to protect their interests by creating a niche for themselves in political life and was preferable to Hindu rule.[93]

Muslims loyal to the British Empire found ways to communicate their position to an English audience. In fact, the Moslem Patriotic League dedicated itself to this cause. At one of its regular gatherings held at the Oriental Institute in Woking, England, the chairman remarked that while Christian nations were 'hurling denunciations against England . . . Moslem nations . . . were offering prayers and thanksgiving in their mosques for the triumph of this country in South Africa'.[94] One British Muslim wrote to the editor of *The Times* testifying to the patriotism among the followers of Muhammad and defying anyone to challenge his loyalty or the loyalty of his family to the British Government in India.[95]

Orientalist approaches

British–Indian as well as other Muslims found a link to England in the form of an Oriental Institute, established in 1884, just outside London in Woking, by Dr. Gottlieb William Leitner.[96] The Institute was affiliated with Punjab University and awarded degrees in its name. It focused on language, culture and history both for those from the 'Orient' wishing to live or travel in Europe and for Europeans who planned to do the same in the East. Most of its students had some connection to the British imperial mission. Attached to the Institute was an Oriental Museum, which Leitner personally supplied with rare books, manuscripts, works of art and antiquities from Egypt to Central Asia and India.[97] The school was known also as the Oriental Nobility Institute, so named because it was intended to educate gentlemen, or those of high caste or birth. Unlike the ayahs and lascars, who found themselves caught in the middle of English class conflict – and often victimised or marginalised as a result – Leitner capitalised on class divisions in an attempt to create a privileged position for his colleagues and students in England.

The Institute also served as a research centre helping scholars to reach a professional audience in England and throughout the British Empire. It published several of Leitner's books as well as journals in Arabic and Sanskrit.[98] Leitner was well-known in the field of Orientalist studies: in addition to his articles, he produced over twenty publications related to his travels in the East, foreign languages, and Islam. Beginning in 1886 and continuing until 1952, the Oriental Institute published a journal; it appeared under various titles, though I refer to it as the *Imperial and Asiatic Quarterly Review and Oriental and Colonial Record (IAQR)*. It was read by those affiliated to the Institute and scholars in the field; it was consulted also by members of the BFASS and was not unknown to the general public.[99]

Most of its articles during the early years focused on the East broadly defined: foreign relations issues, royal personages, and cultural and historical studies.[100] Through this publication scholars who were either Muslims themselves or were sympathetic to the faith challenged the dominant discourse in England regarding Islam. They taught their audience about the religion and presented it in a positive light in articles with such titles as 'The Moslim Call to Prayer' and 'Toleration in Islam';[101] similarly, 'The Muharram' described the purpose and meaning of the processions seen in the streets of London.[102] One article argued that the play *Mahomet* should be banned in England because the content was hostile to Muslims and because the act of portraying the prophet on stage is blasphemous.[103] Another defended the Ottoman Empire against Western criticism by explaining that Turkish society is neither corrupt nor in a state of decay, but rather was in a period of 'transition and development'.[104]

One writer for this journal, Rafi-ud-Din Ahmad, challenged an assumption that remained at the heart of the gendered politics of empire, both at home and abroad, that the woman under Islamic law was oppressed compared to the English woman. To make his argument he contrasts the legal position of women in England during the first half of the nineteenth century to that of Muslim women since the time of Muhammad's revelation. He focuses first on property rights, noting that unlike the married English woman the Muslim wife may own property, enter into legal contracts and demand a marriage dower from her husband; in addition, she is entitled to a certain share of her husband's estate on his death as well as maintenance while he is living. Unlike the woman under English law she may, in certain circumstances, divorce her husband and still receive custody of her young children and financial support from him.[105]

Ahmad turned the discourse of the anti-slavery workers against the British Government by arguing that it was the English woman rather than the Muslim who truly was enslaved. He employed the same types of example that English feminists were using to illustrate the need for reform. He referred to the famous Caroline Norton affair, in which Mrs Norton's husband legally claimed the profits from her book sales, and stated: 'surely one of the principal tokens of slavery is, that the slave has to work for the benefit of another ... and that the fruits of his exertions can be taken forcibly with the sanction of the law to enrich another'. He then related the story of a woman who had been injured seriously in a railway accident but legally could not sue the railway company for damages because her husband had deserted her, and she had no one to represent her interests in court. He stated that while a Muslim woman may sue her debtors and even her husband, the English wife needed her husband's consent, just like the 'slave' in ancient Rome who legally had 'no *persona*'.[106] Ahmad attended a meeting in London on the topic of the English woman's relationship to the Church and the State, and when he explained the legal rights that women had in Islam 'the surprise of the audience knew no bound'.[107]

Leitner similarly tried to reach the English public to dispel negative attitudes about Islam. In his talk published as *Muhammadanism: Being the Report of an Extempore Address Delivered at South Place Chapel, Finsbury on Sunday Afternoon, January Sixth, 1888*, he began by discussing his education at a mosque school in Istanbul, his travels and his study of Arabic. He explained that in order to understand Islam knowledge alone is inadequate:[108] sympathy is necessary, for sympathy 'is the key to the meaning of knowledge', and without it even the finest scholars misjudge the religion. He then discussed the social virtues of Islam, its laws and traditions regarding women, and the concept of *jihad*. He concluded by stating that Judaism, Christianity and Islam are 'sister-faiths' having a common origin and he expressed the hope that 'the day will come when Christians will honour Christ more by also honouring Muhammad'.[109]

Leitner further involved himself in English public life by calling attention to the plight of the *Kafirs*, a people living in an especially mountainous region of the Hindu Kush in Afghanistan who were being attacked and sold into slavery by the amir of Afghanistan's troops. Leitner networked with MPs and a number of organisations based in England, including the BFASS.[110] Although he opposed the BFASS's tendency to portray Islam in a negative light, he spoke on the topic of the Kafirs at several BFASS meetings and was willing to work with the group in order to achieve common goals. Through his activities Leitner showed that, contrary to BFASS rhetoric, sympathy with Islam did not preclude anti-slavery activity. The BFASS, in turn, worked on behalf of the Kafirs, addressing itself to Lord Salisbury and the amir of Afghanistan regarding the issue.[111]

The words and actions of Leitner and others affiliated with the Oriental Institute challenged the dominant imperialist ideology in relation to Islam; yet these men also understood that the many cross-cultural contacts that made the Institute possible resulted from Britain's position as a world power. They did not oppose British imperial ambitions, but rather sought to redefine them in a way that would be more favourable to Muslims and Muslim interests. One issue of the *IAQR* even began with a poem celebrating imperialism, in which reference was made to the 'great Empire whose behest is owned by millions East and West' and which went on to describe the importance of battling common enemies and upholding 'justice' and 'well-ordered laws' in order to keep the Empire strong.[112] By identifying themselves with the imperial mission, these students and scholars helped to create a place for Islam in England.

The mosque at the Oriental Institute became a centre for Muslims in the London area and stood as a visible reminder of an Islamic presence in England and its potential contribution to English life.[113] Its unique architectural style (figure 4) demanded notice, especially by those travelling from London on the South-Western Railway.[114] Muslims and others gathered there for social events and lectures as well as religious activities.[115] In addition, it had the support of Christian ministers who in 'a truly Christian spirit' encouraged provision for the spiritual needs of Muslims in England.[116] A journalist commented: 'It is one of the signs of the times that enlightened Christians unite with pious Mohammedans on what is common ground in their respective faiths ... Dr. Leitner has, on his return to this country, resumed his efforts on behalf of toleration and to promote an accurate knowledge of Eastern languages and creeds.'[117] These sentiments were shared by

4 The Shah Jehan Mosque at the Oriental Institute in Woking, England from *The Illustrated London News* (9 November 1889).

IAQR writers, one expressing the hope that his work would 'bring about a friendly feeling between Englishmen and the Mahomedans who come in contact with them'.[118]

The mosque was named after Shah Jehan (now spelt Shah Jahan) in honour of the *begum* of Bhopal, who personally paid for two-thirds of the cost of the building and whose influence made its erection possible. Shah Jehan also used the written word to represent her faith to an English audience by publishing a narrative of her pilgrimage to Mecca,[119] one passage of which relates her visit to the slave market there. The fact that she neither condemns nor defends slave-trading, but treats it as only a minor aspect of her pilgrimage and marginal to her experience as a Muslim woman, calls into question the dominant imperialist discourses of British officials, the BFASS, feminists and others in English society, who understood women in Islam as necessarily oppressed because of the institutions of slavery and the harem, which they believed reinforced each other.[120] She ruled for more than twenty years and was described as having 'broken through the stern barriers that surround her sex in that religion', a statement that regards her situation as exceptional, but nevertheless acknowledges the possibility of female empowerment in a Muslim society.[121]

Shah Jehan's stance in relation to the Empire was, in certain respects, similar to that of the British–Muslim scholars and statesmen discussed above. Like them, she took advantage of class privilege in order to create a more prominent place for Islam in England. Also like them, she saw British imperialism as not so much a tool of oppression as rather offering an opportunity to promote her own interests and faith within a global political system. In her letters to Queen Victoria, she expressed a passionate loyalty to the British crown,[122] and she began her book with a dedication to the queen and even stated that her 'earnest prayer to Almighty God is that I may be enabled to show my unswerving allegiance to Her Majesty'.[123]

Like Shah Jehan, and the students and scholars affiliated to the Oriental Institute, a number of non-Muslims addressed an English audience and presented perspectives that contradicted the dominant imperialist ideology, which assumed English society and culture to be superior to an Islamic world in dire need of reform. They found ways to sympathise with and develop an appreciation of Islam, usually through travel or literature. They valued visits to distant lands as enriching experiences and were interested in learning about other traditions and belief systems. They acquired new knowledge and developed favourable impressions of the Muslims they encountered abroad.

The mid-to-late nineteenth century saw the growth of popular tourism, made possible by Great Britain's imperial political and economic position in the world, as well as advances in communication and transportation achieved during this period. Entrepreneurs such as Thomas Cook arranged tours, which provided, for the first time, opportunities for large numbers of middle-class English people to travel to the Muslim countries of the Middle East. As a result of these changes, the travel narrative reached a broader segment of English society during this period than previously.[124]

English travellers could appreciate Islamic art and architecture, especially foreign mosques. One noted the 'lofty grace impossible to describe' of a mosque in Cairo;[125] another referred to the 'particularly fine' painted windows through which light entering the mosque 'mellowed to the most exquisite softness'.[126] Still other reports describe the rich embroideries, lamps set in emeralds, ostrich eggs inscribed with verses from the Qur'an and the magnificence of the buildings in general.[127] Some visitors responded to the more austere structures, one praising the 'grand simplicity' of both a mosque and the service held within it.[128] Illuminated Qur'ans made an impression on English observers: while religious authorities associated with the BFASS denounced the book as blasphemy, a Christian clergyman admired a collection of antique Qur'ans, noting that they were 'richly decorated with Arabesque scrolls' and that their writing exhibited a 'great beauty of form'.[129]

Even travellers more interested in sight-seeing than in Islam could not help being affected by the religious practices and beliefs they encountered. All were required to remove their shoes before stepping on ground considered holy and behave with reverence while inside a mosque. One Christian woman visiting a mosque related having the opportunity to hear a recitation of the Qur'an and witness Muslim worshippers observe the ritual of prayer.[130] Another who previously had expressed hostility to Islam nevertheless found herself moved when watching a group of 'dancing dervishes': she explained that the 'whole thing was so solemn, and they appeared to be so completely absorbed in what they were doing that a certain air of devotion and reverence reached even the mind of the spectators'.[131]

English travellers tended to be impressed by the open devotion of Muslims to God and to their religion. As one travel writer noted: 'they see the Lord's hand working all about them, the name of God is in their names, they call upon God in every mouthful of words'.[132] A clergyman compared Muslim practices favourably with those of English people who confined their religion within church walls and he contrasted the 'manly dignity' and 'humble reverence' of the Muslim man praying publicly to what he considered the usual shameful behaviour of Englishmen during services of worship. Finally, he praised the 'simple earnestness' of the Muslim as compared to the 'doubt' and 'indifference' so commonly encountered in England.[133] Similarly, another clergyman observed that Christians should learn from Muslims and proclaim their faith openly instead of behaving as if ashamed of it.[134] Others noted the piety, hospitable nature and outstanding character of individual Muslims with whom they came in contact. One of the clergy referred to above described a dignified young dervish as 'the very model of John the Baptist'.[135] The view expressed in these writings is that English Christians should improve themselves by learning from the example of Muslims, not vice versa.

Scholars and writers of all kinds who appealed to an English audience acknowledged Muslim contributions to humanity. Thomas Carlyle explained how the 'Hero–Prophet' Muhammad brought a poor sheep-herding people from darkness to light, so that within one century a civilisation emerged reaching from Delhi to Granada, 'glancing in valour and splendour and a light of genius'.[136] Similarly, Lane-Poole's historical narrative of the Moors in eighth-century Spain celebrated their accomplishments.[137] An encyclopaedia noted Islam's contributions to philosophy, medicine, geography and poetry, commenting on the religion's role in the development of science and art in the West and explaining that Muslims were the 'enlightened teachers of barbarous Europe' from the ninth to the thirteenth centuries.[138]

English Orientalist literature was able to foster an appreciation of Islam.[139] As Robert Southey explained regarding his work *Thalaba*: 'My intention is to show off all the splendour of the Mohammedan belief... to preserve the costume of place as well as of religion'.[140] Some Orientalists respected Muslim scholars as colleagues and consulted their work.[141] Translations such as that of *The Book of the Thousand Nights and a Night* by Sir Richard Burton exposed English readers to literature from Muslim societies as well as testifying to a genuine interest in and respect for the culture on the part of the scholars who undertook the extremely difficult task of translating the Arabic originals.

Burton was the most famous traveller to present Islam in a sympathetic light to the English reader.[142] With the financial support of the Royal Geographical Society of London, he embarked on a journey to Mecca in 1853, posing as a wandering 'Darwaysh'. To do this he 'plunged' himself 'into the intricacies of the faith', performed ablutions, recited prayers, gave alms and fasted during Ramadan; in short, he lived the life of a devout Muslim during his travels. He recorded his experiences for an English audience in his *Personal Narrative of a Pilgrimage to al-Madinah and Meccah*,[143] in the course of which he gave detailed descriptions of mosques and shrines, and of Mecca itself, as well as discussing Muslim practices and beliefs. He responds to criticism by asking why, when the two religions were so similar, many Christians find his pilgrimage offensive: 'Do they [Muslims] not also venerate Abraham, the Father of the Faithful? Did not Locke, and even greater names, hold Mohammedans to be heterodox Christians?'[144]

Burton's experiences could have threatened commonly accepted beliefs about the differences that separated English people from Muslims, for in one sense he *became* rather than just pretended to be a wandering Muslim dervish. Given that the Islamic world is no more unified than the Western one, his success in playing the role of one who by definition exists on the margins of society should not be surprising. Also, while Burton may not have had a spiritual experience, he was a Muslim during this period in that he professed his belief in the existence of one God and in Muhammad as his prophet, and conformed his actions to that belief. In this respect he was no different from the follower of any religion who performs ritual but lacks sincerity of heart.

ISLAM IN ENGLAND

Considering Burton's hajj from this perspective dissolves the border dividing Englishness and Islam.

Contemporaries took a different approach, however, by depicting Burton as one of England's many hero–adventurers willing to risk life and limb for the good of the Empire. He was praised as a master of disguise who could masquerade as a Muslim on pilgrimage while remaining all the while English. For example, in her biography of her husband Isabel Burton stated:

> To accomplish a journey to Mecca and Medinah quite safely in those days (1853) was almost an impossibility, for the discovery that he was *not* a Mussulman would have been avenged by a hundred Khanjars. It meant living with his life in his hand, and amongst the strangest and wildest companions, adopting their unfamiliar manners, and living for perhaps nine months in the hottest and most unhealthy climate, upon repulsive food, complete and absolute isolation from all that makes life tolerable, from all civilization, from all his natural habits – the brain at high tension, never to depart from the *rôle* he had adopted.[145]

This perspective assumes and reinforces the belief in a unified English culture as well as an equally unified Islamic world existing at the margins of the British Empire. As a result, while new images of Muslims, and even of Mecca, became diffused in English society through Burton's writings, the idea of Islam as essentially foreign to England was simultaneously reinforced. According to the popular interpretation of his travels, Burton crossed cultural boundaries, but the boundaries themselves remained intact.

Burton's own writings regarding his hajj and the English discourses sympathetic to Islam discussed above may have contradicted the dominant imperial rhetoric about English superiority, but they did not challenge imperialism or British foreign policy in Egypt. They functioned within the context of the Empire just as did the words of English anti-slavery activists:[146] they reinforced the understanding of Islam as an alternative system of beliefs and alliances that existed in distant lands of the Empire, or in the East generally, which could be appreciated by English people but was decidedly not English. Muslim ceremonies in the streets of London, Quilliam's community in Liverpool, the *objets d'art* in Leitner's Oriental Institute and the mosque in Woking all remain noticeably absent from the types of writing described in this section. The people who produced them chose to direct their creative and intellectual energies to educating themselves about and representing Islam as practised abroad, not in England.

Conclusion

This chapter has examined certain historical developments during the late nineteenth century which called into question the idea that an English nation existed at the centre of the Empire and could influence Islamic societies on the peripheries, helping them to reform and providing a model for improvement, but that Islam had no place in England and nothing of value to offer its people. A Muslim presence there and a number of English women and men who were appreciative of the religion and saw in it qualities that could benefit their own lives and their country threatened to undermine a basic assumption of the dominant imperialist ideology discussed in chapters two to four. Consideration of these new influences, which altered the face and composition of English society, and the identities that were created in relation to them, sheds light on imperial politics within the metropole by revealing how alternative perspectives could contribute to and be accommodated within the English nation, while at the same time helping to define its limits.

The increasing importance of the British Empire and of Islam within it for the English people during this period created new circumstances that made alternative perspectives necessary. The type of contact they had with Islam was unprecedented. No longer did it take place only beyond England's borders, for immigration to and trade in that country, both of which were closely linked to Great Britain's imperial status, contributed to the creation of environments which allowed a Muslim presence. A group of recently converted English Muslims established a community in the growing city of Liverpool, the premier port of the Empire. In addition, so many lascars and ayahs arrived in England, usually via East India Company ships, that shelters were built for them. Even the ways in which these immigrants were understood by English people had to do with imperial ideology, for often they were represented as inhabiting colonial spaces.

In addition to these new communities, other processes contributed to the changing nature of Anglo-Muslim relations during the late nineteenth century. British–Muslim statesmen associated with the Raj and travellers from the East began to make their presence known and exert their influence in English society in ways not seen previously. They participated in the intellectual life of the newly established Oriental Institute and contributed to its publication. Some of them, such as Sayyid Amir Ali, made an effort to reach English people and educate them on the subject of Islam. They worshipped at the new mosque in Woking, erected through the financial support of Shah Jehan, the begum of Bhopal, who also had ties with the British crown. Finally, growing international political and economic networks resulting from

Britain's position in the world, as well as the rise in literacy and technical advances facilitating travel, made it possible for more English people than in the past to gain exposure to Islam as practised abroad, either through direct contact or second-hand through accounts in the many new books and articles published on the topic.

New circumstances provided opportunities for and in certain cases even demanded that historical actors reconsider their understanding of the relationship between Englishness and Islam, but how they did so could vary considerably. Certain individuals proved to be especially creative in this respect, drawing on ideas culturally available and reinterpreting them through action to contribute original perspectives. For example, W. H. Quilliam used his knowledge of Arabic and Islam acquired during his travels, as well as his understanding of the Victorian reforming impulse and other values closely associated with English national identity, to win converts to Islam and lead a community of believers in Liverpool. He networked with temperance and other organisations to present the faith in a new light and as a remedy for England's social ills. He took advantage of the place created in that country for the wearing of Eastern or Islamic dress by previous generations of Orientalist mimics in order to express visually his new religious identity.

Sayyid Amir Ali also presented Englishness and Islam as compatible, but for different reasons. Amir Ali was influenced by the movement in India to foster Anglo-Muslim understanding, but he drew on his own experiences and certain perspectives that had resonance in English society, such as Enlightenment concepts, in order to produce a body of original writings on the subject for an English readership, both scholars and general readers. His ideas had much to do with the role he had created for himself as a British–Muslim statesman, serving Her Majesty's Government in a number of positions and working to create a more prominent place for Muslims and the Muslim organisations he helped to found.

Sir Richard Burton provides another example of extraordinary initiative and creativity within the larger imperial cultural system. He benefited from existing ideas about the English hero of empire and the scholar–adventurer involved in exploration and the acquisition of knowledge for the good of the nation. However, his hajj never could have been accomplished without resourcefulness, skill and a willingness to incorporate new concepts and practices in daily life. The commonly accepted interpretation of his well-publicised journey was also imaginative. Burton's life and actions could have been seen as blurring the boundaries between what was considered English and what was considered Islamic. Instead, contemporaries reinforced this division by portraying him as a patriotic hero who remained English despite his close association with Muslims and Islam.

While Burton, Amir Ali and Quilliam were exceptional in terms of talent and privilege, their stories illustrate what thousands of people such as British Muslim professional men, immigrants and ordinary English travellers did to a lesser degree: they reconciled Islam and Englishness in creative ways that reflected their specific situations and made their actions meaningful. Factors such as class and gender, as well as language barriers, meant that in England lascars and their English wives, for example, could not hope to have the same influence and impact as did the three discussed above. Yet through public processions and ceremony they were able to express their belief in Islam as a universal faith that belonged in England as much as it belonged in the Middle East or South Asia. How others who came into contact with these Muslims regarded them – and in doing so defined the English nation and their relationship to it – also required thought. They could accept them by finding inspiration in the tradition of English liberalism, with its emphasis on religious tolerance, as did those who praised the Woking mosque. Alternatively, they could extend familiar ideas about colonial savages in need of reform to describe Muslims as well as the urban poor.

As these new ideas and identities evolved through the words and actions of individuals, cultural exchange happened within a global system. The reference to colonial savages illustrates how concepts associated with imperial politics abroad found their way into English domestic life, recreated in different forms, and invested with additional connotations and meanings. The Muslims discussed in this chapter developed their beliefs and political orientations in different parts of the world. British Muslim statesmen and scholars such as Sayyid Amir Ali had loyalties to the Raj; moreover, they had been influenced by the movements to foster Anglo-Muslim unity in India. This background impacted on their understanding of their faith and its place in the Empire.

Quilliam, on the other hand, was indifferent and at times hostile to British imperial expansion. He cultivated alliances with the Ottoman sultan, and initially was more interested in Muslims in Ottoman territories and North Africa than those in South Asia. Leitner, however, easily made the transition from his schooling in Arabic in Istanbul to links with British India through the Oriental Institute. Indeed the books, manuscripts and *objets d'art* that he procured for the museum reflected his travels and experiences, from northern Africa to Central and Southern Asia. Leitner and Muslims living in England during this period understood the disadvantaged position of Islam in that country and drew power from identifying with the different parts of the Islamic world with which they had connections. They may have felt obscure or out of place at times, living among people who so often did not seem to understand them, yet they could engage in a kind of Orientalism by remembering or imagining great palaces, mosques and religious celebrations in distant lands and cities where minarets dotted the skyline and the call to prayer filled the morning air.

Because those who sought to present Islam in a favourable light in English society operated within an imperial cultural system, they realised that they had to counter the negative representations of it produced by missionaries, government officials, BFASS activists and others. Quilliam did so by likening Muslims to English abolitionists, contending that Islam frees the soul from the worst type of slavery: addiction to alcohol. He tried to discredit Christianity as essentially irrational and presented his own faith as the reasonable alternative. Certain lascars, on the other hand, responded to the proselytism of LCM missionaries by stressing the similarities between the two religions. Like English Christians, Sayyid Amir Ali saw the consistency of his faith with Enlightenment ideas about equality and liberty and asserted that true Islam discourages slavery. Like scholars of the Oriental Institute, he adopted the discourse of English feminists to make the case that, contrary to what BFASS supporters and others may have said, the English woman was treated more like a slave than the Muslim woman. These positive representations of Islam created for an English audience, then, are to be understood as facets of ongoing debates, formed in relation to opposing viewpoints and therefore incomplete in isolation, or outside of the specific political context.

The incomplete nature of individual representations and their dependence on other ideas and systems of meaning is especially evident when considering the relationship between lascar sailors and people in England who came in contact with them. How they were regarded was never solely about the sailors themselves but was about larger political issues and debates. For middle-class reformers they came to represent simultaneously both the perceived threat of the disenfranchised, rootless underclass and the un-Christianised *heathens* in the Empire; and how they were treated had to do with competing efforts to define the nation. In addition, bonds with each other formed by Muslim immigrants and identities that reflected those bonds were created as the result of the exclusion and marginalisation they experienced in English society. Consideration of their situation sheds light on the process through which ethnic and national identities developed together and in relation to each other.

The identities that formed in relation to the increasingly important place of Islam in English society during the late nineteenth century were highly unpredictable and situational: they arose from particular historical circumstances that had not existed previously. Yet social conditions alone did not determine which ideas would be embraced, how and by whom. For example, while the changes taking place in the city of Liverpool may have created an environment that allowed the establishment of an English Muslim community, only a minority of Liverpudlians chose to convert, and those who did were not of one social type but came from different backgrounds, in terms of both class and gender. Even a commitment to Christianity did not necessarily predispose people to see Islam in a negative light: some Christians expressed respect for Muslims and identified with them as people of faith. In addition, individuals were inconsistent in how they perceived both themselves and others: each had distinctive ways of identifying herself or himself based on factors such as race, class, gender, nation and religion, and which one would have primacy at any given time was impossible to know beforehand. Sometimes Quilliam effectively reconciled the British and Muslim aspects of himself, while at other times his faith became more important than his loyalty to the Government. Similarly the English people who admired Islam when travelling abroad did not always transfer those feelings to Muslims in England.

Even people who shared a given ideology or worked for the same cause were drawn to it for different reasons. Quilliam's followers, lascars, ayahs, scholars, statesmen and royal personages all found meaning in Islam, practising their religion in England and representing their faith to others there through their words and actions. They had little else in common, however: they spoke different languages and came from different parts of the world. Their roles and expectations varied considerably. Even though, as educated people who kept abreast of current events, Quilliam, Amir Ali, Leitner and Burton were no doubt aware of one another, each cultivated the role of an authority on Islam in English society and therefore tended to focus on his own experiences and interpretations. Perhaps the most striking example of the way that people from different backgrounds and perspectives could orient themselves around a common goal or belief system, in this case appreciation for Islam and the conviction that it had a legitimate place in England, would be the establishment of the Oriental Institute and the mosque in Woking. These institutions were made possible by the efforts of a male Hungarian scholar of Jewish descent who was sympathetic to Islam and had served the British Government and a female Muslim ruler from South Asia who had an alliance with and personal loyalty to Queen Victoria.

Engaging with these differences and emphasising them is crucial to an understanding of Anglo-Muslim identity politics in the imperial metropole during this period. For the image of the unified, monolithic, Islamic world, so frequently found in contemporary English discourse on the topic, served to reinforce the belief in the unified English nation despite the contested nature of Englishness and the fact that national identity was formed through perceived differences. This chapter's discussion of the ways in which competing class-based English national identities developed in opposition to each other, while they simultaneously relied on the shared assumption that Muslim communities were more a part of the Empire than of the nation, although for different reasons, illustrates this process.

The English nation and the identities associated with it were characterised by a constantly shifting border between England and the Empire which helped to define the nation. Where that border would be at any given time depended on the actions of individuals and the specific political circumstances. Quilliam vacillated between challenging the legitimacy of this border by promoting a British–Muslim identity and the compatibility of Islam and Englishness, on one hand, and reinforcing the border but positioning himself on the other side of it by asserting the superiority of Islam and proclaiming his loyalty to it as paramount, on the other. British Muslims such as Sayyid Amir Ali and the scholars and students associated with the Oriental Institute well understood contemporary identity politics and did not make the argument that they or their religion were English, but rather appealed to national pride in the Empire in order to assert a place for their faith in England, a strategy that produced a more porous border but did not challenge its existence. Finally, the positive representations of the religion created by both Muslims and non-Muslims for an English audience had an inherent radical potential because they called into question English superiority and therefore the benefits and legitimacy of the boundaries meant to separate the English nation from imperial spaces, although ultimately those perspectives were accommodated within the dominant ideology and political system.

Notes

1 The English had experienced some exposure to Islam prior to this time through visits by Muslims, foreign travel by British citizens, plays, literature and sermons. In addition, an English translation of the Qur'an was published in the seventeenth century. For more on this topic see Samuel C. Chew, *The Crescent and the Rose: Islam and England during the Renaissance* (Oxford: Oxford University Press, 1937); M. A. Badawi, *Islam in Britain* (London: Ta Ha, 1981); Muhammad Mumtaz Ali, *The Muslim Community in Britain: An Historical Account* (Malaysia: Pelanduk Publications, 1996); and Nabil Matar, *Islam in Britain 1558–1685* (Cambridge: Cambridge University Press, 1998).

2 Discussion of lascar diets dictated by 'religious prejudices' appears in 'Papers in Relation to the Care of Lascars: 1793–1818', in the Marine Department Papers on

THE HAREM, SLAVERY AND BRITISH IMPERIAL CULTURE

Lascars 1793–1818, part 1 (L/MAR/C/902) and part 2 (L/Mar/C/902), Oriental and India Office Collections (henceforth IOR for India Office Records), British Library. The word lascar comes from the Urdu word *lashkar* or its derivative *lashkari*, which usually refers to soldiers but was used for sailors as well: R. W. Burchfield (comp.), *The Compact Oxford English Dictionary: Complete Text Reproduced Micrographically*, 2nd edn (Oxford: Clarendon Press, 1991), p. 943 (p. 666 of multi-volume edition). For a thorough discussion of lascars in Britain see Rozina Visram, *Ayahs, Lascars and Princes: Indians in Britain 1700–1947* (London: Pluto Press, 1986), pp. 34–54; she notes (p. 34) that lascar sailors did not serve on British ships in very large numbers prior to 1780.

3 Jean Sutton, *Lords of the East: The East India Company and its Ships* (London: Conway Maritime Press, 1981), p. 94.

4 *Lascars and Chinese: A Short Address to Young Men, of the Several Orthodox Denominations of Christians, Pointing Out to Them a Sphere of Great Utility, Probable Usefulness, and Where Their Services Are Much Wanted* (London: H. Teape, 1814), p. 4.

5 The estimate of 12,000 is given in 'Native Visitors from Africa and Asia', *London City Mission Magazine (LCMM)*, 55 (September 1890), 220; estimates of 10,000 are more common and appear repeatedly in the *LCMM*. Much of the available information on lascar sailors comes from the records of the LCM, an organisation dedicated to missionary activity in the area. In addition to the LCM, the Lascar Mission, a branch of St Luke's Church, was established in Canning Town: Visram, *Ayahs, Lascars and Princes*, p. 52.

6 In 1876 there were 7,175 Muslim lascars as compared to 763 Hindus, Buddhists and Christians, and the numbers were similar for 1877: 8,079 to 700: 'London City Mission Work among the Mohammedan Population of London', *LCMM*, 51 (March 1876), 47; and 'Missionary to the Asiatics and Africans', *LCMM*, 42 (August 1877), 169. Throughout the *LCMM* reference is made to missionaries who either wrote or were quoted as stating that most lascars were Muslims.

7 It was supported by contributions from individuals, the London Missionary Society, the Baptist and Moravian Missionary Societies, the East India Company and His Highness the Maharajah Duleep Sing, knight grand commander of the Star of India. The ceremony accompanying the laying of the building's first stone included His Royal Highness the prince consort and 'a large assemblage of Noblemen, Ladies, Gentlemen, and Oriental visitors of rank, besides two hundred and thirty natives of India, Africa, and China': Joseph Salter, *The Asiatic in England: Sketches of Sixteen Years Work Among Orientals* (London: S. W. Partridge, 1873), pp. 1, 10, 12. The *Illustrated London News* published several articles reporting the Strangers' Home as a great humanitarian success. The 'respectable' nature of its contributors and the comfort and protection it offered residents are noted: see *ibid.*, 30 (28 February 1857), 194; 28 (14 June 1858), 670; and 52 (7 March 1868), 237.

8 Salter, *The Asiatic in England*, pp. 67, 71; the estimate of 5,709 is given in IOR L/P&J/12/59.

9 While most of the residents were Muslims, it was open to all destitute lascar sailors regardless of religion. The reference to 200 was Salter's: *The Asiatic in England*, p. 68; the lascar's statement is on p. 232.

10 *Ibid.*, pp. 70–1; mention of the Qur'an and the sketches of Mecca and Medina are in Joseph Salter, *The East in the West: Work Amongst the Asiatics and Africans in London* (London: S. W. Partridge, 1895), p. 153.

11 The ayahs are discussed in the following *LCMM* articles: numbers in 'Mission to Asiatics and Africans', subsection 'Our Ayahs', 53 (September 1888), 197–209; quote and reference to religion in 'Mission to Asiatics and Africans', subsection 'The Ayahs', 63 (May 1898), 89–97; photograph of a group of ayahs in 'From the Ends of the Earth: A Record of Work Among Foreigners in London', 63 (November 1898), 260. Visram notes that the practice of bringing ayahs and Indian servants to England probably began in the eighteenth century or earlier: *Ayahs, Lascars and Princes*, pp. 11–33.

12 'Mahommedan Jubilee', *Gentleman's Magazine* (May 1805), 479.
13 'Mission to Asiatics and Africans', subsection 'The Muharram', *LCMM*, 53 (September 1888), 200–1; and 'The Muharram', *ibid.*, 57 (March 1892), 52.
14 'Interment of a Lascar', *Gentleman's Magazine* (January 1823), 80.
15 Salter, *The East in the West*, pp. 135–7.
16 William Berrington, sermon at St Paul's Cathedral entitled 'The Great Blessings of Redemption from Captivity' (1722), pp. 3 and 22, quoted from Linda Colley, *Captives: Britain, Empire and the World, 1600–1850* (London: Jonathan Cape, 2002), p. 79.
17 Colley, *Captives*, p. 79; she describes these processions on pp. 78–80.
18 'Mission to Asiatics and Africans', *LCMM*, 57 (March 1892), 49–50. Scholars and other writers for an English audience also noted similarities in the traditions and beliefs of Christians and Muslims. For example, Muhammad Casim Siddi Lebbe explains how the Virgin Mary is much revered in Islam in 'An Account of the Virgin Mary and Jesus as Given by Arabic Writers', *Orientalist*, 1 (1884), 17.
19 Between 1815 and 1945 more immigrants came to England than during any other period, except for the Norman invasion: Panikos Panayi, *Immigration, Ethnicity and Racism in Britain, 1815–1945* (Manchester: Manchester University Press, 1994), p. 23; see also Colin Holmes, *John Bull's Island: Immigration and British Society, 1871–1971* (London: Macmillan, 1988).
20 For discussion of this Act and related issues see Bernard Gainer, *The Alien Invasion: The Origins of the Aliens Act of 1905* (London: Heinemann Books, 1972).
21 Ian Baucom, *Out of Place: Englishness, Empire, and the Locations of Identity* (Princeton, NJ: Princeton University Press, 1999), pp. 60–2. The reference to missionaries comes from Susan Thorne, '"The Conversion of Englishmen and the Conversion of the World Inseparable:" Missionary Imperialism and the Language of Class in Early Industrial Britain', in Frederick Cooper and Ann Laura Stoler (eds), *Tensions of Empire: Colonial Cultures in a Bourgeois World* (Berkeley: University of California Press, 1997), pp. 238–62, at 247.
22 Thorne, '"The Conversion of Englishmen"', pp. 249, 252.
23 Visram describes the miserable living and working conditions experienced by both lascars and ayahs as well as cases in which they were mistreated: *Ayahs, Lascars and Princes*, pp. 15–19, 35, 40–8. As a result approximately 10 per cent of the lascar sailors who arrived in England prior to the establishment of the Strangers' Home died there: 'Report of a Meeting for the Establishment of a "Strangers' Home", for Asiatics, Africans, South-Sea Islanders and Others, Occasionally Residing in the Metropolis' (March 1855), p. 12.
24 Marriage between formerly non-Muslim English women and immigrant Muslim men is mentioned in Muhammad Mashuq Ally's *The Growth and Organization of the Muslim Community in Britain* (Birmingham: Centre for the Study of Islam and Christian–Muslim Relations, 1979), pp. 1–2; this practice is noted also by Salter and other LCM missionaries.
25 Salter, *The East in the West*, pp. 34–5.
26 It was not until the 1960s and 1970s in England that a 'black identity [which included the majority of Muslims living there] haltingly emerge[d] . . . constructing solidarities and allegiances' among members of various marginalised groups: Catherine Hall, *White, Male and Middle-Class: Explorations in Feminism and History* (New York: Routledge, 1992), p. 19. Even this movement had more to do with entering contemporary politics under the banner of blackness than it did with accurately representing the diverse backgrounds and situations of its supporters, producing what Hanif Kureishi has called 'cheering fictions': Stuart Hall, 'New Ethnicities', in David Morley and Kuan-Hsing Chen (eds), *Critical Dialogues in Cultural Studies* (Routledge: London, 1996), pp. 441–49, quotation of Kureishi at 449.
27 The *Ahmadīyah* movement began in British India in 1889 and has since established mosques and missionary centres in Africa, Asia and Europe. While Ahmadis consider themselves Muslims, they have been persecuted by other Muslims for

their beliefs. Significantly, in 1984 when their religious observances were made illegal in Pakistan, the movement's leader, like Ahmadis before him, moved to London: Yohanan Friedmann, 'Ahmadīyah', in John Esposito (ed.), *The Oxford Encyclopedia of the Modern Islamic World* (Oxford: Oxford University Press, 1995), vol. 1, pp. 54–7.

28 They resided in the West Derby Road area in Liverpool, Edward Square in Tyneside, the Bute Town area in Cardiff and in the east end of London, especially Poplar, Shadwell and Wapping. The term *zawiya* may be used to describe a room for prayer or a larger institution that includes a school and even a hostel for guests. The English zawiyas of the nineteenth century were probably simple with a few rooms or perhaps a house.

29 Muhammad Mashuq Ally, *Growth and Organization of the Muslim Community*, pp. 5–6.

30 Salter, *The Asiatic in England*, pp. 220–3, and 'The Recent Work in Various Parts of Great Britain of the Missionary to the Asiatics, Africans and South Sea Islanders', *LCMM*, 32 (January 1867), 5–8.

31 Salter, *The Asiatic in England*, p. 190.

32 J. A. Picton, *Memorials of Liverpool Historical and Topographical Including a History of the Dock Estate* (London: Longmans, Green & Co., 1873), vol. 1, p. 636; also see Thomas Baines, *History of the Commerce and Town of Liverpool and the Rise of the Manufacturing Industry in the Adjoining Counties* (London: Longman, Brown, Green & Longmans, 1852).

33 Baines, *History of the Commerce and Town of Liverpool*, pp. 743–5.

34 Frank Neal, *Sectarian Violence. The Liverpool Experience, 1819–1914: An Aspect of Anglo-Irish History* (Manchester: Manchester University Press, 1988), p. 1.

35 Baines, *History of the Commerce and Town of Liverpool*, p. 811.

36 Picton, *Memorials of Liverpool*, vol. 1, pp. 588, 623. Ibrahim Pasha was the eldest son of Muhammad Ali; he died in 1848, during his father's lifetime. Muhammad Said strengthened economic ties with Western European powers and conceded to the construction of the Suez Canal.

37 For Irish immigrants see Baines, *A History of the Commerce and Town of Liverpool*, p. 678; and Neal, *Sectarian Violence*; for Chinese immigrants see Holmes, *John Bull's Island*, pp. 32–3, 52–3.

38 Baucom, *Out of Place*, p. 58; this statement is quoted from John Ruskin's discussion of images of the Victorian city and the threat of urbanisation.

39 'Men who are Talked About: Abdullah Quilliam', the *Porcupine* (21 November 1896) and 'Sheikh Abdullah Quilliam', *ibid*. (7 April 1900), Liverpool Public Record Office (henceforth LPRO).

40 Captain Scott, 'Mr W. H. Quilliam and His Varied Life', *Liverpool Freeman* (8 July 1905), LPRO. This article is in a collection of newspaper clippings discussing famous Liverpool men.

41 *Ibid.* and 'Sheikh Abdullah Quilliam'.

42 Scott, 'Mr W. H. Quilliam and His Varied Life', and B. G. Orchard, *Liverpool's Legion of Honour*, LPRO.

43 'Disappearance of a Liverpool Solicitor', *Porcupine* (31 October 1908), LPRO.

44 For example, Sir Robert Sherley, who engaged in military and diplomatic pursuits in the Ottoman Empire and Persia during the early seventeenth century, had one such portrait painted; also the journalist James Silk Buckingham commissioned Henry William Pickersgill to produce a portrait of himself and his wife in 'Oriental costume' in 1816.

45 Matar, *Islam in Britain*, p. 15.

46 The reference to Lady Mary Wortley Montagu is in Alev Croutier, *The Harem: The World Behind the Veil* (New York: Abbeville Press, 1989), p. 179. Montagu, who was well known in literary circles, published observations from her travels (1763–67) in which she expressed sympathy with Islam and an ability to identify with Muslim women in *The Turkish Embassy Letters* (London: Virago, 1994). Robert Blake, *Disraeli* (New York: St. Martin's Press, 1967), p. 80; also see Robert

Blake, *Disraeli's Grand Tour: Benjamin Disraeli and the Holy Land 1830–31* (New York: Oxford University Press, 1982).

47 Kathleen Wilson notes that mimicry could neutralise the radical potential of the 'other': 'The Island Race: Captain Cook, Protestant Evangelicalism and the Construction of English National Identity, 1760–1800', in Tony Claydon and Ian McBride (eds), *Protestantism and National Identity: Britain and Ireland, c.1650–c.1850* (Cambridge: Cambridge University Press, 1998), p. 273. Mimicry could also further the imperial project by defining the nation in relation to those excluded from it, as discussed in chapter three.

48 The information regarding these titles and honours are in the articles: 'Men Who Are Talked About'; 'Mr W. H. Quilliam and His Varied Life', 4; 'Sheikh Abdullah Quilliam'; Scott, 'Quilliam and Life', 1; and 'Disappearance of a Liverpool Solicitor'; all are in the LPRO.

49 J. H. McGovern, the architect who designed the alterations for the Institute, describes the Liverpool mosque in 'Saracenic Architecture: A Paper Read Before the Literary Society of the Liverpool Moslem Institute, January 15, 1896', reprinted in the *Islamic World* (April 1896), 364, 366, 367, 369. This paper is in a larger collection entitled 'Lectures on Saracenic Architecture', which includes a photograph of the interior of the Liverpool Muslim Institute and an extract from the *Crescent* regarding plans for the erection of a cathedral mosque in that city: 'Men Who Are Talked About'. Also see Peter Clark, *Marmaduke Pickthall: British Muslim* (London: Quartet Books, 1986), p. 39.

50 Yehya-en-Nasr Parkinson, 'The Liverpool Muslim Movement', *Islamic Review*, 2 (1914), 167.

51 J. H. McGovern provided detailed architectural plans. The proposed site for the new mosque was purchased by the trustees of the Liverpool Muslim Congregation, and in 1898 the plans were forwarded to Quilliam in Istanbul, so that he could submit them to the Sultan with a request for approval and financial assistance. 'Proposed Mosque in Liverpool', *Crescent* (28 March 1900); 'The Erection of a Cathedral Mosque in Liverpool', clipping from LPRO; article discussing plans for cathedral mosque in *Liverpool Mercury* (19 April 1898) (reprinted in previous clipping); and McGovern, 'Saracenic Architecture', pp. 367–8.

52 'Disappearance of a Liverpool Solicitor'.

53 Parkinson, 'The Liverpool Muslim Movement', 167.

54 'Sheikh Abdullah Quilliam'; Clark, *Marmaduke Pickthall*, p. 39; and various stray, unidentified newspaper clippings from the LPRO kept with the other materials related to Quilliam and the community. The Strangers' Home is mentioned briefly.

55 *Fanatics and Fanaticism: A Lecture Delivered by W. H. Abdullah Quilliam* (Liverpool: Crescent Printing and Publishing Co., 1898), p. 1 of the Preface to the 3rd edn, LPRO.

56 ibid., pp. 20, 62–6.

57 Mrs R. L. Bensly, *Our Journey to Sinai: A Visit to the Convent of St Catarina* (Oxford: Religious Tract Society, 1896), p. 70.

58 Letter to the editor from Robert Cust, late member of Her Majesty's Civil Service, 'The Drink Question in India', *The Times* (19 December 1887).

59 Naomi Shepherd, *The Zealous Intruders: The Western Rediscovery of Palestine* (San Francisco, CA: Harper & Row, 1987), p. 170.

60 See Lilian Lewis Shiman, *The Crusade Against Drink in Victorian England* (New York: St. Martin's Press, 1988) and Norman Longmate, *The Waterdrinkers: A History of Temperance* (London: Hamish Hamilton, 1968).

61 The first temperance society in England was formed in that city in 1830, and similar organisations soon followed: Longmate, *The Waterdrinkers*, p. 33. The movement became so popular there that Toxteth Park was regarded as the largest area of prohibition in England: Shiman, *The Crusade Against Drink*, pp. 158–9.

62 Immigration and overcrowding meant that by the first half of the nineteenth century Liverpool had the highest density of people per square mile in England. In 1842 it was declared the 'unhealthiest' town in the country and could be found at

the top of every index measuring poor living conditions: quoted in Neal, *Sectarian Violence*, pp. 1–4. In addition, its many Irish immigrants escaping the famine arrived destitute.
63 Shiman, *The Crusade Against Drink*, p. 2.
64 For example, a Manx proverb is mentioned in Quilliam, *Fanatics and Fanaticism*, p. 7.
65 *Footprints of the Past: A Series of Lectures Demonstrating How the Discoveries of Geologists and Archaeologists Are Conformable with the Islamic Faith* (Liverpool: Crescent Publishing Co., 1907). The lectures collected in this book were delivered earlier in the year at the British Muslim Institute and published in the newspaper the *Crescent*, LPRO. Thomas Walker Arnold presents a similar perspective, 'Islam is a religion that is essentially rationalist in the widest sense of this term considered etymologically and historically': *The Preaching of Islam: A History of the Propagation of the Muslim Faith* (Westminster: A. Constable & Co., 1896), p. 418.
66 'The Origin of Easter', lecture 6 in Quilliam's *Footprints*, pp. 137–58.
67 'Buddhism in Christianity', lecture 5 in *ibid.*, pp. 115–35.
68 See *ibid.*, lectures 1–3, pp. 1–97.
69 *slamic Review* (1914), 32.
70 W. H. Quilliam, 'Men you Know LXIX – Islam', *Liverpool Review* (13 December 1902), LPRO.
71 For Unitarianism in England see Earl Morse Wilbur, *A History of Unitarianism in Transylvania, England, and America* (Cambridge, MA: Harvard University Press, 1952), especially chapters 16–19; also of interest David Robinson, *The Unitarians and the Universalists* (Westport, CT: Greenwood Press, 1985).
72 Colley notes that religious divisions among Britons could foster sympathy for Islam, and that 'renegades', or converts living in the Mediterranean during the eighteenth century, often were former Catholics or Protestant dissenters: *Captives*, pp. 121–5.
73 The reference to working men is from Parkinson, *Islamic Review*, 2 (1914), 167; and the reference to the women is in Mumtaz Ali, *Muslim Community in Britain*, p. 24.
74 For example, see Frank Neal, *Sectarian Violence*.
75 They are *Liverpool Mercury*, *Liverpool Review*, *Porcupine* and *Liverpool Freeman*.
76 As no single, unified 'Islamic Movement' existed in England during this time, this phrase most likely refers to Quilliam's activities and his community: 'Sheikh Abdullah Quilliam'.
77 Orchard, *Liverpool's Legion of Honour*.
78 Clark, *Marmaduke Pickthall*, p. 39.
79 Ali, *Muslim Community in Britain*, p. 2.
80 The first quoted statement is from the Preface of Salter's *East in West*, and the second is from his *The Asiatic in England*, p. 255.
81 Sir Almeric Fitzroy (clerk to the Privy Council in 1909), *Memoirs* (London: Hutchinson) vol. 1, entries for 18 and 22 of November 1909, pp. 386–387; and 'Obituary: Mr Ameer Ali. Moslem Judge and Leader', *The Times* (4 August 1928). As I noted in the Introduction, there are a number of spellings for his name, and unless citing a specific title, as in this obituary, Sayyid Amir Ali will be used each time for consistency and to avoid confusion.
82 Sayyid Amir Ali, *Islamic History and Culture*, reprinted (Delhi: Amar Prakashan, 1981), p. 1. Because Amir Ali's ideas sometimes contradicted those of other authorities on the faith, his arguments should be understood as one position in ongoing debates within Muslim societies, as well as in England. Information about Amir Ali as well as a collection of some of his writings are in Khursheed Kamal Aziz, *Ameer Ali: His Life and Work* (Lahore: Publishers United Ltd, 1968). Additional publications by Amir Ali, which represented Islam to an English audience, include: *A Critical Examination of the Life and Teachings of Mohammed* (London: Willliams and Norgate, 1873); 'Islam and Canon MacColl', *Nineteenth Century* (November 1895), 778–85; 'The Influence of Women in Islam', *ibid.* (May 1899),

755–74; 'The Caliphate: A Historical and Juridical Sketch', *Contemporary Review* (June 1915), 681–94; 'The Caliphate and the Islamic Renaissance', *Edinburgh Review* (January 1923), 180–95; 'The Modernity of Islam', *Islamic Culture* (January 1927), 1–5. For a more extensive list which includes his many works on the role of Muslims in Indian politics and international affairs, see Appendix 4 in Aziz, *Ameer Ali*, pp. 666–9.
83 Sayyid Amir Ali, 'Islam and its Critics', *The Nineteenth Century*, 37 (September 1895), 361–80.
84 Sayyid Amir Ali, 'Bondage (Slavery)', in *The Spirit of Islam: A History of the Evolution and Ideals of Islam with a Life of the Prophet* (London: Chatto & Windus, 1964 [1891]), pp. 258–67, at 267. Here Amir Ali discusses the circumstances of enfranchisement and explains that marriage between slaves and freemen is allowed, that true Islam makes no distinction on the basis of race or colour and that Muhammad specifically forbade mutilation. Furthermore, the status 'slave' was to be conferred only on prisoners of war after a struggle in self-defence.
85 Sayyid Amir Ali, 'The Real Status of Women in Islam', *Nineteenth Century*, 30 (September 1891), 387–99, reprinted in *Islamic History and Culture*, pp. 1–15. Amir Ali presents a similar argument in chapter 5, 'The Status of Women in Islam', in *The Spirit of Islam*, pp. 222–57, focusing on polygamy, its history and its widespread practice outside of Islam.
86 For example, a writer for *Contemporary Review* who tried to discredit the religion and portray it as oppressive to women refuted Amir Ali's statements regarding the equality of wives: Malcolm MacColl, 'The Musulmans of India and the Sultan', *ibid.*, 71 (February 1897), 280–94, at 283. Previously, Edward Sell had challenged the statements of Amir Ali in 'The New Islam', *ibid.*, 64 (August 1893), 281–93.
87 Sir Frederic J. Goldsmid, 'The Mohammedan Idea of Slavery', MSS Brit. Emp. S. 24 J. 33, BFASS.
88 FOBPP, Dispatch from Sir E. Baring to Earl Granville, February 1884 (vol. 60, p. 2).
89 Amir Ali acted as chairman for the mosque fund: *Sunday Times and Sunday Special* (London) (26 April 1927), p. 10, col. 2. The prospect of building a mosque in London had been discussed since the 1880s.
90 In fact, Amir Ali's arguments 'found their way into the thinking of the English-educated Muslim': Peter Hardy, *The Muslims of British India* (Cambridge: Cambridge University Press, 1972), p. 105.
91 *Ibid.*, pp. 102–3; and David Lelyveld, *Aligarh's First Generation: Muslim Solidarity in British India* (Oxford: Oxford University Press, 1996). Ahmad Khan was born into a family of civil servants in Delhi. He served as a judge before founding the college. The institution educated people like himself, literate north Indian Muslim men from the *ashrāf* class employed in law, education, and government service. Lelyveld, pp. 3, 123–5. Ahmad Khan also wrote *Essays on the Life of Muhammad* (Lahore: Premier Book House, 1968 [1870]) for an English audience.
92 Hardy, *The Muslims of British India*, pp. 104, 113. For discussion of the various ways in which Muslim intellectuals on the Indian subcontinent understood their relationship with the English and the West in general see Aziz Ahmad, *Islamic Modernism in India and Pakistan 1857–1964* (London: Oxford University Press, 1967).
93 See Hardy, *The Muslims of British India*, especially chapter 4, pp. 92–115. Ahmad Khan involved himself in contemporary politics and worked to improve the position of Muslims and to a lesser extent Indians generally in the British administration and that country while, at the same time, opposing Indian nationalism: Lelyveld, *Aligarh's First Generation*, pp. 305–13.
94 'The Moslem Patriotic League', *The Times* (11 April 1900), p. 8C.
95 Letters to the editor, both entitled 'Indian Mussulmans', *The Times* (28 September 1871), p. 10C, and (4 October 1871), p. 12B, and both signed 'A Mahomedan'. The writing style as well as the title and the name suggest that these two letters were from the same person. This issue of Indian–Muslim loyalty to the queen was a subject of concern for the English Victorians and formed the theme of the

contemporary book by Wilson Hunter, *The Indian Musalmans* (Delhi: Indological Book House, 1969 [1871 and 1876]). In this work Hunter discusses the different factions and divisions among Indian Muslims and the doctrinal conflicts regarding the correct approach towards the British Government. He concludes by stating that while the majority of them believe that they are bound by their own laws not to rebel, this obligation lasts only as long as their spiritual rights and privileges are protected. Furthermore, it is the responsibility of the British Government to make sure that it does not neglect to provide protection, noting that it had been remiss in the past

96 Leitner was a Hungarian scholar of Jewish descent who became a British subject, served as an interpreter to the British commissar in the Crimea with the rank of colonel, and studied at King's College, London where he later became a professor of Arabic and Islamic law. After spending time in India, Leitner returned to England and established the Institute at his own expense. He was considered by many to be Jewish, even though he stated that he was a member of the Church of England when applying for naturalisation in 1862: William Rubinstein, 'The Secret of Leopold Amery', *Historical Research*, 73 (June 2000), 173–96, at 178.

97 *A Short Catalog of the Contents of the Leitner Museum at Woking with Illustrations* (Woking, England: Oriental Institute, 1901).

98 J. R. and S. E. Whiteman, *Victorian Woking: Being a Short Account of the Development of the Town and Parish in the Victorian Era* (Castle Arch, Guildford: Unwin Brothers Ltd, 1970), p. 50.

99 Mention of it is made in *ASR* (August–September 1896), 233–5.

100 One later article discusses the lascar sailors mentioned previously: J. Walsh, 'The Empire's Obligation to the Lascar', *IAQR*, 30 (July–October 1910).

101 Herbert Baynes, 'The Moslem Call to Prayer', *IAQR*, 17 (January–April 1904), 109–10, and Abdullah al-Mâmûn al-Suhrawardy, 'Toleration in Islam: The Charter of the Prophet Muhammad to the Christians, and that of the Caliph Ali to the Parsees', *IAQR*, 19 (January–April 1905), 152–61.

102 H. E. Mirza Muhammad Ali, 'The Muharram Celebration', *IAQR*, 1 (January–April 1891), 193–4.

103 Nawwáb A'bdurrashîd Khán, 'The Play "Mahomet" in England', *ibid.*, 195–205, at 195.

104 Ibrahim Hakki, 'Is Turkey Progressing?' *ibid.*, 3 (January–April 1892), 265–78, at 278.

105 Rafi-ud-Din Ahmad, 'Are English Women Legally Inferior to their Mahomedan Sisters', *ibid.*, 1 (January–April 1891), 410–29.

106 *Ibid.*, p. 416.

107 *Ibid.*, p. 412.

108 Published in Woking by the Oriental Nobility Institute (1889).

109 Leitner, *Muhammadanism*, pp. 3, 12. Appended to this talk are six other letters and essays which also focus on Islam. Several had appeared in contemporary publications such as *The Times*, the *Daily Telegraph* and the *Bombay Gazette*.

110 He worked with the Aborigines' Protection Society, the Peace Society, the Indian National Congress, and the Anthropological Institute.

111 The Kafirs' situation received some attention from the press: in addition to the *IAQR* and the *ASR*, their story was covered by *The Times*, the *Church Milt. Intelligencer* (July 1896), the *Calcutta Review* (July 1865), the *Saturday Review* (18 January 1896), the *Globe* and the *Morning Post*. For discussion of the Kafirs and reprints or references to the above-mentioned articles see *ASR*: (July 1874), 66, 73–4; (January–February 1896), 7, 15–34; (August–September 1896), 233–35; and (October–December 1896), 302–4.

112 C. L. Tupper, 'Bonds of Empire', *IAQR*,13 (January–April 1902), 1.

113 Worshippers included Her Majesty's two Indian attendants. The mosque officially closed along with the Institute in 1899 on Leitner's death. It was visited and used occasionally for worship until it's re-opening in 1912 by Kwaja Kamel-ud-Din, the Ahmadi Muslim missionary, mentioned previously, who established the Woking

Muslim Mission the following year. General information about the mosque and the Oriental Institute is from: Alan Crosby, *A History of Woking* (Sussex: Phillimore & Co., 1982), pp. 114–16; 'The First Mosque in England', *Illustrated London News* (November 1889); Iain Wakeford, 'Mosque Centenary', *Woking History Journal*, 1 (1989), 27; and Whiteman, *Victorian Woking*, pp. 49–52.

114 Its design combines various styles of architecture, including Cairene, 'Deccan' and Mogul. It was inspired by buildings that Leitner encountered on his travels and illustrations from the book *Art Arabe*, borrowed from the India Office Library. Leitner furnished the mosque with 'exquisite' wood carvings collected during a trip to Kashmir: *Illustrated London News* (9 November 1889).

115 Festivals held during the nineteenth century are mentioned both by Crosby, *History of Woking*, p. 115 and in the *Islamic Review*, 2 (1914), 453, 557; references to the 'Woking mosque lectures' appear in the *Islamic Review*.

116 'First Mosque', *Illustrated London News* (November 1889). The Bishop of Winchester visited it as well: *Islamic Review*, 2 (1914), 87, 145.

117 'First Mosque'.

118 Ahmad, 'Are English Women Legally Inferior', p. 429.

119 Nawab Sikander Begum of Bhopal, *A Pilgrimage to Mecca*, trans. and ed. Mrs Willoughby-Osborne (London: William Allen & Co., 1870).

120 In Leitner's letter 'Muhammadanism and Slavery' in *Muhammadanism* he notes that the Begum of Bhopal bought several slaves for the sole purpose of freeing them, p. 17.

121 *Women and Work* (20 November 1875), 3.

122 Shah Jehan, Begum of Bhopal, Letter to Queen Victoria, 1871 (41567, f. 49; also see letters to Lord Ripon, 1881 and 1882 (43628, f. 79; 42631, f. 18, Manuscripts Division, British Library.

123 Begum of Bhopal, *A Pilgrimage to Mecca*; the dedication is in the opening pages.

124 Shepherd, *The Zealous Intruders*, pp. 170–92; and Piers Brendon, *Thomas Cook: 150 Years of Popular Tourism* (London: Secker & Warburg, 1991). Included in this trend were English women who visited Muslim harems. Their writings have been discussed at length by Billie Melman: *Women's Orients. English Women and the Middle East, 1718–1918: Sexuality, Religion and Work* (London: Macmillan, 1992); see also chapter four, this book.

125 Amelia B. Edwards, *A Thousand Miles Up the Nile* (London: Routledge & Sons, 1890), p. 18.

126 Mrs Baille, *A Sail to Smyrna: or, An Englishwoman's Journal; Including Impressions of Constantinople, a Visit to a Turkish Harem and a Railway Journey to Ephesus* (London: Longmans, 1873), p. 149.

127 For examples of such descriptions see: Emily A. Beaufort, *Egyptian Sepulchres and Syrian Shrines Including Some Stay in the Lebanon, at Palmyra, and in Western Turkey* (London: Longman, 1861), vol. 2, pp. 150, 156, 158; Mrs W. M. Ramsay, *Everyday Life in Turkey* (London: Hodder & Stoughton, 1897), pp. 270–1; and Reverend George Townsend, *A Cruise in the Bosphorus, and in the Marmora and Aegean Seas* (London: SPCK, c.1890), p. 144.

128 Annie Jane Harvey, *Turkish Harems and Circassian Homes* (London: Hurst & Blackett, 1871), pp. 22–3.

129 Reverend Charles Bell, *A Winter on the Nile, in Egypt and in Nubia*, 2nd edn (London: Hodder & Stoughton, 1889), p. 276.

130 Mrs Bensly, *Our Journey to Sinai*, pp. 22–3.

131 Beaufort, *Egyptian Sepulchres and Syrian Shrines*, vol. 2, pp. 419–24, at 420.

132 Charles M. Doughty, *Travels in Arabia Deserta* (London: J. Cape, 1888), p. 517.

133 Reverend E. L. Cutts, *Christians Under the Crescent in Asia* (London: SPCK, 1877), p. 46.

134 Rev. Bell, *A Winter on the Nile*, p. 29.

135 Rev. Cutts, *Christians Under the Crescent in Asia*, p. 82.

136 Thomas Carlyle, *Heroes and Hero Worship* (London: 1840) quoted by Quilliam in *Fanatics and Fanaticism*, p. 63.

137 Stanley Lane-Poole with Arthur Gilman, *The Moors in Spain* (London: T. Fisher Unwin, 1888); Lane-Poole also published a collection of essays about Islam for the general reader, some of which were his articles that had been printed in the *Edinburgh Review* or the *Saturday Review*. They generally present the religion in a positive light: *Studies in a Mosque* (London: W. H. Allen & Co., 1883)
138 'Mahommedanism', *Chambers Encyclopedia*, cited by Quilliam in *Fanatics and Fanaticism*, pp. 63–4.
139 Mohammed Sharafuddin explores the ways in which English Orientalist literature could promote cross-cultural understanding in *Islam and Romantic Orientalism: Literary Encounters with the Orient* (London: I. B. Tauris, 1994).
140 *Ibid.*, p. 44, from Jack Simmons, *Southey* (London: Collins, 1945), p. 64.
141 Dale Eickelman, *The Middle East and Central Asia: An Anthropological Approach* (Englewood Cliffs, NJ: Prentice-Hall, 1998), pp. 40, 46.
142 Burton was a famous Orientalist scholar–adventurer. For more information about his life and impact see: Isabel Burton, *The Life of Captain Sir Richard F. Burton* (London: Chapman & Hall, 1893); Edward Rice, *Captain Sir Richard Francis Burton: The Secret Agent Who Made the Pilgrimage to Mecca, Discovered the Kama Sutra, and Brought the Arabian Nights to the West* (New York: Charles Scribner's Sons, 1990) and Frank McLynn, *Burton: Snow upon the Desert* (London: John Murray, 1990).
143 Captain Sir Richard Burton, Isabel Burton (ed.), *Personal Narrative of a Pilgrimage to Al-Madinah and Meccah* (New York: Dover Publications, Inc., 1964 [1893]), vols 1 and 2.
144 Letter signed Richard F. Burton (followed by the Arabic *al-hajji 'Abd Allah*, meaning 'hajji, servant of God'), London, 31 March 1879, reprinted in Preface to the third edition (p. xxii) of *Personal Narrative*.
145 Isabel Burton, *Life*, vol. 1, p. 169.
146 Similarly, Kathryn Tidrick has shown that Arabophilia contributed to British attempts to govern or exercise influence in the Middle East during the early twentieth century: the official policy and approach towards British mandates in the area were informed in part by the widespread belief that English men were endowed with an understanding of and a natural affinity with Arabs, especially the 'noble' and 'gentlemanly' Bedouins: K. Tidrick, *Heart-Beguiling Araby* (Cambridge: Cambridge University Press, 1981). This attitude is best illustrated by the life and career of T. E. Lawrence, the legendary 'Lawrence of Arabia', whose successful campaigns in the Middle East during the First World War, close contact with the Bedouins and practice of wearing Arab dress all made him a symbol of the 'benevolent imperialism' of the early twentieth century: Lawrence James, *The Golden Warrior: The Life and Legend of Lawrence of Arabia* (London: Weidenfeld & Nicolson, 1990), p. 277.

CHAPTER SIX

Conclusion

This book has examined the formation of English national identities in relation to Islam during the late nineteenth century through the lens of four historical developments: British anti-slavery efforts in occupied Egypt; the activities of the BFASS in regard to that campaign; gender conflicts and debates in English society; and the creation of a place for Islam in England in the form of newly established Muslim communities and outspoken advocates for and sympathisers with the faith. Considering these four narratives together helps to illuminate the process of cultural exchange within an imperial system characterised by increasingly aggressive British involvement in the Islamic world and more frequent and intimate contact between English people and Muslims. Through encounters in Egypt, new understandings of English national identity were created which had as much to do with domestic issues as they did with foreign policy. These new understandings, in turn, informed competing versions of Englishness, so that second- or third-hand accounts of Islam and the harem were reproduced in English society, where they were invested with additional meanings and political purchase. No constant or linear relationship existed between the development of one conception of English national identity with regard to Islam and another. Rather, the ideologies that emerged through these movements influenced each other in unexpected ways, usually through the interplay of reinforcement and opposition.

This interplay seems especially obvious where British officials and BFASS members were concerned. Her Majesty's officers were motivated by the belief in the essential immorality of slavery, a belief which had become a part of English society and culture through the work of anti-slavery activists even before this specific campaign. The activists, on the other hand, drew inspiration from the efforts of those stationed in Egypt and helped to publicise their correspondence and reports, making them available to an English audience. The two groups shared similar beliefs about Englishness, including the duties of abolitionism, responsibilities of empire, and proper gender roles. Indeed the eventual success of this campaign could not have been accomplished without their mutual reinforcement. Yet officers identified strongly with their Government and their role in its service. They sometimes resented the interference of private citizens who, they complained, put moral zeal ahead of diplomacy and tact, and they disliked female involvement in a sphere that they tried to maintain as a masculine domain. BFASS organisers tended, however, to view themselves as the upholders of true English virtue. They associated their activism with Christian beliefs and acted as watchdogs lest British officials be tempted to compromise what they considered to be the nation's ideals.

Individuals active in both aspects of this campaign took part in contemporary English gender debates; creating and advocating an ideal of proper English gender roles could not involve a politically neutral stance in a society deeply, sometimes violently, divided on the issue. For the majority of the anti-slavery workers, the campaign served to counter feminist criticism of patriarchal domesticity and a male-dominated public sphere. They, along with other conservatives such as missionaries and a number of anti-vice activists, could agree with feminists insofar as they acknowledged that ill-treatment of women took place and should be stopped. However, they presented a protective, or custodial, approach as the answer.

The liberal feminists drew from accepted ideas, associating liberty, justice and individual freedom with English national identity in order to argue that such patriarchal relationships were, in fact, at the root of female oppression. If anti-slavery workers were Anglicising the Egyptians by eliminating female, or harem-oriented, slavery, as they claimed, then feminists would take the project one step further by Anglicising the gender relationships that allowed the subjugation of women in England. They adopted and therefore helped give power to anti-slavery imperialist ideology, particularly negative representations of Islam and the harem, but they did so to suit their own ends. They expressed this perspective in the course of agitation for causes such as women's education, suffrage and property law reform. In addition, some feminists worked within the BFASS, which allowed them to contribute to the campaign while asserting a public role for themselves in the imperial nation state.

Proponents of anti-vice legislation and reform borrowed from BFASS imagery, and as a result efforts to advance one cause helped to raise awareness and support for the other. Sarah and Sheldon Amos dedicated themselves to both, treating them as part of the same overall mission of coming to the aid of fallen women. Associating English prostitution

CONCLUSION

with female slavery in Egypt through the use of the term 'white slavery' proved to be an effective strategy for mobilising reformers. It appealed to, and therefore recreated and reinforced, a sense of national identity based on race and sensationalised the issues by emphasising the brutality of prostitution and the sexual side of the slave trade. In addition, a creative tension existed between conservative and feminist elements in both campaigns: they worked together and reinforced certain shared assumptions, such as the idea that the exploitation of women was Eastern or Islamic and not truly English; yet both groups hoped that their efforts ultimately would serve to promote their particular version of proper gender relationships.

These approaches that relied on negative depictions of the Islamic world were, to a certain extent, reactions to cultural feminist interpretations and other positive images of the harem inspired by the tradition of Orientalism. In order for anti-slavery workers to generate support for a cause that involved transgressing the boundaries of the harem and interfering with private family life in Egypt, they had to convince potential contributors that the institution was illegitimate. They attempted to disassociate it from the English home and to counter popular images of it as a place of feminine empowerment and beauty by describing it as confining, oppressive, even evil. Those who promoted conservative patriarchal gender roles then could contribute to the campaign without calling into question the value of the private domestic sphere in England. Liberal feminist representations of the harem also were created in opposition to those of the cultural feminists, both because of the former's sympathy with the anti-slavery movement and because a number of them saw the celebration of a separate feminine sphere as an obstacle to their goal of establishing a more prominent place for women in English public life.

Those who presented Islam in a light favourable to an English audience entered these ongoing debates and spoke to current concerns, realising that they could ignore neither the anti-slavery rhetoric nor its role and that of images of the harem in English gender politics. Those ideas shaped perceptions of the religion in that country. W. H. Quilliam likened Muslims to English abolitionists, and Sayyid Amir Ali maintained that true Islam condemns slavery. Some connected to the Oriental Institute argued that historically, in law and in practice, the English woman had been more of a slave than the Muslim woman. They even employed the arguments of liberal feminists by citing cases of injustice experienced by females in England. The status of women and the abolition of slavery were not issues of central concern to the public lives and careers of these individuals. Rather they addressed topics and developed arguments in response to anti-Islamic sentiment in England.

Each of these different voices, or perspectives, should be understood as existing in conversation with the others. Individuals had to make themselves and their actions meaningful in ways that contemporaries – their opponents, supporters and those they hoped to win over to their point of view – would understand and appreciate. Consequently they borrowed heavily from and constructed their positions with regard to one another. All drew from existing ideas about Englishness, Islam and the British imperial mission, such as the British hero of empire, the tradition of English abolitionism or the secluded harem. Some found inspiration in shared beliefs in Christianity or affinity to Enlightenment thought. Each perspective, from that of the British officer in Cairo to that of the suffragist in London, is to be regarded as incomplete in isolation because it developed in the context of an imperial cultural system and in relation to the alternative points of view within that system.

This need to borrow, engage and respond is apparent especially when we consider the discourses sympathetic to Islam produced for an English audience. In addition to the examples given previously, Sayyid Amir Ali's discussion of such Enlightenment concepts as liberty and Quilliam's speeches educating reformers about the compatibility of Islam with the temperance movement were shaped by the social milieu. The same arguments would not have been as relevant to the concerns of, for example, most Egyptians at that time. Even the lascars, who were among the least political of the historical actors discussed, formed bonds of ethnicity in response to the experience of exclusion from the English nation, despite differences among them.

Yet these historical actors did not respond to every influence in the larger culture. One of the first steps in the process of creating identity and meaning involves weighing available ideas and deciding which to engage with and which to ignore. British officials and BFASS members consistently disregarded evidence that contradicted the anti-slavery ideology they had created. They continued to view Islam and the harem as *requiring* slavery, even though the latter was suppressed and eventually eliminated, while the former remained intact. They tended also to dismiss arguments favourable to Islam, treating a more sympathetic or complex understanding of the religion as incongruous with their political goals. Likewise, cultural feminist interpretations of the harem had no use for BFASS materials. Muslims, however, who hoped to influence public opinion in England, had less freedom in this respect. They operated at the centre of an imperial system characterised by English hegemony and therefore had to address the dominant discourses if they hoped to have an impact.

Because identities develop in relation to specific social situations, they are created in the present and change as historical circumstances

CONCLUSION

change. The belief in the essential immorality of slavery and their duty to eradicate it had not always characterised English national identity, but rather emerged through abolitionist efforts during the eighteenth and nineteenth centuries. This principle was re-conceptualised and extended to include female and harem-oriented slavery during the late nineteenth century with the increased involvement of the British Government in the Islamic world and the occupation of Egypt. Similarly, defining prostitution and vice as contrary to the English nation, despite the fact that these practices had existed in that society for generations, and labelling them as Eastern, or Islamic came into being through the anti-vice movement linked to anti-slavery efforts. Finally, the ways of understanding the place of Muslims in relation to the English nation – from drawing on the tradition of liberal tolerance to regarding them, like the urban poor, as heathens within to conceding that Islam had a place in that country as the centre of the Empire – were created in the light of the new presence of outspoken Muslims and their communities established during this same period.

For individuals also identities were temporary, constantly forming and re-forming. For example, sometimes W. H. Quilliam expressed allegiance to the British crown, with which he pronounced his faith compatible. Yet when political circumstances arose that put these two loyalties in conflict, he opposed the Government and encouraged his Muslim brethren to do the same. Furthermore, identities could change as subjects moved from one imperial territory to another: English travellers who found common ground with and even admired Islam when abroad could be indifferent to that faith as practiced in their own country.

This fluidity of identity also resulted from the dynamics between ideology and action, as identities were mediated through organised loyalties, such as the British Government, reforming societies or the Oriental Institute, and efforts to further their political agendas. Identities and the systems of belief associated with them influenced activities by giving them meaning in ways understandable to others, though they were produced also through new experiences and encounters. For example, British officials had a sense of their role and mission when they arrived in Egypt, but they re-created and redefined that role in the course of suppressing the slave trade. They patrolled steamer traffic, the Red Sea and caravan routes. They came into conflict with the hudud and Muslim religious authorities, and they put in place alternative legal systems. Through the decisions these officers made and the policies they pursued, Islam and the harem assumed new meaning for them, informing their understandings of appropriate gender roles and their place as individuals in the English nation and British Empire.

Similarly, BFASS members spent considerable time and energy recreating English abolitionist identities in a way that would include an obligation to the slave in the harem as well as the plantation slave, and they did so by organising and pooling their resources. They worked with British officials, sent deputations abroad, and established and maintained the CHFWS. A critically important aspect of the development of this new belief system involved efforts to appeal to the English public through meetings and lectures, and the production and dissemination of printed materials such as the *ASR*.

The importance of considering the relationship between issues covered in the more traditional historical narrative such as reform movements, foreign policy and immigration, on one hand, and Orientalist representations of the harem and the Islamic world, topics usually associated with literary and cultural studies, on the other, can not be overstated. Recent scholarship has tended to place disproportionate emphasis on the role of Orientalist art and literature in providing an ideological foundation for Western imperialism. As this study has shown, even in the case of British imperial foreign policy directly related to the harem, such Orientalist depictions of that institution played a minor role. The systems of meaning produced by British officers in Egypt and by BFASS members served to counter them. Images of the enchanting and luxurious harem informed BFASS rhetoric only to the extent that activists used especially harsh language condemning the institution in order to overshadow them.

When we examine these Orientalist images of the harem in the light of the other systems of meaning available in English society and British imperial culture for understanding this institution, it becomes clear that these ideas were the exception rather than the rule. Cultural feminist attraction to the harem, for example, rejected the dominant imperial ideology in its various versions presented by British officials, BFASS supporters, liberal feminists and others. Their perspectives even went so far as to ignore the contemporary ideal of the democratic nation state, a concept necessary with regard to the other positions and one of central importance to both the imperial project and the process of negotiating power relationships in English society. Instead, they found inspiration in the traditions of pre-revolutionary aristocratic practices.

Orientalism, a term which during the nineteenth century referred also to an interest in or study of the East in general, could encourage identification with Islam. Of all the available approaches and discourses in English society it was the most sympathetic regarding Islam, short of those that inspired conversion, and even Quilliam's conversion was made more acceptable by the Orientalist tradition of mimicry. People with varied backgrounds, perspectives and religious identities from both the East and the West produced Orientalist writings. Institutions such as the Muhammadan Anglo-Oriental College and the Oriental Nobility Institute, as well as the *IAQR*, promoted the study of Orientalism as a positive contribution to scholarship, one which would help to create a more influential role for Muslims in England and throughout the British Empire. In addition, when non-Muslim English people felt a sincere appreciation for the harem or the art, architecture and literature of the Islamic world, they could transcend, even if only momentarily, familiar boundaries of race, nation, and religion.

Certainly Orientalist perspectives functioned in an imperial cultural system characterised by English hegemony as well as by the increasing the importance of Islam within it. Identification and appreciation could give way to more hierarchal relationships, and the former could be used to justify and romanticise the latter. Perhaps the most important factor contributing to the power of British imperialism during this period was that it could accommodate a variety of people and points of view. Each of the four developments discussed in this book and the historical actors involved in them played a role in the British imperial project. The officials who suppressed slavery in Egypt identified with their positions in the service of Her Majesty's Government. BFASS members viewed the British occupation of Egypt and the opportunities that it provided as a calling, a responsibility on the part of English citizens to dedicate themselves to abolition. They used imperialist rhetoric to rally support for their cause and even pressured authorities to be more vigilant and aggressive with regard to foreign policy in Egypt. The women and men who engaged in English gender debates lent their support to imperialist ideology by reproducing it and identifying themselves and their actions with it, often investing it with additional moral force in the process.

Muslims in England also were associated with the Empire. Lascars had worked on East India Company ships, and ayahs cared for the children of company employees. English people often regarded them as inhabiting colonial spaces which involved them in the imperial politics of the metropole. British Muslim men had built their careers through imperial institutions, and even Quilliam, who sometimes expressed anti-government sentiment, benefited from Great Britain's status as a world power.

While all of these people participated in the experience of empire and contributed to its influence and the widespread acceptance of imperial ideology, their reasons for doing so differed dramatically. They were in conflict with each other about the very terms and concepts that they all used and so often treated as clear and obvious: Englishness; proper English gender roles; the British imperial mission;

and the place of Islam within the Empire. Each group particularised these ideas in ways suitable to its own ends. Members of the BFASS acted as part of an extra-parliamentary political culture that asserted an understanding of Englishness as representing certain ideals and values that their Government could not always be relied on to uphold. They also tended to view efforts in Egypt in a missionary spirit not shared by British officials more concerned with diplomacy and practical matters. Feminists, conservatives and others involved in gender debates found an arena in which to compete to further their individual agendas as well as common ground in their mutual support of anti-slavery efforts in Egypt.

Muslims in England and those sympathetic to the faith presented alternative versions of empire through words and actions which communicated the belief that Islam was compatible enough with English society to exist comfortably within it and even to make a positive contribution to it. They challenged English hegemony characterised by the rigid division between the English centre of empire and Muslim peripheries and by the idea that English culture should influence and reform the Islamic world, but not vice versa. Each of the groups discussed here, from Muslims in England to officials in Egypt, reconciled its own concerns with imperial concerns in order to assert a place within this global network of relationships.

Not only were the ideologies of different movements particularised to suit the imperial context, but individuals within these movements particularised them as well, reconciling Islam and Englishness in ways that reflected their specific situations and made their actions meaningful. As each chapter has detailed, women and men of diverse background and viewpoint were drawn together for a variety of reasons. Not all of the British officials or BFASS contributors whose efforts produced new versions of Englishness were themselves English: they came from different areas of the British Isles, the British Empire and the world. Workers may have donated to the BFASS because they identified with the slaves, while the organisation's leadership tended to rely on maternal–paternal class-based approaches.

Liberal feminists took part in this campaign despite the conservative ideas about English gender roles it promoted, and feminist movements crossed class and gender lines; even Scottish and Irish feminists participated in English campaigns. Finally, Muslims living in England hailed from all over the Empire and the world, from South Asia to Northern Africa; some had been born in England. Quilliam identified himself as Manx, British and Muslim. Muslims could be sailors, ayahs or even royal personages, and they did not always share the same understanding or interpretation of Islam.

CONCLUSION

How people chose to identify themselves at any point in time, whether they would give primacy to class, gender, race, nation or religion, and how they would then interpret that identity and translate it into action was impossible to predict, for individuals were not predisposed to react to situations or events in one way or another. Social circumstances always provided support for a number of interpretations of the self in relation to Islam, Englishness and the Empire, and they did not determine which one would be chosen and which equally viable options would be rejected. English people could identify with the white slave in Egypt or regard her as essentially different depending on how they chose to understand race, whether as determined primarily by physical characteristics or in terms of nation as defined through culture, language and belief systems. Similarly, class could be used to help create a place for Islam in England as in the establishment of the Oriental Nobility Institute and in the appreciation for the educated British–Indian gentlemen living in London. However, it could also serve to exclude and marginalise Muslims from the English nation, as in the case of the lascar sailors who often were thought to represent the uncivilised underclass existing in imperial spaces and in need of reform. Thus a bourgeois sense of English national identity ensured neither sympathy with nor animosity towards Islam.

Even the belief in a certain religious or ideological system did not predispose individuals to interpret Islam in one way or another. For example, while Cardinal Lavigerie conducted anti-slavery activity in such a manner that some contemporaries accused him of attempting to lead an anti-Muslim crusade, other Christians identified with Muslims as people of faith and expressed admiration for their piety and devotion. The idea of the closed harem seemed an affront to suffragists and other feminists who embraced Enlightenment ideals about individual liberty, autonomy and the transparent civil society. For W. H. Quilliam, however, Enlightenment thought played a central role in his conversion to Islam, from his initial interest in Unitarianism and Deism, and his attempt to examine different religions and objectively weigh the value of each to his understanding and presentation of his newfound faith as essentially reasonable.

The fact that so many possibilities, so many ideas and ways of interpreting them, existed within this British imperial cultural system testifies to the importance of agency. Activists involved in each of the movements discussed, from anti-slavery efforts to anti-vice agitation to the various feminist campaigns, invested considerable time and energy in creating new systems of meaning to effect change. They remained a minority within the larger society, and their identification with such movements was a conscious choice that involved rejecting other, more popular, points of view. Muslims in England also were in the minority. Those who had made the decision to immigrate to that country and those English people who converted to Islam were the exception, not the rule. Their words and actions show extraordinary initiative. Those sympathetic to Islam who appealed to an English audience tended to be especially creative, from the theatrical processions of the lascars to the prolific writing of Sayyid Amir Ali to the manipulation of roles by Richard Burton.

Even the British officials, who seemed merely to be following orders, made decisions in the course of the anti-slavery campaign that allowed them to create their own unique understanding of themselves and their relationship to the nation and empire. They very well could have chosen not to identify with their government's agenda in Egypt by turning a blind eye to the transport of female slaves as some, in fact, did. Alternatively, they could have decided not to go beyond their prescribed duties by taking precautions to limit the independence of freed female slaves. Either course of action would have changed fundamentally the version of the British imperial mission and English gender roles that they created and promoted.

Part of the English experience of imperialism in the Islamic world – for British officials particularly, but for others as well – involved identification with the Muslim male and masculinist power structure. Indeed, this power structure and the threat of it were used to bolster the position of traditionalists with regard to the increasingly influential feminist movements. British officers prided themselves on having certain attributes in common with Muslim men that allowed them to win the latter's respect and govern in that part of the world. For generations Orientalist mimics had appropriated the power of the Muslim from the East through portraiture, speech, and dress. Similarly, titles such as 'pasha' and 'bey', and in the case of Richard Burton 'hajji', were used by British officers for the benefit of an English audience and for each other as much as for contacts abroad.

W. H. Quilliam took advantage of these practices. The tradition of mimicry provided an opportunity for him to express his faith visually by appearing in what was recognised as Islamic dress. He also used his influential position in England to make numerous connections and acquire titles from Muslim rulers in Turkey, Persia and Northern Africa. Quilliam and others, such as Sayyid Amir Ali and to a lesser extent Gottlieb William Leitner, understood English identification with Islam and saw in it what most at the time did not see, an intellectual space that had the potential of transforming Anglo-Muslim relations by allowing the creation of a place for Islam in that society and nation. As Sayyid Amir Ali maintained, if the British Empire was a

CONCLUSION

great power with millions of subjects who were followers of the prophet, than its capital city should have a mosque of sufficient grandeur to reflect the circumstances.

In summation, identification and the projection of inferiority were not mutually exclusive attitudes, but part of the same imperial ideology. The belief in the backwardness of Muslim institutions preserved English hegemony and imperial hierarchies, while the establishment of commonalities and shared interests served to justify extensive British involvement in the Islamic world. The idea of imperial greatness was based on both a duty to reform and a certain amount of respect and admiration for occupied peoples. As a result, the British officer could call himself a pasha while working to undermine the existing power structures in Egypt, and see no contradiction – such interplay between identification and conflict, from competing class-based versions of English national identity to feminists and their opponents working together in the cause of anti-slavery, has been a theme throughout the book. Thus the forging of alliances through the perception of difference existed on a number of levels in the British imperial cultural system, from the home and family to the nation to the international political arena, each of which overlapped and informed the others.

The border separating the English nation from the rest of the Empire and the Islamic world was constantly drawn and redrawn by historical actors in relation to specific circumstances in the course of political campaigns, identity formation and cultural exchange. For British officials and BFASS members engaged in suppressing the slave trade in Egypt, Englishness constituted the core of the Empire, while Muslims lived in its peripheries. English culture could and should, according to them, be exported to Egypt, but not vice versa. Missionaries and other conservatives shared this view. For liberal feminists and anti-vice activists, however, Muslim tendencies existed at both the centre and the peripheries of the Empire. For them, references to Islam were not so much about the religion, but rather a way of signifying behaviour that they considered uncivilised, which included prostitution, vice and injustices to women indigenous to English society, as well as slave-trading in Egypt. Because the English nation so often was defined in contrast to imperial spaces and to Islam, the evocation of images of that religion provided a powerful means for activists to communicate as to who and what they believed should be excluded from it and eliminated.

Others presented alternative perspectives that did not assume a dichotomy between English superiority and Muslim inferiority. For a number of Muslims, including the lascars and ayahs, beliefs about what separated Englishness from Islam were irrelevant: their faith was universal. Likewise cultural feminists saw a certain ideal of femininity as transcending the boundaries of nation or religion, and new discourses produced for an English audience encouraged identification with that faith. British–Muslim statesmen and Shah Jehan took a more strategic approach. They manipulated the border between nation and empire by asserting a place for Islam in England; yet they also reinforced it by accepting the idea that their faith was British but not English. Finally, Quilliam and Burton understood the malleable, porous and essentially fictive nature of this dividing line. They crossed it and created personas based on their connection with Islam *and* their ties to the English nation, while at the same time re-creating this boundary in different ways through their words and actions.

Because of the increased and more intimate contact that English people had with Muslims and Islam during the late nineteenth century – the result of a new and aggressive foreign policy and of immigration – aspects of Islam found their way into English culture and society. In this respect the border remained porous regardless of how often it was drawn and redrawn. Encounters with the harem and the hudud in the course of anti-slavery efforts brought new images of the institution to an English audience, adding to the more familiar travel and missionary accounts that proliferated during this period. Muslim celebration and ceremony could be seen on the streets of the larger cities and seaport towns, and a mosque was erected in Woking. In addition, followers of the prophet presented arguments to convert English Christians, and unique perspectives appeared regarding the faith, such as the writings of Sayyid Amir Ali and those related to Burton's hajj.

A greater number of opportunities for exposure to Islam did not, however, guarantee a better understanding of this religious and social system. The English person interested in learning about it was faced with multiple and contradictory representations, each asserting its own importance and truth. In fact, when I began to consider this research project I was intrigued by how many nineteenth-century books and articles published in England on the topic, regardless of the particular background or agenda of the author, would begin by assuring the reader that, despite widespread confusion about Islam, his or her writing would clarify and explain, an approach adopted year after year, decade after decade.

English people of the late nineteenth and, indeed, many in the early twenty-first century struggle with this issue, in part because Islam has had so many different meanings in the West, produced by Muslims and non-Muslims alike. How it was regarded at any given time depended on the specific circumstances and individual interpretations. In addition to religious and spiritual matters, perceptions of Islam had to do with foreign policy, gender debates, and the politics of nation and eth-

CONCLUSION

nicity. Different depictions of this faith, both positive and negative, circulated within British imperial culture. Each attempt to explain it definitively and examine it objectively outside the context of current events and debates would be undermined by many conflicting accounts; and narratives intended to clarify became part of the dynamics of creation and exchange. Thus, understanding the impact and significance of Islam in the West involves recognising this process and its role in politics, societal change and the formation of competing national identities.

Yet lack of clarity provides opportunity. Actions that led to real change became meaningful and therefore possible because women and men created and oriented themselves around new, ever-evolving, identities based on varying conceptions of Englishness, Islam and the British imperial mission. They established a place for Islam in England, effected reform in that country and eliminated slavery in Egypt. Encounters between non-Muslim English people and Muslims allowed both for identification and for the perception of difference, though typically a combination of the two approaches. Understanding the wide range of possibilities and the power of individual agency as evidenced in this study in the history of Western–Muslim, or more specifically Anglo-Muslim, relations could help us in the postcolonial era to create new roles for ourselves that more effectively address the concerns and problems of the modern world and to avoid some of the negative aspects of our collective past. Certainly Western involvement in and attempts to reform Muslim countries of the Middle East, immigration and ethnicity in Europe and the United States, and the importance of understanding the position of women and feminism in a global context are all matters of pressing concern, as relevant today as they were during the late Victorian period.

APPENDICES

Appendix 1

Table A1 Number of slaves manumitted, 1877–97

	1877–81	1882–86	1887–91	1892–97
African female	3,579	5,254	616	240
African[a] male	1,410	3,656	389	137
Circassian female	43	92	11	1
Circassian male	16	24	–	–
Female	17	242	239	74
Male	42	38	69	29
Eunuch	2	–	–	–
Non-specific	–	4,703	–	–
Totals	5,109	14,009	1,324	481

Note:
[a] 'African' here refers to those slaves from Central and East Africa, usually identified in reports as 'Negro', Abyssinian, Nubian, or Sudanese.
No information was given indicating whether these slaves were adults or children.

Sources:
Foreign Office Records (BPP unless otherwise indicated):
Sir E. Baring to Earl Granville, Feb. 1884 (vol. 60, p. 4); Memorandum from R. Borg, July 1880 (vol. 58, pp. 85–6); 'Return Showing the Number of Slaves Manumitted at the Several Bureaux, and the Manner in Which They Have Been Provided For. Quarter Ended Jan. 31, 1880', from R. Borg, February 1880 (vol. 58, p. 44); same return form for the quarter ending 30 April 1880, R. Borg, May 1880 (vol. 58 p. 59); 'Return of Slaves Liberated by the Egyptian Authorities at Alexandria Between 1 August 1877 and 31 July 1878' (v. 58, p. 26); 'Return Showing the Number of Slaves Manumitted at the Bureaux Hereunder, and the Manner in Which They Have Been Provided For, Year Ended 31 July, 1878' (vol. 58, p. 34); same return form for the quarter ended 31 October 1878 (vol. 58, p. 44); 'Statement Respecting the Slaves Liberated by the Alexandria Office of the Department for the Suppression of the Slave Trade, during the Month of November, 1878' (vol. 58, p. 50); 'Slaves Emancipated Through the Intervention of Her Majesty's Vice-Consulate at Larissa and Volo', enclosure in letter dated May 1881 (vol. 59, p. 137); Vice-Consul Borg to Mr Cookson, July 1881 (vol. 59, pp. 44–5); 'Return of Slaves Who Have Sought Refuge in, or Who Have Been Manumitted Through, the Intervention of Her Majesty's Consul at Jeddah, during the Quarter Ended 31 March 1881' and same form for 30 June 1881 and 30 September 1881 (vol. 59, pp. 132–5); 'Return Showing the Number of Slaves Manumitted at the Several Bureaux, to the End of January 1884', which includes information for 1882 and 1883 (vol. 60, p. 3; this document is also in FO 84/1675); 'État des esclaves libérés par les bureaux d'affranchissement du service de la répression de la traite. – depuis le 1 Janvier, 1885, jusqu'a` fin Décembre 1885', and the same form for 1886 (vol. 60, pp. 11–12); FO CP 541/30/Turkey, 1887–89; FO CP 541/27/Turkey 1884–86.

APPENDICES

BFASS collection Egypt (G-25):
Sir E. Baring to the Marquis of Salisbury, received 21 February 1886; "État mensuel-démontrant le nombre des esclaves affranchis pendant le mois de (Mai, Mars, Feb., Jan., Avril)', 1892; 'État nominal des esclaves importés pendant le saison du pèlerinage de 1886'; form from the Ministry of the Interior, Repression of Slave Trade Department, No. 41, April 1897; same form for July and October 1896, November 1890, and March, April, May, September, October, November and December 1888.

Appendix 2

Table A2   BFASS members' and contributors' places of residence

Aberdeen	Colchester	Heworth	New York	Sydenham
Alexandria	Coventry	Halifax	North Shields	Sudbury
Alton	Cowbridge	Highbury	Norwich	Sunderland
Ambleside	Croydon	Highgate	Nottingham	Surbiton
Aspley	Darlington	Hitchin	Oxford	Sydenham
Banbury	Daventry	Holloway	Paris	Sydenham Hill
Barnsley	Demerara	Horspools	Peckham	Tadcaster
Baschurch	Denmark Hill	Houghton	Peckham Rye	Teignmouth
Bath	Deptford	Huddersfield	Pickering	Thornton
Bedford	Derby	Ipswich	Plaistow	Torquay
Berkhampstead	Devon	Islington	Plymouth	Tottenham
Bingley	Devizes	Isle of Wight	Preston	Truro
Birmingham	Derwent Hill	Ivybridge	Rawden	TunbridgeWells
Birstwith	Dorking	Kelso	Reading	Tyneholme
Blackburn	Dublin	Kensington	Red Hill	Ulverstone
Blackheath	Dunfermline	Kendal	Redditch	Upper Clapton
Bolton	Eastbourne	Kent	Regents Park	Vienna
Bradford	Eatington	Kingsbridge	Reigate	Walthamstow
Bridgnorth	Edinburgh	Kirkliston	Rio de Janeiro	Wandsworth
Bridgwater	Essex	Lancaster	Ripon	Warren Point
Bridport	Edenderry	King's Lynn	Rochester	Warwick
Brighton	Exeter	Leeds	Roehampton	Watcombe
Bristol	Exmouth	Leighton	Rushmore	Waterford
Bromley	Evesham	Lewes	Rydal	Wellington
Budleigh	Falmouth	Leytonstone	Salterton	Westbury
Burley-in-Wharfedale	Frenchay	Liskeard	Scarborough	Weston-super-Mare
Cairo	Glasgow	Leicester	Sheffield	Whitehaven
Camberwell	Goole	Leamington	Shotley Bridge	Wigan
Cambridge	Great Bealings	Liverpool	Shrewsbury	Wimbledon
Carlisle	Gloucestor	Leighton	South Benton	Winchmore Hill
Charlbury	Heavitree	Moorfields	Southhampton	Wincobank Hill
Chelmsford	Hampstead	London	Spalding	Winscombe
Chelsea	Harlow	Luton	St Austell	Wisbeach
Chislehurst	Helston	Morton	St Lucia	Woodbridge
Cirencester	Hensol Castle	Neath	Staines	Worcester

Table A2 (cont.)

Clapham Com.	Hereford	Newcastle	Stanstead	Workington
Clifton	Hertford	Newbury	Stoke Newington	York
Coalbrookdale	Harrogate	Manchester	Stratford	
Cork	Harrow	Manningham	Swansea	

Sources: Information given throughout the *ASR* and the BFASS collections; the majority of members and contributors lived in and around London, Bristol, Bath, or Birmingham.

SELECT BIBLIOGRAPHY

Archives and special collections of primary source materials

American University in Cairo Rare Books and Special Collections Library
Bodleian Library of Commonwealth and African Studies at Rhodes House, University of Oxford : British and Foreign Anti-Slavery Society Collections
British Library: India Office Records, Manuscript Collection, Newspaper Division
Church Missionary Society Archive, Special Collections, University of Birmingham, UK
Dar al-Kutub, Cairo
Fawcett Library, London
Liverpool Public Record Office
London City Mission records
National Archives, Kew, Richmond, Surrey: Foreign Office Records and Correspondence
New York Public Library: Asian and Middle Eastern Division
Schomburg Center for Research in Black Culture: Rare Books Division

Books and articles used for secondary source material

Ackermann, Robert John, *Heterogeneities: Race, Gender, Class, Nation, and State* (Amherst: University of Massachusetts Press, 1996)
Adams, James Eli, *Dandies and Desert Saints* (Ithaca, NY, and London: Cornell University Press, 1995)
Ahmed, Leila, *Women and Gender in Islam: Historical Roots of a Modern Debate* (New Haven, CT, and London: Yale University Press, 1992)
Anderson, Benedict, *Imagined Communities: Reflections on the Origin and Spread of Nationalism* (London: Verso, 1983)
Ashcraft, Richard, *Revolutionary Politics and Locke's Two Treatises of Government* (Princeton, NJ: Princeton University Press, 1986)
Austen, Ralph, 'The Mediterranean Islamic Slave Trade Out of Africa: A Tentative Census', *Slavery and Abolition: A Journal of Comparative Studies*, 13 (April 1992), 214–48.
Al-Azmeh, Aziz, *Islams and Modernities* (London: Verso, 1993)
Al-Tirmanini, 'Abd al-Salam, *al-Riqq Madihu wa Hadiruhu* (Kuwait: al-Majlis al-Watani al-Thaqafa wa al-Funun wa al-Adab, 1979)
Badran, Margot, *Feminists, Islam, and Nation: Gender and the Making of Modern Egypt* (Princeton, NJ: Princeton University Press, 1995)
Baer, Gabriel, *Studies in the Social History of Modern Egypt* (Chicago, IL, and London: University of Chicago Press, 1969)
Balibar, Etienne and Immanuel Wallerstein, 'The Construction of Peoplehood: Racism, Nationalism, Ethnicity', in E. Balibar and I. Wallerstein (eds), *Race,*

SELECT BIBLIOGRAPHY

Nation, Class: Ambiguous Identities, trans. Chris Turner (London: Verso, 1991)

Baron, Beth, *The Women's Awakening in Egypt: Culture, Society, and the Press* (New Haven, CT, and London: Yale University Press, 1994)

—— 'The Making of the Egyptian Nation', in Ida Blom, Karen Hagemann and Catherine Hall (eds), *Gendered Nations: Nationalisms and Gender Order in the Long Nineteenth Century* (Oxford: Berg, 2000)

Baucom, Ian, *Out of Place: Englishness, Empire, and the Locations of Identity* (Princeton, NJ: Princeton University Press, 1999)

Bhabha, Homi, *The Location of Culture* (London and New York: Routledge, 1994)

—— 'The Other Question: Difference, Discrimination, and the Discourse of Colonialism', in Houston Baker Jr, Manthia Diawara and Ruth Lindeborg (eds), *Black British Cultural Studies: A Reader* (Chicago, IL, and London: University of Chicago Press, 1996), 87–106

Bloom, William, *Personal Identity, National Identity and International Relations* (Cambridge: Cambridge University Press, 1990)

Brockliss, Laurence and David Eastwood (eds), *A Union of Multiple Identities: The British Isles, c.1750–c.1850* (Manchester and New York: Manchester University Press, 1997)

Burton, Antoinette, *Burdens of History: British Feminists, Indian Women, and Imperial Culture, 1865–1915* (Chapel Hill and London: University of North Carolina Press, 1994)

—— *At the Heart of the Empire: Indians and the Colonial Encounter in Late-Victorian Britain* (Berkeley: University of California Press, 1998)

Cabrera, Miguel, 'On Language, Culture, and Social Action', *History and Theory*, 40 (December 2001), 82–100

Chatterjee, Indrani, *Gender, Slavery and Law in Colonial India* (Oxford: Oxford University Press, 1999)

Clark, Anna, 'Queen Caroline and the Sexual Politics of Popular Culture in London, 1820', *Representations*, 31 (summer 1990), 47–68

Cohn, Bernard, *Colonialism and its Forms of Knowledge: The British in India* (Princeton, NJ: Princeton University Press, 1996)

Colley, Linda, *Britons: Forging the Nation 1707–1837* (New Haven, CT, and London: Yale University Press, 1992)

—— *Captives: Britain, Empire and the World, 1600–1850* (London: Jonathan Cape, 2002)

Crick, Bernard (ed.), *National Identities: The Constitution of the United Kingdom* (Blackwell: Oxford, 1991)

Cuno, Kenneth, 'Ambiguous Modernization: The Transition to Monogamy in the Khedival House of Egypt', in Beshara Doumani (ed.), *Family History in the Middle East: Household, Property, and Gender* (Albany: State University of New York Press, 2003)

Davidoff, Leonore and Catherine Hall, *Family Fortunes: Men and Women of the English Middle Class, 1780–1850* (Chicago, IL: University of Chicago Press, 1987)

Dawson, Graham, *Soldier Heroes: British Adventure, Empire and the Imagining of Masculinities* (London and New York: Routledge, 1994)

SELECT BIBLIOGRAPHY

Dodd, Philip, 'Englishness and the National Culture', in Robert Colls and Philip Dodd, (eds), *Englishness: Politics and Culture 1880–1920* (London: Croom Helm, 1986)

Erdem, Y. Hakan, *Slavery in the Ottoman Empire and its Demise, 1800–1909* (London: Macmillan Press Ltd, 1996)

Gates, Henry Louis Jr, (ed.), *'Race', Writing, and Difference* (Chicago, IL: University of Chicago Press, 1986)

Geertz, Clifford, *The Interpretation of Cultures* (New York: Basic Books, 1973)

Gilroy, Paul, *The Black Atlantic: Modernity and Double Consciousness* (Cambridge: Harvard University Press, 1993)

Grant, Alexander and Keith Stringer (eds), *Uniting the Kingdom? The making of British History* (London and New York: Routledge, 1995)

Grewal, Inderpal, *Home and Harem: Nation, Gender, Empire, and the Cultures of Travel* (Durham, NC, and London: Duke University Press, 1996)

Hall, Catherine, *White, Male and Middle-Class: Explorations in Feminism and History* (Cambridge: Polity Press, 1992)

—— *Civilising Subjects: Metropole and Colony in the English Imagination, 1830–1867* (Chicago, IL, and London: University of Chicago Press, 2002)

Handler, Richard, 'Is "Identity" a Useful Cross-Cultural Concept?' in John R. Gillis (ed.), *Commemorations: The Politics of National Identity* (Princeton, NJ: Princeton University Press, 1994)

Hardy, P., *The Muslims of British India* (Cambridge: Cambridge University Press, 1972)

Hatem, Mervat, 'Through Each Other's Eyes: The Impact on the Colonial Encounter of the Images of Egyptian, Levantine–Egyptian, and European Women, 1862–1920', in Nupur Chaudhuri and Margaret Strobel (eds), *Western Women and Imperialism: Complicity and Resistance* (Bloomington: Indiana University Press, 1992)

Hilal, 'Imad Ahmad, *al-Raqiq fi Misr fi al-qarn al-tasi' 'ashara* (Cairo, 1999)

Hendricks, Margo and Patricia Parker (eds), *Women, 'Race' and Writing in the Early Modern Period* (London and New York: Routledge, 1994)

Holcombe, Lee, 'Victorian Wives and Property: Reform of the Married Women's Property Law, 1857–1882', in Martha Vicinus (ed.), *A Widening Sphere: Changing Roles of Victorian Women* (Bloomington: Indiana University Press, 1977)

Holton, Sandra Stanley, *Feminism and Democracy: Women's Suffrage and Reform Politics in Britain, 1900–1918* (Cambridge: Cambridge University Press, 1986)

Hourani, Albert, *Arabic Thought in the Liberal Age 1798–1939* (Oxford: Oxford University Press, 1962)

Husayn, 'Abd al-Ghafar Muhammad, *Bina' al-Dawla al-Haditha fi Misr* (Cairo: Dar al- Ma'arif, 1981)

Ibrahim, 'Abd Allah 'Abd al-Raziq, 'al-Juhud al-Dawliyya li-Ilgha' al-Riqq fi Ifriqiyya', *al-Majalla al-Tarikhiyya al-Misriyya*, 32 (1985), 181–219.

Jones, Gareth Stedman, *Outcast London: A Study in the Relationship Between Classes in Victorian Society* (Oxford: Clarendon Press, 1971)

Kale, Madhavi, '"When The Saints Came Marching In:" The Anti-Slavery

Society and Indian Indentured Migration to the British Caribbean', in Martin Daunton and Rick Halpern (eds), *Empire and Others: British Encounters with Indigenous Peoples, 1600– 1850* (London: University College London Press, 1999)

Kearney, Hugh, *The British Isles: A History of Four Nations* (Cambridge: Cambridge University Press, 1989)

Kelsall, Malcolm, 'The Slave-Woman in the Harem', *Studies in Romanticism*, 31 (fall 1992), 315–31

Lelyveld, David, *Aligarh's First Generation: Muslim Solidarity in British India* (Oxford: Oxford University Press, 1996)

Lewis, Bernard, *Race and Slavery in the Middle East: An Historical Enquiry* (Oxford: Oxford University Press, 1990)

Lewis, Reina, *Gendering Orientalism: Race, Femininity and Representation* (London and New York: Routledge, 1996)

Lutfi al-Sayyid, Afaf, *Egypt and Cromer: A Study in Anglo-Egyptian Relations* (New York: Frederick A. Praeger, 1969)

Lutfi al-Sayyid Marsot, Afaf, *A Short History of Modern Egypt* (Cambridge: Cambridge University Press, 1985)

MacKenzie, John M., *Propaganda and Empire: The Manipulation of British Public Opinion, 1880–1960* (Manchester: Manchester University Press, 1984)

MacKenzie, John, 'Essay and Reflection: On Scotland and the Empire', *International History Review*, 15 (1993), 661–880

—— 'Empire and National Identities: The Case of Scotland', *Transactions of the Royal Historical Society*, 6th series (Cambridge: Cambridge University Press, 1998), vol. 8

Matar, Nabil, *Islam in Britain 1558–1685* (Cambridge: Cambridge University Press, 1998)

Melman, Billie, *Women's Orient. English Women and the Middle East, 1718–1918: Sexuality, Religion and Work* (London: Macmillan, 1992)

Melucci, Alberto, *Nomads of the Present: Social Movements and Individual Needs in Contemporary Society*, ed. John Keane and Paul Mier (Philadelphia, PA: Temple University Press, 1989)

—— 'The Process of Collective Identity', in Hank Johnston and Bert Klandermans (eds), *Social Movements and Culture* (Minneapolis: University of Minnesota Press, 1995), vol. 4, pp. 41–63

Midgley, Clare (ed.), *Gender and Imperialism* (Manchester: Manchester University Press, 1998)

Miers, Suzanne, *Britain and the Ending of the Slave Trade* (London: Longman, 1975)

Mitchell, Timothy, *Colonising Egypt* (Cambridge: Cambridge University Press, 1988)

Mukhtar, Muhammad, *Bughyat al-Marid fi Shira' al-Jawari wa Taqlib al-'Abid: al- Awda' al-Ijtima'iyya li al-Raqiq fi Misr 642–1924* (Cairo: Khalid Mukhtar and Muhammad Mukhtar, 1997)

Mustafa, Ahmad 'Abd al-Rahim, *Misr wa al-Mas'ala al-Misriyya min 1876 ila 1882* (Cairo: Dar al-Ma'arif bi-Misr, 1966)

SELECT BIBLIOGRAPHY

Oldfield, J. R., *Popular Politics and British Anti-Slavery: The Mobilisation of Public Opinion Against the Slave Trade 1787–1807* (Manchester: Manchester University Press, 1995)

Panayi, Panikos, *Immigration, Ethnicity and Racism in Britain, 1815–1945* (Manchester: Manchester University Press, 1994)

Perkin, Harold, *The Origins of Modern English Society 1780–1880* (London: Routledge & Kegan Paul, 1969)

Philipp, Thomas, 'Feminism and Nationalist Politics in Egypt', in Lois Beck and Nikki Keddie (eds), *Women in the Muslim World* (Cambridge: Harvard University Press, 1978)

Pick, Daniel, *Faces of Degeneration: A European Disorder, c.1848–c.1918* (Cambridge: Cambridge University Press, 1989)

Platt, Gerald, 'Thoughts on a Theory of Collective Action: Language, Affect, and Ideology in Revolution', in Mel Albin (ed.), *New Directions in Psychohistory* (Lexington, MA: Lexington Books, 1980)

Pocock, J. G. A., *Virtue, Commerce and History: Essays on Political Thought and History, Chiefly in the Eighteenth Century* (Cambridge: Cambridge University Press, 1985)

—— 'British History: A Plea for a New Subject', *New Zealand Journal of History*, 8 (April 1974), reprinted in *Journal of Modern History*, 47 (December 1975), 601–21

Poovey, Mary, *Uneven Developments: The Ideological Work of Gender in Mid-Victorian England* (Chicago, IL: University of Chicago Press, 1988)

Powell, Eve Troutt, *A Different Shade of Colonialism: Egypt, Great Britain, and the Mastery of the Sudan* (Berkeley and Los Angeles: University of California Press, 2003)

Ramadan, 'Abd al-'Azim, *Awraq fi Ta'rikh Misr* (Cairo: al-Hay'a al-Misriyya al-'Amma li al-Kitab, 1995).

Rendall, Jane, *The Origins of Modern Feminism: Women in Britain, France and the United States, 1780–1860* (London: Macmillan, 1985)

Roach, Joseph, *Cities of the Dead* (New York: Columbia University Press, 1996)

Robbins, Keith, *Great Britain: Identities, Institutions and the Idea of Britishness*. (London: Longman, 1998)

Said, Abdul Aziz and Meena Sharify-Funk (eds), *Cultural Diversity and Islam* (New York: University Press of America, 2003)

Said, Edward, *Orientalism* (New York: Pantheon Books, 1978)

—— *Culture and Imperialism* (New York: Alfred A. Knopf, 1993)

Sharafuddin, Mohammed, *Islam and Romantic Orientalism: Literary Encounters with the Orient* (London: I. B. Tauris, 1994)

Sinha, Mrinalini, *Colonial Masculinity: The 'Manly Englishman' and the 'Effeminate Bengali' in the Late Nineteenth Century* (Manchester: Manchester University Press, 1995)

Smyth, Jim, *The Making of the United Kingdom, 1660–1800: State, Religion and Identity in Britain and Ireland* (London: Longman, 2001)

Stocking, George, *Victorian Anthropology* (New York: Free Press, 1987)

Taussig, Michael, *Mimesis and Alterity: A Particular History of the Senses* (New York and London: Routledge, 1993)

SELECT BIBLIOGRAPHY

Thompson, E. P., *The Making of the English Working Class* (London: Victor Gollancz, 1963)

Thorne, Susan, '"The Conversion of Englishmen and the Conversion of the World Inseparable:" Missionary Imperialism and the Language of Class in Early Industrial Britain', in Frederick Cooper and Ann Laura Stoler (eds), *Tensions of Empire: Colonial Cultures in a Bourgeois World* (Berkeley: University of California Press, 1997)

Tidrick, Kathryn, *Heart-Beguiling Araby* (Cambridge: Cambridge University Press, 1981)

Tignor, Robert, *Modernization and British Colonial Rule in Egypt, 1882–1914* (Princeton, NJ: Princeton University Press, 1966)

Toledano, Ehud, *The Ottoman Slave Trade and its Suppression: 1840–1890* (Princeton: Princeton University Press, 1982)

—— *Slavery and Abolition in the Ottoman Middle East* (Seattle and London: University of Washington Press, 1998)

Toledano, Ehud, 'Shemsigul: A Circassian Slave in Mid-Nineteenth-Century Cairo', in Edmund Burke (ed.), *Struggle and Survival in the Modern Middle East* (Berkeley: University of California Press, 1993)

Tucker, Judith, *Women in Nineteenth-Century Egypt* (Cambridge: Cambridge University Press, 1985)

Turbiyyn, Ahmad, *Tarikh Misr wa al-Sudan al-Hadith wa al-Mu'asir* (Beirut: Muwassasat al-Risala, 1994)

Turley, David, *The Culture of English Antislavery, 1780–1860* (London and New York: Routledge, 1991)

Visram, Rozina, *Ayahs, Lascars and Princes: Indians in Britain 1700–1947* (London: Pluto Press, 1986)

Walkowitz, Judith, *Prostitution and Victorian Society: Women, Class and the State* (Cambridge: Cambridge University Press, 1980)

—— *City of Dreadful Delight: Narratives of Sexual Danger in Late-Victorian London* (Chicago, IL: University of Chicago Press, 1992)

Weinstein, Fred, *History and Theory After the Fall: An Essay on Interpretation* (Chicago, IL, and London: University of Chicago Press, 1990)

Welch, William M., *No Country for a Gentleman: British Rule in Egypt, 1883–1907* (New York: Greenwood Press, 1988)

Wilson, Kathleen, *The Sense of the People: Politics, Culture and Imperialism in England, 1715–1785* (Cambridge: Cambridge University Press, 1995)

—— *The Island Race: Englishness, Empire and Gender in the Eighteenth Century* (London and New York: Routledge, 2003)

Wood, Gordon, 'Ideology and the Origins of Liberal America', *William and Mary Quarterly: A Magazine of Early American History and Culture*, 44 (July 1987), 628–40

Wurgaft, Lewis D., 'Identity in World History: A Postmodern Perspective', *History and Theory: Studies in the Philosophy of History*, 34 (1995), 67–85

Yeğenoğlu, Meyda, *Colonial Fantasies: Towards a Feminist Reading of Orientalism* (Cambridge: Cambridge University Press, 1998)

Young, Robert, *Colonial Desire: Hybridity in Theory, Culture and Race* (London and New York: Routledge, 1995)

SELECT BIBLIOGRAPHY

Zakriya, Jamal, Shawqi al-Jamal and Salah al-Hamarna, *Mas'alat al-Riqq fi Ifriqiyya: Buhuth wa Dirasat* (Tunis: al-Munazzama al-'Arabiyya li al-Tarbiya wa al-Thaqafa wa al-'Ulum, 1989), 19–70

Zonana, Joyce, 'The Sultan and the Slave: Feminist Orientalism and the Structure of Jane Eyre', *Signs*, 18 (1993), 592–617

INDEX

Note: 'n.' after a page reference indicates the number of a note on that page

'Abduh, Muhammad 57, 67 n.97
Aborigines' Protection Society 84, 194 n.110
Ackerman, Robert John 152 n.124
Act of Emancipation 1834 103 n.42
Adams, James Eli 64 n.3
al-Afghani, Jamal al-Din 67 n.97
Afghanistan 164, 176
agency 5, 6, 62–3, 104, 115, 142–3, 169, 183–4, 205–6, 209
agricultural slavery 15
Ahmad, Aziz 193 n.92
Ahmad, Rafi-ud-Din 174–5
Ahmadi Muslims 159
Ahmad Khan, Sayyid 173, 193 n.93
Ahmed, Leila 24 n.19
Alexander, William 147 n.18
Alexandria 33, 53, 131
Ali, Chiragh 173
Ali, Muhammad Mumtaz 187 n.1
Aliens Act 1905 157
Allan, Sir William, *Slave Market in Constantinople* 127–8
Allen, Charles 109 n.65
All-India Muslim League 170
Ally, Muhammad Mashuq 189 n.24
al-Tirmanini, 'Abd al-Salam 27 n.49, 150 n.91
American Revolution 72
Amin, Qasim 67 n.97
Amir Ali, Sayyid 28 n.61, 51, 170–3, 182–3, 185–7, 199–200, 206, 208
Amos, Sarah 47, 84, 90–2, 94, 103, 110 n.86, 130, 132–3, 144, 198
Amos, Shelon 90, 94, 132–3, 198
Anderson, Benedict 22 n.7
d'Anjou, Leo 107 n.7
Anthropological Institute 194 n.110
Anti-Slavery Reporter (ASR) 70, 74–7, 79–84, 87–8, 90, 93–4, 98–100, 102, 105, 202
anti-vice movement 130–5, 141, 142, 143, 144, 198–9, 201, 207

Apffel-Marglin, Frédérique 149 n.49
Apter, Emily 152 n.126
Arberry, A. J. 27 n.47
Armitage, David 23 n.13
Arnold, Thomas Walker 192 n.65
Arnot, Fred 76
Ashcraft, Richard 22 n.8
Assiout 113 n.148
Atlantic world 5
Austen, Ralph 29 n.76
ayahs 156–60, 182, 203
Ayah's Home 156
Aziz, Khursheed Kamal 192 n.82
Al-Azmeh, Aziz 24 n.21, 109 n.63

Badawi, M.A. 187 n.1
Badran, Margot 68 n.121
Baer, Gabriel 28 n.64, 28 n.65
Bakabur, 'Umar bin Salim 'Umar 24–5 n.23
Balibar, Etienne 21 n.2
Baring, Sir Evelyn *see* Cromer, Lord
Baron, Beth 24 n.19
Baucom, Ian 3, 23–4 n.15
Beachey, R. W. 24 n.18, 27 n.50, 67 n.100
Beaufort, Emily A. 195 n.127
Beckford, William, *Vathek* 138
Bentham, Jeremy 83
Bhabha, Homi 108 n.51
Bird, Isabella L. 146 n.18
Blackstone, Sir William 116
Bloom, William 23 n.9
Blunt, Lady Anne 152 n.108
Book of the Thousand Nights and a Night, The 138, 144, 180
borders 5–6, 20, 21, 24 n.16, 105, 127, 140, 141, 144–5, 154, 156, 158, 181, 182, 187, 203–4, 207–8
bourgeois household 57, 61–2, 82, 104
Braddick, Michael 23 n.13
Brinton, Jasper Yeates 66 n.68

[220]

INDEX

British and Foreign Anti-Slavery Society (BFASS) 2, 22 n.3, 32–3, 47, 59, 70–106, 197–8, 200, 202–4, 207
   Amir Ali, Sayyid 172
   anti-vice movement 133
   conservative stance 124, 125–6, 127–8, 129–30, 142
   members' and contributors' places of residence 211–12
   Orientalism 144, 174, 176
British Muslim Association 164
British Red Crescent Society 170
Brockliss, Laurence 29–30 n.79, 30 n.81, 30 n.82, 30 n.83
Buckingham, James Silk 166, 190 n.44
Burton, Antoinette 23 n.15, 145 n.4
Burton, Isabel 181
Burton, Sir Richard 15, 49, 138, 180–1, 183–4, 186, 206, 208

Cabrera, Miguel 23 n.11, 69 n.125
Cairo 10, 16, 33, 38, 53, 56, 100, 127, 178
Cairo Home for Freed Women Slaves (CHFWS) 33, 45, 56, 84–91, 102–3, 132, 202
Caisse de la Dette Publique 32
Cambridge University 119–20
Cannadine, David 29 n.78
Canning, Stratford 46
caravans, slave 38–9, 53, 59
Carlyle, Thomas 179–80
Central National Mohammedan Association 170
Chartism 73
Chatterjee, Indrani 69 n.124
Chew, Samuel C. 187 n.1
child slaves 14, 34, 36, 81
Christianity 71, 75–7, 103, 124–6, 157, 165–8, 171–2, 176, 179–80, 186, 200
Church Missionary Society 126
Clark, Anna 145 n.2
class issues 17, 44, 72–3, 89, 102, 104, 122, 158–60, 174, 178, 205
Clouston, T. S., MD 148 n.36
Cobbe, Frances Power 121
Cohn, Bernard 25 n.26
Colley, Linda 26 n.36, 26 n.39, 111 n.125, 145 n.2, 192 n.72
conservative stances 124–30, 142, 199
Contagious Diseases (CD) Acts 130, 132
Cook, Thomas 166, 178

couverture 116–17
Crescent 164
Crewe, Mrs 85–8
Crick, Bernard 30 n.85
Criminal Law Amendment Act 1885 130–1
Cromer, Lord (earlier Sir Evelyn Baring)
   'Abduh, relationship between 57
   Amir Ali, Sayyid 172
   Amos, Sarah 90–2
   anti-slavery campaign 47, 51, 52, 55
   autocratic style 7–9
   BFASS 99
   Cairo Home for Freed Women Slaves 84–5
   conformity to expectations 5
   conservative stance 124, 127, 129
   Government as Muslim power 29 n.77
   judicial system 48
   male slaves 15
   Sudanese slavery 88
   on unified Egyptian society 11
   women's suffrage movement 43
Crosby, Alan 195 n.113
Cry From the Depths, A 1, 121–2
Cuno, Kenneth 67 n.102, 68 n.122
Curzon, Earl 129

Dangerfield, George 147 n.21
Davidoff, Leonore 29 n.74
Dawson, Graham 3, 64 n.9
Deism 168
Della Sala, Count Edward 53–4, 98
Derby, Earl of 39
Disraeli, Benjamin 162
diversity *see* heterogeneity, diversity and lack of predisposition
Dodd, Philip 21–2 n.2
Drescher, Seymour 107 n.7
Dufferin, Lord 8, 82

East India Company 69 n.124, 155, 156, 182, 203
Eastwood, David 29–30 n.79, 30 n.81, 30 n.82, 30 n.83
education, women's access to 119–20
Eltis, David 106 n.6
Enlightenment 71, 147 n.31, 171, 200, 205
Erdem, Y. Hakan 24 n.18
ethnicity 159

[221]

INDEX

eunuch slaves 14–15, 81, 93
Evangelicals 71

Fawcett, Millicent Garrett 132, 152 n.111
femininity, genteel 135–40, 141, 208
feminism 43, 57, 60, 63, 84, 115–23, 126, 129–30, 140–4, 175, 185, 198–200, 202, 204, 207–8
France 93, 96–7

Gallagher, John 26 n.34
Garrison, William Lloyd 113 n.147
Gates, Henry Louis Jr 28 n.68
Geertz, Clifford 106 n.1, 111 n.114
genteel femininity 135–40, 141, 208
Gilroy, Paul 23 n.13
Gladstone, William Ewart 82, 92
Gordon, General Charles George 70, 79, 92, 98
Gordon, Lady Duff 125
Gramsci, Antonio 63 n.1
Grant, Alexander 29 n.78, 30 n.85, 30 n.86
Granville, Earl 77, 82, 172
Grewal, Inderpal 23 n.15, 149 n.49
Grosrichard, Alain 152 n.125

Halbersleben, Karen 113 n.147
Hall, Catherine 3, 29 n.74, 189 n.26
al-Hamarna, Salah 26 n.35
Handler, Richard 23 n.9
Hanum, Melek 126–7, 144
Hardy, Peter 29 n.77, 193 n.90
Hardy, Thomas 73
Harris, John 106 n.6
Harrison, Brian 150 n.76
Hatem, Mervat 149 n.49
Hendricks, Margo 28 n.68
heterogeneity, diversity and lack of predisposition 4, 6–7, 16, 23 n.10, 24 n.21, 54, 58–9, 63, 70–1, 78, 85–6, 96–7, 102, 105–6, 134–5, 143–4, 152 n.124, 159, 186, 189 n.26, 202–5, 209
higher education, women's access to 119–20
Hilal, 'Imad Ahmad 26 n.35, 27 n.48, 68 n.123, 111–12 n.127
Holcome, Lee 146 n.12
Holton, Sandra Stanley 145 n.3, 147 n.31
Hourani, Albert 25 n.30, 67 n.97
House of Commons 119

human rights movement 73
Hunter, Wilson 194 n.95
Husayn, 'Abd al-Ghafar Muhammad 64 n.5
Hutchins, Francis 25–6 n.33, 26 n.34

identity
  definition of 2–6
  temporary, incomplete and situational nature of 4, 16–17, 23 n.9, 23 n.10, 34, 58–9, 71, 102, 104, 141–4, 158, 169, 184–7, 197–202, 205, 209
immigration to Britain 155–60, 161, 182
Imperial and Asiatic Quarterly Review and Oriental and Colonial Record (*IAQR*) 174, 176, 176, 203
India 8, 10, 150 n.75, 161, 170–3, 183, 184
Indian National Congress 194 n.110
Ireland/Irish identity *see* Scotland, Ireland, and Wales/Scots, Irish, and Welsh identities and/or the British Isles
Islamic practices, traditions of jurisprudence, and beliefs with regard to slavery in Egypt 11–13, 57
Ismail, Khedive 9, 12, 52, 67 n.100
Istanbul 10, 12, 88, 131, 164

al-Jamal, Shawqi 26 n.35
Jehan, Shah 177–8, 182, 208
Jiddah 35, 50, 51, 88, 113 n.148
John, Michael 29–30 n.79, 30 n.83
Jones, Gareth Stedman 151 n.101
judicial system and jurisprudence 12, 46–9, 60–1

Kafirs 176
Kale, Madhavi 69 n.124, 109 n.71
Kamel-ud-Din, Kwaja 159, 194–5 n.113
Kearney, Hugh 29 n.78, 30 n.83
Kelsall, Malcolm 146 n.9, 149 n.49
Kinglake, Alexander 127
kul slavery 28 n.64
Kureishi, Hanif 189 n.26

lack of predisposition *see* heterogeneity, diversity and lack of predisposition
Ladies' Land League 146 n.7
Ladies' National Association for Repeal of the Contagious Diseases Acts 116, 146 n.7

INDEX

Lane, Edward 138
Lane-Poole, Stanley 133, 180
lascars 155–60, 182, 184, 185, 200, 203, 205, 206
al-Latif, 'Abd 173
Lavigerie, Cardinal 75, 76, 89–90, 96, 205
Lawrence, T. E. 196 n.146
Leitner, Dr. Gottlieb William 173–6, 184–6, 195 n.114, 195 n.120, 206
Lelyveld, David 193 n.91, 193 n.93
Leneman, Leah 145–6 n.5, 146 n.7
Levine, Philippa 145 n.2, 150 n.90, 151 n.96
Lewis, Bernard 28 n.71
Lewis, John Frederick 144
   Harem, The 138–9
   In the Bey's Garden, Asia Minor 138, 139
   Reception, The 139
Lewis, Reina 151 n.102
Liberal Party 118
liberating slaves in Egypt according to Islamic principles, tradition of 13
Liddington, Jill 145 n.3
Liverpool, Muslim converts' community 160–70, 182, 183, 186
Liverpool Manx Society 167
Liverpool Muslim Congregation 191 n.51
Liverpool Muslim Institute 164, 165
Locke, John 71
London City Mission (LCM) 108 n.41, 155–8, 185
London Female Preventive and Reformatory Institution 132
London mosque proposal 172
Lutfi al-Sayyid, Afaf 25 n.32
Lutfi al-Sayyid Marsot, Afaf 64 n.5

MacKenzie, John M. 22 n.4, 30 n.80
mamluks 28 n.64, 52
Manning, Cardinal 74, 92
Mansour, Princess 85
manumission 13–14, 32–3, 35, 44–7, 55–6, 93, 210
   Cairo Home for Freed Women Slaves 33, 45, 56, 84–91, 102–3, 132, 202
marriage 116–17, 122, 125, 159
Married Women's Property Act 1870 117
Married Women's Property Committee 117

Matar, Nabil 187 n.1
Maza, Sarah 111 n.124
McClintock, Anne 151 n.101
McGovern, J. H. 191 n.49, 191 n.51
McWilliams-Tullberg, Rita 148 n.32
Mecca 10, 50–1, 61, 74, 180–1
Meinig, D. W. 23 n.13
Melman, Billie 146 n.16, 151 n.102, 152 n.108, 195 n.124
Melucci, Alberto 23 n.9
Men's League for Opposing Women's Suffrage 129
Midgley, Clare 107 n.7, 148 n.41
Miers, Suzanne 24 n.18, 106–7 n.7
Mill, John Stuart 116, 146 n.16
mimicry 64 n.2, 68 n.108, 79, 108 n.51, 162–4, 183, 191 n.47, 202, 206
miscegenation 135
Mitchell, Timothy 29 n.74
monogenesis 135
Montagu, Lady Mary Wortley 153 n.127, 162, 190 n.46
Montesquieu, Charles Louis de Secondat 71
Moore, Thomas, *Lalla Rookh: An Oriental Romance* 138
Morgan, David 147 n.31
Moslem Patriotic League 173
Muhammadan Anglo-Oriental College 203
Muhammadan Literary and Scientific Society of Calcutta 173
Mukhtar, Muhammad 26 n.35, 28 n.61, 111–12 n.127
Murphy, Cliona 145–6 n.5, 146 n.7
Mustafa, Ahmad 'Abd al-Rahim 64 n.5

National Association for the Repeal of the Contagious Diseases Acts 130
National Union of Women's Suffrage Societies 116, 118
National Vigilance Association (NVA) 131, 133
Neal, Frank 192 n.74
Norris, Jill 145 n.3
Norton, Caroline 175
Nussbaum, Felicity 153 n.127

Oldfield, J. R. 106 n.4
Oriental Institute 173–4, 176, 177, 178, 182, 184, 186, 199–201

INDEX

Orientalism 3, 143, 144, 173–81, 184–5, 199, 202–3, 206
Oriental Museum (Oriental Nobility Institute) 174, 184, 203, 205
Owen, Roger 25 n.30
Owens, Rosemary Cullen 146 n.5
Oxford, University of 119

Panayi, Panikos 189 n.19
Parker, Patricia 28 n.68
Pasha, Ibrahim 161, 190 n.36
patriarchy 43, 45–6, 60, 62, 63, 116, 129, 131, 142, 144
Peace Society 194 n.110
Perkin, Harold 107 n.13
Philipp, Thomas 24 n.19
physical abuse of women 121–2
Pick, Daniel 151 n.101
pilgrims 42, 50–1, 74
Platt, Gerald 22 n.8, 23 n.10
Pocock, J. G. A. 22 n.8, 29 n.78
polygamy 26 n.38, 38, 76–7, 80, 125, 137–8
Ponsonby, Lord 32
Poovey, Mary 66 n.64
Powell, Eve Troutt 28 n.71, 112 n.127
predisposition, lack of *see* heterogeneity, diversity and lack of predisposition
property rights 72, 116–17, 175
prostitution 44, 130–5, 141, 143, 144, 198–9, 201
Punjab University 174

Quakers 71
Quilliam, Captain John 162
Quilliam, William Henry 21, 160, 162–70, 183–7, 199–206, 208
al-Qurtubi, Muhammad 12

race 16–18, 44, 94–6, 103, 134–5, 143, 158, 205
Ramadan, 'Abd al-'Azim 64 n.5
Razuq, Muhammad 26 n.35
Red Crescent Society 170
Red Sea slave traffic 35–8, 59, 99
Reform Act 1832 73
Rendall, Jane 145 n.1
Rice, C. Duncan 113 n.147
Richmond, J. C. B. 64 n.5
Roach, Joseph 23 n.13
Robbins, Keith 30 n.83, 30 n.85
Robinson, David 192 n.71

Robinson, Ronald 26 n.34
Royal Geographical Society 78, 180
Ruskin, John 138–9, 157

Said, Abdul Aziz 24 n.21
Said, Edward 22 n.5, 23 n.12
Said, Muhammad 161, 190 n.36
Salisbury, Lord 97, 176
Salter, Joseph 158
Schaefer Bey, Colonel 54, 56, 68 n.111, 82, 90, 99, 110 n.86
Scotland, Ireland, and Wales/Scots, Irish, and Welsh identities and/or the British Isles 2, 20–1, 29 n.78, 29 n.79, 30, 54, 58, 70–1, 78, 97, 101, 106, 111 n.125, 112 n.132, 113 n.147, 116, 145–6 n.5, 146 n.6, 146 n.7, 172, 204, 211–12
seclusion 40, 43, 57, 126–7
Sell, Edward 193 n.86
Service for the Abolition of the Slave Trade 53, 55
Shafiq, Ahmad 51–2, 107 n.20
Shah Jehan Mosque, Woking 19, 170, 176–7, 182, 186, 208
Sharafuddin, Mohammed 196 n.139
shari'a 26–7 n.42
Sharif, 'Ali Pasha 112 n.127
Sharify-Funk, Meena 24 n.21
Sharp, Granville 71
Simon, Suzanne 149 n.49
Sinha, Mrinalini 150 n.75
Slave Trade Department 55, 56, 90, 93, 99
Smyth, Jim 30 n.84, 30 n.87
social Darwinism 9
Société Antiesclavagiste de France 96
Society for the Abolition of the Slave Trade 71
Society for Promoting Christian Knowledge (SPCK) 126
Somersett case (1772) 71
Southey, Robert 180
Spencer, Herbert 9
Stead, W. T. 130, 132, 151 n.101
steamer traffic 37–8, 42, 59
Stocking, George 28 n.70, 147 n.18
Stoler, Ann Laura 151 n.101
Strangers' Home for Asiatics, Africans and South Sea Islanders 155
Stringer, Keith 29 n.78, 30 n.85, 30 n.86
Sublime Porte 32, 40, 41, 83

[224]

INDEX

Sudan 81, 88, 100, 169
suffragists and suffragettes 43, 116, 117–19, 129, 205
Summary Jurisdiction (Married Women) Act 1895 121
Suppression of the Slave Trade in the Red Sea 35

Taussig, Michael 24 n.16
Tawfiq, Khedive 52–3, 57
Taylor, Harriet 116
temperance movement 165–7, 168–9
Temperley, Howard 113 n.147
Thomas, Nicholas 23 n.13
Thompson, E. P. 21 n.2
Thorne, Susan 23–4 n.15
Tidrick, Kathryn 196 n.146
Tignor, Robert 25 n.26
al-Tirmanini, 'Abd al-Salam 27 n.49, 150 n.91
Toledano, Ehud 26 n.37
tourism 178–9
trial of the pashas 93–4
Tucker, Judith 110 n.86
Turbiyyn, Ahmad 25 n.32
Turkey 15, 39, 83, 119, 120, 122, 131, 136, 137, 151 n.99, 174
Turley, David 107 n.7

Unitarianism 168

'veiled protectorate' system 8
veiling 40–1, 42, 43, 57, 126–7
Victoria, Queen 68 n.116, 85, 178
Visram, Rozina 188 n.2, 188 n.11, 189 n.23
Vivian, Lord 49, 55, 89

Wakeford, Iain 195 n.113
Wales *see* Scotland, Ireland, and Wales/Scots, Irish, and Welsh identities and/or the British Isles

Walkowitz, Judith 29 n.74, 150 n.79, 151 n.101
Wallerstein, Immanuel 21 n.2
Walvin, James 107 n.7, 107 n.13
Weinstein, Fred 23 n.10
Welch, William M. 25 n.24
Welsh identity *see* Scotland, Ireland, and Wales/Scots, Irish, and Welsh identities and/or the British Isles
Wesleyans 71
Whateley, Mary L. 85, 124, 126, 147 n.28, 149 n.66
Whiteman, J. R. and S. E. 195 n.113
'white slavery' (prostitution) 130–5, 141, 143, 145, 199
Wilkite radicalism 72
Wilson, Kathleen 3, 112 n.138, 114 n.169, 191 n.47
Winnicott, Donald Woods 22 n.7
Woking
  Muslim Mission 195 n.114
  Oriental Institute 173–4, 176, 177, 178, 182, 184, 186, 199–201
  Oriental Museum (Oriental Nobility Institute) 174, 184, 203, 205
  Shah Jehan Mosque 19, 170, 176–7, 182, 186, 208
Wollstonecraft, Mary 116, 147 n.31
Women's Social and Political Union 116
women's suffrage movement 43, 116, 117–19, 129, 205
Wood, Gordon 22 n.8
Wurgaft, Lewis D. 24 n.17

Ye[g]eno[g]lu, Meyda 153 n.127
Young, Robert 28 n.70
Young Men's Literacy and Mutual Improvement Society 108 n.41

Zakriya, Jamal 26 n.35
Zonana, Joyce 146 n.9, 148 n.4

EU authorised representative for GPSR:
Easy Access System Europe, Mustamäe tee 50,
10621 Tallinn, Estonia
gpsr.requests@easproject.com

www.ingramcontent.com/pod-product-compliance
Ingram Content Group UK Ltd.
Pitfield, Milton Keynes, MK11 3LW, UK
UKHW041920140426
5217IPUK00013B/240